MANAGEMENT, WORK AND ORGANISATIONS

Series editors: **Gibson Burrell**, Warwick Business School
Mick Marchington, Manchester School of Management, UMIST
Paul Thompson, Department of Human Resource Management, University of Strathclyde

This series of textbooks covers the areas of human resource management, employee relations, organisational behaviour and related business and management fields. Each text has been specially commissioned to be written by leading experts in a clear and accessible way. The books contain serious and challenging material, take an analytical rather than prescriptive approach and are particularly suitable for use by students with no prior specialist knowledge.

The series is relevant for a number of business and management courses including MBA and post-experience courses, specialist masters and postgraduate diplomas, professional courses, and final-year undergraduate courses. These texts have become essential reading at business and management schools worldwide.

Published:

Paul Blyton and Peter Turnbull   **The Dynamics of Employer Relations** (2nd edn)
J. Martin Corbett   **Critical Cases in Organisational Behaviour**
Marek Korczynski   **Human Resource Management in Service Work**
Sue Ledwith and Fiona Colgan (eds)   **Women in Organisations**
Karen Legge   **Human Resource Management**
Stephen Procter and Frank Mueller (eds)   **Teamworking**
Helen Rainbird (ed.)   **Training in the Workplace**
Michael Rowlinson   **Organisations and Institutions**
Harry Scarbrough (ed.)   **The Management of Expertise**
Adrian Wilkinson, Mick Marchington, Tom Redman and Ed Snape   **Managing with Total Quality Management**
Diana Winstanley and Jean Woodall (eds)   **Ethical Issues in Contemporary Human Resource Management**

Forthcoming:

Richard Badham   **The Management of Change**
Pippa Carter and Norman Jackson   **Critical Issues in Organisational Behaviour**
Keith Grint   **Leadership**
Irena Grugulis   **The Learning Organisation**
John Purcell and Peter Boxall   **Strategies in Human Resource Management**
Jill Rubery and Damian Grimshaw   **Employment Policy and Practice**
Hugh Scullion and Margaret Lineham   **International Human Resource Management**
Graham Sewell   **Demystifying Management**

Series Standing Order

If you would like to receive future titles in this series as they are published, you can make use of our standing order facility. To place a standing order, please contact your bookseller or, in case of difficulty, write to us at the address below with your name and address and the name of the series. Please state with which title you wish to begin your standing order. (If you live outside the UK we may not have the rights for your area, in which case we will forward your order to the publisher concerned.)

Standing Order Service, Macmillan Distribution Ltd,
Houndmills, Basingstoke, Hampshire RG21 6XS, England

TRESHAM INSTITUTE LRC
060153

HUMAN RESOURCE MANAGEMENT IN SERVICE WORK

Marek Korczynski

palgrave

© Marek Korczynski 2002

All rights reserved. No reproduction, copy or transmission of
this publication may be made without written permission.

No paragraph of this publication may be reproduced, copied or
transmitted save with written permission or in accordance with
the provisions of the Copyright, Designs and Patents Act 1988,
or under the terms of any licence permitting limited copying
issued by the Copyright Licensing Agency, 90 Tottenham Court
Road, London W1T 4LP.

Any person who does any unauthorised act in relation to this
publication may be liable to criminal prosecution and civil
claims for damages.

The author has asserted his right to be identified
as the author this work in accordance with the
Copyright, Designs and Patents Act 1988.

First published 2002 by
PALGRAVE
Houndmills, Basingstoke, Hampshire RG21 6XS and
175 Fifth Avenue, New York, N. Y. 10010
Companies and representatives throughout the world

PALGRAVE is the new global academic imprint of
St. Martin's Press LLC Scholarly and Reference Division and
Palgrave Publishers Ltd (formerly Macmillan Press Ltd).

ISBN 0–333–77440–X hardback
ISBN 0–333–77441–8 paperback

This book is printed on paper suitable for recycling and
made from fully managed and sustained forest sources.

A catalogue record for this book is available
from the British Library.

Library of Congress Cataloging-in-Publication Data
has been applied for.

10 9 8 7 6 5 4 3 2 1
11 10 09 08 07 06 05 04 03 02

Printed in Great Britain by
Creative Print & Design (Wales), Ebbw Vale

TRESHAM
060153
KETTERING
658·3 KOR
INSTITUTE

To Eva, the little girl with the big heart

Contents

List of tables

List of tables

Acknowledgements

A lot of the energy for writing this book came from reading a number of outstanding and stimulating books on service work and on consumption written over the last two decades. Among these books I would like to highlight (and recommend) the following. The wisest books offering the most profound insights were often the detailed ethnographies which married a sensitivity to the experience of service workers with a wider theoretical awareness. Here, Deidre Wicks' *Nurses and Doctors at Work*, Robin Leidner's *Fast Food and Fast Talk*, Nancy Foner's *The Caregiving Dilemma* stand out. Susan Benson's *Counter Culture*, as well as having the best title, showed that important insights can be generated from a historical study, in this case of department store work. Each of these books, in its own way, explores the interplay between routinisation and the service worker's experience of, often deeply socially embedded, relationships with service recipients. Two essential recent edited collections on service work are Cameron Macdonald and Carmen Sirianni's *Working in the Service Society*, and Andrew Sturdy, Irena Grugulis and Hugh Willmott's *Customer Service*. Steve Herzenberg, John Alic and Howard Wial's *New Rules for a New Economy* represents an important political economic examination of the USA as a service economy. On customers and consumption, Yiannis Gabriel and Tim Lang's *The Unmanageable Consumer* remains an outstanding overview and I would suggest that the collection of classic pieces put together by Martyn Lee, *The Consumer Society Reader* (Blackwell, 2000), makes up an excellent companion piece. Colin Campbell's *The Romantic Ethic and the Spirit of Modern Consumerism*, and George Ritzer's *Enchanting a Disenchanted World* are deeply stimulating explorations of consumption.

In addition to the writing of others I am indebted to comments from and conversations with colleagues from Loughborough University and beyond, most notably, Pete Ackers, Seamus Allison, Gibson Burrell, Laurie Cohen, Dan Cornfield, Irena Grugulis, Ed Heery, Ursula Holtgrewe, Mick Marchington, Peter Prowse, Kerstin Rieder, Karen Shire, Andrew Sturdy, May Tam, Paul Thompson and Adrian Wilkinson. Thanks also to Sarah Brown and Keith

Povey at the publishers. The biggest thanks go to Kathy and Eva here in West Bridgford, Nottingham.

Finally, I would like to thank the students at Loughborough who have contributed to the second-year module, Human Resource Management in Service Industries, which has been a joy to teach. I also offer an open invitation to fellow university teachers to contact me at m.korczynski@lboro.ac.uk to offer comments or criticisms and/or to open a dialogue about useful ways to help the teaching of this subject. I am happy to share my ideas on this, and am interested in hearing other people's ideas.

Marek Korczynski

CHAPTER 1

Service work

Introduction

All advanced economies are dominated by service industries. While we may never live in economies in which 'everyone will serve someone else and no one will be making anything' (Rohantyn, 1984), most people in employment work in a service industry. Over 10 per cent of the UK workforce are employed in the retail sector (Jarvis and Prais, 1989), and 'more Americans now work in physicians' offices than in auto plants, in laundries and dry cleaners than in steel mills' (Herzenberg *et al.*, 1998, p. 3). The trend in advanced economies towards service industries from manufacturing and agriculture is still continuing. Between 1974 and 1994 service sector employment rose by 9 per cent to 73 per cent in the USA, by 13 per cent to 71 per cent in Australia, and from 50 to 60 per cent in Japan (OECD, 1996). Castells (1996, ch. 4) estimates that in the UK in 1990 service sector employment stood at 70 per cent.

Despite this, many of the dominant concepts and metaphors used to analyse employment are rooted in manufacturing. For instance, one of the key themes for debates in recent decades has been around the existence and nature of post-Fordism. We are told both literally and metaphorically that the machine that changed the world is that most emblematic of manufactured items, the car (Womack *et al.*, 1990). Important debates about high-performance work systems and about 'lean production' ways of working continue to revolve around research in manufacturing workplaces. In some analyses the main point of interest regarding service industries concerns how far work organisation there is lagging behind that in manufacturing (Poynter, 1999). Employment in manufacturing industries is implicitly seen as the norm to which employment in services will gravitate (Appelbaum and Batt, 1994).

This book is an attempt to move away from this way of thinking. It focuses on the nature of employment in services. The main reason it does this is not the numerical importance of employment in services but the fact that *there are unique factors in service work that make its separate analysis essential*. There are a number of these factors, which are drawn out below in the discussion of what service work is, but the most important is that in a lot of service work there is direct contact with the *customer*. Here customers become an important part of the social relations of the workplace. As Whyte (1946, p. 123) puts it, 'when workers and customers meet... that relationship adds a new dimension to the pattern of human relations in industry.' Employment which has traditionally been seen as dominated by the dyadic management–worker relationship must be seen as potentially influenced by the three-way relationship involving management, workers and customers. There is good reason to agree with the conclusion to Benson's (1986, p. 288) insightful study of an American department store: 'Taxonomies of management practice derived primarily from manufacturing may not be readily applicable to service industries with their more complicated social reality and greater variability.' The task, then, is to develop analysis that can aid understanding of the specific nature of service work.

Because the role of the customer is the most important *unique* aspect of service work, this book's main focus is on those jobs involving direct customer contact. Specifically, the book is primarily concerned with customer contact jobs in the mass-customised and medium-customised market segments. So, for example, the book concentrates on the work of customer service reps in call centres, tellers in banks, and nurses and nursing aides in hospitals, rather than doctors, management consultants, lawyers or other 'knowledge workers' who have significant contact with customers. As such the book focuses on what MacDonald and Sirianni (1996, p. 3) have called 'the emotional proletariat'. As the numbers employed in service work generally have grown, so have the numbers employed in direct customer contact jobs. Indeed, Hochschild (1983, p. 11) estimates that as many as half of American women in paid employment are in customer contact jobs requiring a degree of emotional labour.[1] This book's focus on customer contact jobs also mirrors the focus of management in recent decades. Managers in many firms have come to see the interaction between their customer service workers and (potential) customers as 'the moment of truth' for the firm (Carlzon, 1987). This is the moment when important impressions of the firms are formed which influence future consumption decisions. Hence management has devoted increasing energy to trying to ensure that their customer service workers act in the appropriate way to customers. Increasingly, management is seeing customer service work as one of the key terrains of competitive advantage or disadvantage for the firm (Schlesinger and Heskett, 1991a).

These are all good reasons to have a book focused on customer service work. Another good reason is that the existing literature on the subject is difficult to comprehend *as a whole*, riven as it is by a schism between two broad approaches that contain very different images of the nature of customer service work.

The first broad school is the *new service management school*, led by a group of influential, mainly American, human resource management (HRM) academics. Here, the argument is that the alienating, assembly line approach to organising service work belongs to the past, and that to deliver the sort of qualities of service that customers want requires an 'empowerment' approach to service work. Schlesinger and Heskett (1992) argue that only by treating workers in a more humane way, by 'de-industrialising the service sector' can managers expect workers to give good quality service to customers. As long as firms can hire the right sort of people with the right customer-focused attitude (Stanback, 1990) and treat their workers well then their customers will receive good service. Schneider and Bowen (1995) have summarised research which apparently shows that customers' perception of the quality of service is significantly correlated with service workers' perception of the climate of their firm. The more favourably service workers view the firm and how management treats them, the more favourable are customer perceptions of the service delivered by these same workers. Within this school, the three-way relationship of service work is a *win : win : win* one. Customers win because they receive qualitatively superior service, workers win because they become empowered to act on their firmly held customer service values, and are freed from the old industrial tyranny, and managers win because customers keep coming back to the firm. This win : win : win story comes through well in Zemke and Schaaf's (1989) discussion of Marriott Hotels. The authors enthuse (p. 118):

> The current Mr. Marriott credits his father with the philosophy of taking care of employees as he wanted them to take care of the customer. 'My father knew if he had happy employees, he would have happy customers and that would result in a good bottom line.'

Against this approach is a range of *critical perspectives* that suggest very different images of customer service work. Unlike with the new service management school it is difficult to speak of a coherent critical school on service work. As Chapter 3 shows, there are important differences between some critical perspectives. However, they do share a common thread in arguing that the contemporary nature of service work is increasingly harmful to workers in a number of ways. Perhaps the best known critical perspective has been expounded by George Ritzer in *The McDonaldization of Society*. This analysis portrays customer service work as variously, fake, invasive, emotionally draining, demeaning, highly routinised and alienating. On the fake nature of customer service work, Ritzer (1999a, p. 116) writes:

> Most of the people we encounter in the new means of consumption are simulations...The blackjack dealer at a Las Vegas casino, the ticket taker at Disney World...the counterperson at McDonald's, and the cashier at Wal-Mart are all

playing well-defined roles. Their employing organisations have developed a series of guidelines about how they are supposed to look, speak, behave, and so forth... There is little or no room for creativity or individuality... The blackjack dealer and the counterperson are simulations – they are fakes.

How are we to make sense of service work when confronted by such contradictory images from the new service management school and from the critical perspectives? Addressing this question is one of the central tasks of this book. The main argument of the book revolves around viewing much of contemporary service work through the lens of the *customer-oriented bur-eaucracy* – a form of work organisation in which there are dual, and potentially contradictory, logics at play. The logics are those of routinisation and efficiency on the one hand, and those of the customer and customer orientation on the other.

Before this argument is elaborated more fully, however, the necessary building blocks need to be in place. First we need to ask: just what is service work and how does it differ from manufacturing? And we also need to consider what different types of service work there are. In addition, this chapter reviews the key competitive contexts driving the reorganisation of service work. The final section of this chapter outlines the structure of the book.

What is service work?

Attempts to draw clear distinctions between manufacturing and services date back over two hundred years. The original theorists and supporters of the emerging capitalist system were keen to draw out these differences because they saw manufacturing as synonymous with capitalism (think of cotton mills, for instance), and services as remnants of the feudal society that they wished overturned (Delaunay and Gardrey, 1992). The following quotation from Adam Smith brings out this praise for the manufacturer and the barely concealed contempt for services. For Smith there were two types of labour (1776, pp. 314–15):

The former, as it produces a value, may be called productive; the latter, unproduct-ive labour. Thus the labour of a *manufacturer* adds, generally, to the value of the materials which he works upon... The labour of a menial servant, on the contrary, adds the value of nothing... The *services* [of the menial servant] generally perish in the very instant of their performance, and seldom leave any trace or value behind them.

As capitalism has developed, however, it has become clear that Smith's approach to distinguishing between manufacturing and service work is flawed. Service sectors are dominant parts of the major capitalist economies; most analysts would agree that much of service labour *is* productive labour. In the middle of the twentieth century writers began to identify the service sector as an increasingly important *tertiary* sector of capitalist economies alongside the primary, agricultural sector and the secondary, manufacturing sector (Fisher, 1935; Clark, 1940; Fourastie, 1949). Daniel Bell (1973) theorised that underlying the growth of the tertiary services sector were inevitable changes in the overall long-term composition of demand in capitalist economies. He pointed to the work of the German economist Christian Engel, famous for the 'Engel curve'. The Engel curve shows that with rising affluence, demand for the primary necessities of life (arising from the primary sector) is soon nearly saturated and over time becomes a smaller part of overall demand. The Engel curve shows that the same is true for demand for products of a secondary necessity, mostly associated with the secondary, manufacturing sector. Therefore, over time the composition of demands proportionally gravitates towards the tertiary services sector. Hence the considerable growth of that sector in all capitalist economies.

But this still leaves us with the question of what it is about services that makes them different from the secondary, manufacturing and primary, agricultural sectors. Here five attributes of services are traditionally highlighted – intangibility, perishability, variability, simultaneous production and consumption, and inseparability.

Intangibility

Manufacturing work creates a tangible product that 'can drop on your feet' (Herzenberg *et al.*, 1998, p. 22). By contrast there is an intangible element to what is produced in service work. The quality of service that diners receive at a restaurant, or the way in which a nurse attends to a patient, cannot be touched. The 'product' here in part involves how the service recipient perceives the service. As Zemke and Schaaf (1989, p. 14) put it, the product in services is 'something more slippery to measure than the physical dimensions of a product'.

Perishability

This refers to the temporally specific nature of service work. Service work cannot be stored in the way that cars can be stockpiled and information filed. As Herzenberg *et al.* (1998, p. 22) state, 'the great bulk of services cannot be produced in advance, shipped and then stored until a customer comes along'.

Variability

Because customer actions within the service interaction may not be tightly prescribed by an organisation, and because customer perception of service may vary by individual, there is more scope for *variability* within customer service work than in work on materials or information. As Fuller and Smith (1991) note, customers tend to be 'idiosyncratic' in their expectations of, actions within and evaluations of service work.

Simultaneous production and consumption

During the service interaction, at the same time, the worker produces and to a degree the customer consumes. By contrast, in manufacturing there is a clear buffer between the activities of production and consumption.

Inseparability

This refers to the way in which the customer takes part in the service process. The customer cannot be separated from the service process. Some authors have gone so far to describe customers as *co-producers* in service work (Lachmann, 2000; Schneider and Bowen 1995).

These attributes can help us think of the important differences between services and manufacturing, but the list is not meant to suggest that all service work has each of the five features. Service work involving work mainly on information rather than on customers will share only a few of the above characteristics. The work of back-office jobs, that is, those with no customer contact, is generally non-perishable, because information and files can be saved to be used another day. Similarly in the work of a hospital clerk who deals with information for the running of the hospital there is a separability of production and consumption. We can say, however, that *customer* service work, where there is direct interaction between a worker and a service recipient, will feature each of these attributes to a degree. It is the presence of the customer in the service labour process that underlies the qualities of perishability, simultaneity and inseparability, while the qualities of intangibility and variability are often attributes of work on information as well as attributes of customer service work.

Another important point to stress is that not all forms of customer service work have the above five attributes to the same degree. Many forms of service work – think of retail work, for instance – do involve an exchange of tangible goods and so cannot be said to involve absolute intangibility. Indeed, we will see below that some typologies of different forms of service work use one or more these attributes as an axis against which to plot forms of service work. If in this sense there are 'degrees' of service work, this should tell us that the distinction between manufacturing and services should be seen as a relative rather than an absolute one. Delauney and Gardrey (1992, p. 120) have suggested that it is necessary for theory 'to abandon the old separation between the secondary and tertiary sectors, and to consider that all activities tend to have both an industrial and a service dimension, although in different proportions'. As Quinn (1992) has pointed out, the majority of jobs in so-called manufacturing industries do not involve work on objects but rather involve work on information or customers. The car design worker does not alter tangible goods, but manipulates information in diagrammatic form. Further down the product chain, the work of the car sales staff involves primarily working on customers. The picture becomes potentially even more muddled when we consider that some types of work officially classified as service work are actually manual jobs which involve work on objects, rather than information or customers. Think of garbage disposal workers, for instance.

The easiest way to avoid confusion in thinking about types of work at this level is to remember that there are three basic media of work – objects, information, and people (US Dept. of Labor, 1991; Barley, 1993). Industries officially classified as manufacturing or services may involve a range of jobs which deal in each of the three media. It is only jobs involving working on people as customers, that is, customer service work, that have all of the five attributes discussed above. It is *customer* service work that is the primary focus of this book.

Types of service work

If a book on HRM in service work is to be useful it must be able to help analysis at two levels. At the higher level of abstraction it should be able to say meaningful things about the nature of employment and management in service work *as a whole*, highlighting factors that are common across all service jobs. The previous section, looking at the ways service work has been differentiated from manufacturing, is at this level. At a lower level of abstraction this book should also help shed light on *specific types* of service work, allowing students and analysts interested in specific types of service work to be aware of the factors that might make that form of service work take on particular characteristics. This section is written at this lower level of abstraction. It deals with how types of work within services have been differentiated by academic writers.

At the most basic level, writers have examined the different occupations of service work. There have been a number of important studies of specific types of customer service occupations that have mainly focused on the nature of the management–worker dyad. Over the last two decades there have also been a number of insightful studies of specific service occupations which have begun to consider the customer as an important part of the social relations of work – studies of health care workers (Foner, 1994), department store workers (Benson, 1986), fast food workers and insurance sellers (Leidner, 1993) and call centre workers (Frenkel *et al.*, 1999) among others. At their best these studies are rich with detail on the lived experience of types of service work, and of micromanagement practices in these workplaces. They can build up engaging and sensitive pictures of the occupations being studied, and are important in reminding us of crucial contextual factors that inform the nature of service work. On their own, however, they can do little to help us have a more *general* understanding of service work.

At the other extreme, there is also a stream of writing that simply uses general categories of work, such as unskilled, semi-skilled and skilled, and applies them across all types of work – service work, information work, and work on objects. While it is clearly important to be able to make generalisations across all types of work, this approach is at too high a level of abstraction for our purposes, glossing over as it does the important distinctive elements of service work. It is one of the kernel arguments of the book that there are important unique elements of service work (the presence of the customer, the intangibility, the simultaneous consumption and production and so on) that suggest the usefulness of its separate analysis. In this regard, it runs directly counter to arguments such as those by Beynon (1992), who suggests that there is little distinctive about service work that warrants its separate analysis.

Another approach to distinguishing types of service work is taken by economists. Here the classic work is that of Singleman (1974). Singleman argued that the service sector was comprised of four distinct subgroups: distributive services (transport, communication, trade), producer services (banking, business services, real estate), social services (health care, education, public and nonprofit services) and personal services (home help, hotels, restaurants, travel, repairs). He argued that the Engel curve was too simplistic in suggesting that spending and employment in services went up proportionally as affluence rose. He used data to show that in fact there were important differences in the relationship with affluence between the *types* of services he elucidated. Although these categories of service work still have currency with economists and even industrial sociologists (Hodson and Sullivan, 1995) it is not clear how the distinctions are useful in considering forms of employment and management practices within services.

Recently, however, there have been a number of attempts to delineate types of service work which do seek to have relevance for the nature of employment and HRM. These typologies generally involve the authors taking one or more of the five distinctive dimensions of service work and plotting types of service work against these dimensions. Leidner (1993), Mills (1986), Fitzgerald *et al.* (1991) and Lashley (1997) have all taken this approach – with remarkably similar results. Each approach is briefly outlined before the commonalities across them are highlighted.

Leidner (1993, p. 26) suggests that there are three main types of 'interactive service work'. The key dimension that underlies her typology is the degree to which the service interaction is separable from the product being sold or delivered – or what was discussed above as the *inseparability* of the customer from the service provided. First, there are jobs with a weak degree of inseparability:

> in some jobs the [service] interaction is a crucial part of the work process *even though it is not part of a product being sold* or provided. The success of salespeople, fundraisers, bill collectors, and survey interviewees depends on the workers' ability to construct particular kinds of interactions.

Second, there are jobs where

> a product exists apart from the interaction, but a particular type of experience is an important part of the service. For example, patrons of Playboy Clubs expected titillation and deference as well as food and drink (Steinem 1983), and airline passengers who buy tickets primarily to get from one place to another, are promised friendly service on their journey.

Finally, there are jobs where

> the interaction is inseparable from the product being sold or delivered – for instance, in psychotherapy . . . or teaching.

Mills (1986) puts forward four criteria for distinguishing types of service work. Two of these criteria implicitly coincide with the dimensions of inseparability and variability. From his criteria he argues that three basic types of service organisations can be identified. First is the 'maintenance-interactive service organisation' where 'the service provider . . . is not so much involved with the production of the service but with dispensing it' (p. 27). Examples include retail organisations, fast food restaurants, and banks. Next is the 'task-interactive service organisation'. Here, 'employees . . . are not only dispensers of the service but, more significantly, are producers [of the service] also' (p. 30). Finally, there are what Mills terms 'personal-interactive service organisations', where the service provided in the interaction is the entire product. Mills cites health care, religious organisation and psychological therapy as examples.

The threefold typology developed by Fitzgerald *et al.* (1991) is derived by plotting service work against six dimensions. These dimensions are:

    (i) customer contact time;
   (ii) extent of customisation;
  (iii) extent to which the employee exercises discretion in meeting customer needs;
  (iv) degree of focus on people or equipment;
   (v) source of value added – front or back office;
  (vi) extent to which focus is on separate product or service process.

The dimension of the degree of customisation closely maps onto variability, while the final dimension pertains to intangibility. The three main types of service work that Fitzgerald *et al.* identify on the basis of these dimensions are 'mass services', 'service shops' and 'professional services'. So for instance, in mass services, there is low contact time customisation and discretion, and the focus is on equipment, the back office and the product. In professional services, contact time, customisation, and discretion are high and there is a people, front-office and service process focus.

Lashley's (1997) analysis builds on the work of Schmenner (1995) and Heskett *et al.* (1990). He argues that useful distinctions, between types of service work can be made, but that there will be slight differences in these distinctions depending on whether one looks through a marketing, an operational management or an HRM lens. For each of these lenses he states that plotting service work against two dimensions or axes leads to identifying four types of service work. For each of the lenses one key dimension is the degree of standardisation/customisation. In his model, the other key dimension varies. From a marketing focus, he suggests that the degree of tangibility is a key dimension, from an operations focus it is the degree of labour intensity and from an HRM focus it is the locus of control. For the sake of simplicity, however, he implicitly suggests that these dimensions will tend to co-vary; that is, service work that has a high degree of tangibility will tend to have low labour intensity and there will be largely external control. This allows Lashley to present an overall model of types of service work as summarised in Table 1.1.

The type of service work in at bottom left (1) is the *service factory* where there is a high degree of standardisation and where labour intensity is low, tangibility is low, and control is externally located. To the right (2), the level of standardisation is still high, but now labour intensity and tangibility are high,

Table 1.1 Lashley's typology of service work, incorporating a marketing and an operations management approach

	Degree of intangibility, and labour intensity	
Degree of customisation	*Low*	*High*
High	(3) Service shop	(4) Professional service
Low	(1) Service factory	(2) Mass service

and control becomes internal. This type of service work is labelled '*mass services*'. Moving to (3), services are highly customised but labour intensity and tangibility are low, while control is external. This is the *service shop*. Finally, at (4), customisation is high, as are intangibility and labour intensity, with control located internally. This is the category of *professional service* work.

Although Leidner, Mills, Fitzgerald *et al.* and Lashley have all used different approaches to developing typologies of service work, there is a great deal of overlap in the resulting categories. As represented in Table 1.2, the authors have an essentially similar type of service work in mind as existing at the lower level of the hierarchy of service work. This is the work typified by the fast food worker where the product (the burger) represents an important buffer between production and consumption, between the producer and the consumer, and where there is an organisational focus on the product being delivered, rather than on the service process of the delivery of that product. This is the form of service work with the least differences from manufacturing work.

As also summarised in Table 1.2, there is also considerable overlap in the type of service work the authors see as occupying the middle level of the hierarchy of service work. Here the service process is an important part of the 'product' being delivered; the organisation has both a back-office and front-office focus; there is an important degree of intangibility. The bottom row of Table 1.2 shows the different labels that have been put to identify work at the upper end of the hierarchy of service work. An archetypal example is the work of the psychiatrist in which the service interaction *is* the product, where the focus is on the process of the interaction rather than on the back office producing a separate product.

Table 1.2 Different labels for similar types of service work

Leidner (1993)	Mills (1986)	Fitzgerald et al. (1991)	Lashley (1997)
Service where there is weak inseparability	Maintenance-interactive service work	Mass services	Service factory
Particular type of experience is part of the product	Task-interactive service work	Service shops	Mass service/ Service shops
Interaction inseparable from product	Personal-interactive service work	Professional services	Professional services

This classification of types of service work can be used to clarify the focus and potential usefulness of this book. The book's main focus is on the first two types of service work, and it will generally exclude from consideration the professional form of service work. A key point is that there has been a migration towards the middle category of service work. Herzenberg *et al.* (1998) have gone beyond the creation of categories of service work and, in a meticulous process, have also estimated the percentage of US service workers in each category. Their category of 'tightly constrained' work system closely corresponds to the Fitzgerald *et al.* 'mass services' and Lashley's 'service factory'. They estimate that only 4 per cent of US service workers can be placed in this category. Their category of 'high skill, autonomous' work system closely matches Fitzgerald *et al.* and Lashley's idea of professional services and Mills's concept of personal-interactive service work. Herzenberg *et al.* place 40 per cent of US service jobs in this category. This means that, in their estimates, 56 per cent of US service workers are located in their middle categories of 'semi-autonomous' and 'unrationalised labour-intensive' work systems. These categories map onto the middle categories of service work summarised in Table 1.2.

Competition and the context of service work

The above discussion begs questions about which factors have driven employers in their restructuring of service work. This section addresses these questions by examining the main competitive contexts of contemporary service work.

Commentators have noted that there has been a considerable intensification in competition in service industries over the last two decades. A number of writers express this in terms of a shift in power from producers to customers (Abercrombie, 1991; Hammer and Champy, 1995; Kumar, 1996, p. 12; Poynter, 1999). DuPuy (1999) makes this point in his book *The Customer's Victory*. He argues that 'we are moving from a long-standing period in which what was scarce was the product, to a period where what is scarce is the customer' (p. 38). Important service industries, such as airlines, telecommunications and financial services, were 'deregulated' in many advanced economies in the 1980s and 1990s (Katz, 1996; Regini *et al.*, 2000). Governments lifted a number of regulations that had limited the operation of market forces in these industries. Competition therefore intensified.

Even in service industries which had only been lightly regulated, and in which therefore deregulation could not have a significant effect, competition intensified, particularly because domestic economies became increasingly subject to globalisation. The pressures of globalised competition have implications for service work, involving as it does direct interaction with customers, that are rather different from those for manufacturing work. Front-line service work involves perishability, inseparability and simultaneous production and consumption. This means that such service work must be located geographically close to the customer. This constraint does not exist for manufacturing, where there is a buffer between production and consumption. In manufacturing, the forces of globalised competition can mean that production may be relocated to another country which has lower labour costs, or else may be undercut by competitor firms operating in that low-labour-cost country (Piore and Sabel, 1984; Burawoy, 1985; Klein, 2000). By contrast, the requirement for service work to be located close to customers leads Herzenberg *et al.* (1998, p. 16) to estimate that 'only about 10 per cent of the service [that is, information and customer handling] workforce holds jobs directly exposed to international competition.'

While there is, therefore, a constraint on the implications of globalised competition for front-line service work, globalisation can still have significant implications. Specifically, the rise of large multinational corporations specialising in service industries has meant that while the front-line work cannot be exported, capital and accompanying management approaches can be imported to compete against local capital and its accompanying management approaches (Segal-Horn, 1989; Goffee and Scase, 1995). A number of commentators have noted this phenomenon of internationalisation in retailing (for instance Fine, 1995; Akehurst and Alexander, 1996; Shackleton, 1998a). Poynter (1999) has argued, more generally, that the dominance of US-owned multinationals has meant that the dominant accompanying management approach has been 'the American model' of service work. Deregulation and the phenomenon of large multinationals competing with each other helps explain commentators noting both the intensification of competition in service industries and the rising levels of capital concentration in some of those same industries (for example, Fine, 1995; Poynter, 1999). The rise of multinationals has eliminated many of the smaller domestic service firms. These multinationals have undertaken more proactive and direct competitive practices than the smaller, often locale-specific, service firms had in the past. Another significant aspect in the structure of global capital has been the merging of firms across previously distinct service industry boundaries. Klein (2000) describes this process as being informed by the search for 'synergy', or systematic opportunities to cross-sell to customers.

Meanwhile, in the public sector, many governments have promoted the restructuring of important service jobs, in health care work and public welfare work for instance, by introducing (quasi) forms of competition (Pollitt, 1990; Osborne and Gaebler, 1992; Smith and Lipsky, 1993; O'Donovan and Casey, 1995; Grimshaw *et al.*, 2000; du Gay, 2000a). In the UK, for instance, Conservative governments introduced a form of internal market system within the public National Health Service, and in the USA welfare provision has involved extensive (competitive) contracting out to nonprofit organisations. Where it has not been possible to introduce forms of competition, management has sought to shift power from (state monopoly) producers to service recipients through other means. Key policies include the redefinition of the citizens who are service recipients as customers, the introduction of 'customer'-related performance measures and the 'empowerment' of these customers, particularly through the establishment of so-called citizen charters. These charters, which should more accurately be termed customer charters, set out expected service standards and establish clear and relatively open complaints procedures. In some cases, service recipients are given cash instead of services and are allowed to purchase the services that they feel suits them (Ungerson, 1999). The overall restructuring of public service work has been informed by a fundamental shift in some governments from a (production-led) role as a model employer to a (consumption-led) one as a model service provider (Heery, 1993).

So far I have outlined the intensified competition and quasi-competition experienced in service industries over the last two decades. But what is the terrain of this competition? Is it a competition of price, or of service quality? Have service firms competed by offering the cheapest and most efficient services, or have they competed by offering superior service quality? The answer is that they have had to compete at both levels *simultaneously*. As Goffee and Scase (1995) put it, the key management dilemma is to provide 'high-quality but affordable services'. 'Store wars' in retailing have been informed by both price competition and service quality competition (Fine, 1995). Heskett *et al.* (1997) have formalised these dual pressures by arguing that contemporary consumption decisions are driven by what they term the 'customer value equation', which is as follows:

$$\text{Customer value} = \frac{\text{(Tangible) results} + \text{Process quality}}{\text{Price} + \text{Customer access costs}}$$

Customers will return to do business with those service firms which offer higher 'customer value' through both lower price and higher service, or process, quality. Not only is customer perception of the service process part of the customer value equation, but it is also becoming a very important part of the equation. Lash and Urry (1994) concur, arguing that 'the quality of services has become of greater importance to people', for 'part of what is consumed is the physical and semiotic context' of the service process (p. 204). Zemke and Schaaf (1989, p. 4) note that in the

1987 Gallup Poll asked 1,045 people what makes them decide not to return to a given restaurant. Number one on the lists of reasons, identified by fully 83 per cent of the respondents, was poor service. Not food quality, not ambiance, not price. Poor service.

In the UK retailing context, du Gay notes that competition based solely on low price is giving way to competition entailing service quality (1996, p. 105). In an overview of the implications worldwide of the forces for change in the telecommunications industry, Katz (1996, p. 10) highlights the dual pressures noted here: 'pressures for costs savings, flexibility, and more customer-oriented service provision are shaping the changes occurring in work and employment relations.' Indeed, the increasing centrality of service quality in the terrain of competition has given rise to a whole set of service management literature dealing with the issue of service quality. This literature is examined in Chapter 4. The greater role of the service process within the value equation flows logically from intensified competition. In situations of weak competition, customers may have had to settle for correct and efficient service outcomes, regardless of the service process. However, with intensified competition customers can increasingly now aim to settle for correct and efficient service outcomes, with a favourable service process as well. The dual terrain of competition is important to bear in mind, for it has significant implications for the organisation of front-line service work, suggesting as it does a migration of service work (below the level of professionals) towards the middle category of service work identified in Table 1.2.

In sum, this review of the competitive context of service work has shown that many service workers are employed by large (Rothman, 1998), often multinational and multi-industry firms which compete on the basis of price and service quality, and often seek to exploit cross-selling opportunities.[2] The book traces the implications of this context for the management and experience of service work (mainly with reference to the UK, the USA and Australia).[3] The following section gives an outline of the book's structure.

Structure of the book

Here I briefly outline the structure of the book and sketch how its main arguments are related to its structure. The reader can consult the concluding chapter for a detailed summary of the main arguments.

The book is about the experience of service work, and it is about the management, particularly the human resource management, of service work.[4] Unlike many other texts focusing on HRM it does not feature separate chapters dealing with the HRM 'cycle' of selection, appraisal, development and rewards (Bratton and Gold, 1999). These areas are certainly examined in the book, but their analysis is located in the context of a wider understanding of the nature of service work. It is a central argument of the book that *it is impossible to understand HRM in service work – the policies pursued, the meaning ascribed by management and the workforce to those policies, and therefore their likely success or failure – without first understanding the nature of service work.* What is the nature of service work, how can we understand the social relations within it and what are the key forces underlying its organisation? These are the key questions that must be addressed before it is possible to see the reasons behind, and the meaning of, individual HRM practices. These questions are not trivial ones to which answers can be quickly fired off. They require careful evaluation. The book is structured to give such an evaluation, which can then also offer an adequate understanding of HRM in service work and the *systematic* contradictions within it between 'hard' and 'soft' policies, and between rhetoric and reality.

Two chapters, therefore, are devoted to examining the main existing perspectives on service work and the implications of their approaches for the content and meaning of HRM. The influential new service management school is examined in Chapter 2, with the following chapter evaluating three important critical sociological perspectives. Important weaknesses are located in each of these approaches. Chapter 4 puts forward two important ideas – the first being that service work cannot be understood without at the outset understanding the customer. With an understanding of the customer established, the chapter then puts forward the second idea, namely that the nature of service work is best understood if examined through the lens of the customer-oriented bureaucracy. Within this concept, service work is seen as structured by management aims for the customer to experience efficient service delivery and to consume the enchanting myth of sovereignty within the service interaction. Here, HRM is conceived of as having a role primarily in trying to establish a (necessarily fragile) social order that can allow the creation of profit. HRM functions at two levels. First, it promotes the necessary efficient and customer-oriented behaviour from the front-line staff. Second, it serves to cope with the inevitable ensuing tensions. If there is a meaningful cycle of HRM in service work, it exists in this (analytical) division between on the one hand the policies designed to give rise to certain behaviours from the workforce and on the other those designed to cope with the ensuing tensions. Chapter 5 illustrates these arguments by providing an overview of the management and experience of three important types of service work – hospitality work, call centre work and health care work. Chapter 6 acknowledges the limits of the concept of the customer-oriented bureaucracy in illuminating front-line work by arguing that sales work, particularly in its extreme forms, tends to be of a fundamentally different nature and requires separate analysis. There are distinct implications for HRM here also.

Chapters 7 and 8 focus in more detail on central aspects in the nature of service work – empowerment, control and emotional labour. In examining these aspects it draws out key implications for a range of HRM practices such as recruitment, culture management, stress management, appraisals, and performance-related pay. The analysis of HRM derived between Chapters 2 and 8 clearly shows that the front-line workforce cannot rely on decisions made by service management to work unambiguously to their benefit. Two chapters are therefore devoted to examining the regulation of service work, with regard to the systematic gendered segregation and disadvantage that exists in many front-line occupations, and with regard to trade union strategy, structure and ideology. The concluding chapter summarises the main arguments of the book, and looks at implications of its analysis for the wider study of HRM. It also considers the implications for overall characterisations of the service economy.

Notes

1   Although also note that there are some significant differences between advanced economies regarding the proportion of the workforce in customer contact jobs. For example, Lash and Urry (1994, p. 109) point out that in the USA and the UK the proportion of the workforce in advanced consumer services sector (that is, a sector with high customer contact) is twice the size it is in Japan and Germany where there is less individualised consumption.
2   Front-line workers, although often working for large organisations, are often located in small workplaces. See Chapter 10 for more on this.
3   The nature of service work, just like other forms of work, will clearly differ between countries according to the nature of their overall political economy. In comparisons of the political economic nature of countries, commentators often group the UK, the USA and Australia together – whether under the label of an 'Anglo-Saxon' model or (with Canada) under that of of a 'service economy model' (Castells, 1996, p. 229). Esping-Andersen (1990) is alone in putting forward an international political economic taxonomy centrally related to service work, suggesting that there are three 'worlds of welfare capitalism' which differ centrally according to the relative distribution of employment in producer services, health/education/welfare services and 'fun' services. It is not hard to place the UK, the USA and Australia together as leaning more heavily towards individualised consumer, 'fun' services than for instance, Germany and Japan. Firms in the UK, the USA and Australia also tend to have similar pressures toward 'short-termism' (Hutton, 1995) in business decisions stemming from pressures for immediate returns to financiers, and have relatively unregulated labour markets. These commonalties make it useful to concentrate the focus of this book on this group of countries. On the other hand, where appropriate, the book does also call on literature relating to other countries. As Lash and Urry (1994, p. 197) note with regard to Esping-Andersen's arguments, while there are distinctions between countries it is still the case (a) that there are significant divergences within individual countries, and (b) that, therefore, there are cases of important similarities of certain industries between different countries.

4   Debates on the definition of HRM have spawned a 'cottage industry' of academic
    writing (Bratton and Gold, 1999, p. 4). In this book, HRM is understood to mean a
    set of management practices and rhetorics concerned with managing the employ-
    ment relationship – mainly, but not exclusively, the 'employment relations'
    (Gospel, 1983) aspect of that relationship. Gospel's concept of the area of 'employ-
    ment relations' closely maps onto the practices identified in the 'cycle of HRM'
    approach (see main text and Frenkel *et al.*, 1999, p. 14), which in turn corresponds
    to the HRM practices prescribed by the new service management school (see
    Chapter 2). This is essentially a *descriptive* definition. An *analytical* approach to
    the meaning of HRM in service work is offered in Chapter 4, and is briefly
    outlined in the final section of this chapter as well.

The new service management school

Insightful analyses of general HRM theory and practice have been conducted elsewhere (Guest, 1990; Sisson, 1994; Legge, 1995; Marchington and Grugulis, 2000). Rather than revisiting these analyses and debates, this chapter focuses in on the literature concerned with HRM in front-line work. This literature has developed since the 1980s from the USA. It offers mainly a normative model of HRM in service work, proposing a model of what HRM in service work *should* be like. While there have been some small differences in emphasis between authors, taken as a whole the literature develops a very similar story line. This chapter first summarises and then evaluates the new service management literature.

The new service management school – an outline

In this section I outline the main ideas of this new service management school – the rejection of the 'old' production line approach to services, and the celebration of a set of new HRM practices, underpinned by the concept of the satisfaction mirror between customers and front-line workers. In this summary I also highlight a contingency substream of the literature, and connect the new service management school with wider management concepts and writers, such as total quality management, business process re-engineering, and Peters and Waterman.

In all of the key contributions to the new service management literature there is an emphasis on discontinuity – on the way in which contemporary approaches to HRM in service work represent a major departure from the past. The 'production line' approach to service management is the main way in which the past is described. The production line approach was most clearly articulated by Levitt, who argued that efficiency in service industries continued to lag behind efficiency in manufacturing primarily because 'we think about service in humanistic terms [but] we think of manufacturing in technocratic terms' (1972, p. 41). To rectify this, Levitt argued, it was necessary to apply clear technocratic principles to service work, to allow a substitution of 'technology and systems for people and serendipity' (1972, p. 41), through:

- the simplification of tasks;
- establishment of a clear division of labour;
- the application of technology and systems as substitutes for service workers;
- the development of tighter and more systematic control of service workers;
- the reduction of discretion in service jobs.

In this way, service work, even if it was located in relatively small, disparate and decentralised locales, could become more like factory work in manufacturing settings where there are 'centralized, carefully organized, tightly controlled and elaborately engineered conditions' (1972, p. 42). Levitt implicitly stressed the tangible outcome aspect of service jobs and downplayed aspects of intangibility.

In his 1976 follow-up article Levitt made the case that in fact many of the leading US service firms were extensively adopting the very strategies he had earlier recommended. Schlesinger and Heskett (1991a) have argued that the production-line approach to services leads to failure because its narrow, low-skilled jobs and emphasis on the use of technology leads to workers either having a poor service attitude or leaving the firm through boredom and dissatisfaction. These in turn lead to customer perception of low service quality and to a lack of customer loyalty. Profit levels fall because, as research suggests, the loyal customer is by far the most profitable form of customer to firms (Reichheld and Sasser, 1990; Reichheld, 1996).

Taking a cue from the rising importance of service quality, the new service management school argues that there is a need for a new set of HRM practices to underpin contemporary service work. A key stepping-stone in this argument is the concept of the customer satisfaction–workforce satisfaction mirror (Zemke and Schaaf, 1989; Barbee and Bott, 1991; Schneider and Bowen, 1993; Bowen and Lawler, 1995; Zeithaml and Bitner, 1996; Heskett *et al.*, 1997).

The basic idea of this mirror is simple. Customers will receive higher-quality service and will be more satisfied when the front-line workforce themselves are satisfied in their jobs. A key part of the mirror is the inter-relatedness of the satisfaction of the two parties. Customers become more satisfied because the workers' satisfaction with their job comes through in the manner in which they treat customers. Another aspect of the reflective mirror is the argument that front-line workers become more satisfied because they are able to satisfy customers. Heskett *et al.* (1997, p. 113) go so far as to suggest that 'the (in)ability to satisfy customers is the primary determinant of front-line workers' job (dis)satisfaction'. The new service management literature also makes reference to research which, it is claimed, shows the existence of this mirror in practice. This research is examined below in the evaluation section.

To foster workforce satisfaction, which can underpin customer satisfaction, the new service management writers prescribe the adoption of a range of HRM practices. As DuPuy (1999, p. 48) puts it, 'HRM [is] a necessary counterpart to the customer's victory' over the production line approach of the past. Again there is a consensus on the sort of 'cycle of capability' HRM practices that should be adopted: careful selection, high-quality training, well-designed support systems, empowerment, teamwork, appropriate measurement, rewards and recognition, and the development of a service culture.

Careful selection

The new service management writers are united in emphasising the need for service mangers to hire front-line workers on the basis of personality traits, or attitudes. Two quotations from senior managers in what Heskett *et al.* (1997, p. 116) regard as world-class service firms express this very clearly:

> It's not technical skills we're looking for, it's nice people. We can train people to do anything technical, but we can't make them nice.

> Hiring starts off looking for people with a good attitude – that's what we're looking for – people who enjoy serving other people.

This approach places little emphasis on technical skills and knowledge, but considerable emphasis on customer-related attitudes and values.

High-quality training

Given the recommended hiring criteria, it is hardly surprising that the new service management writers argue that firms should provide wide-ranging and high-quality training of technical skills and knowledge for their newly hired workforce. 'Examples of technical skills and knowledge are working with accounting systems in hotels, cash machine procedures in a retail store, underwriting procedures in an insurance company, and any operational rules the company has for running its business' (Zeithaml and Bitner, 1996, p. 316). In addition, it is recommended that firms should train their front-line workforce in the interactive skills that will lead to high customer satisfaction with service encounters. Schneider and Bowen (1995, p. 133) argue that 'newcomers are sponges which absorb whatever is thrown at them'. Consequently, it is vital for firms to direct the informal learning of the culture of the service workplace. The culture that is learned should be a customer-oriented one; it is best reproduced by putting newly hired workers in close contact with high-performing, service-oriented existing workers.

Well-designed support systems – information, facilities

Given the argument of Heskett *et al.* (1997) that the ability to satisfy customers is perhaps the primary determinant of front-line workers' job satisfaction, it is no surprise that these writers emphasise the need for well-designed support systems. Such systems of information technology (IT), and the firm's physical facilities are necessary, if not sufficient, to deliver quality service. As Zeithaml and Bitner (1996, p. 322) put it, 'without customer-focused internal support and customer-oriented systems, it is nearly impossible for employees to deliver quality service no matter how much they want to'. For many front-line jobs, information technology is likely to be a key support system. This is because, in order to gain most value from the 'moments of truth' (Carlzon, 1987) when customers contact the firm, management is likely to invest heavily in IT. IT allows the front-line worker to access very rapidly a wide range of information that may be necessary to deliver satisfaction to the customer.

Empowerment

There is a clear consensus within the new service management literature that it is important for front-line workers to be empowered in their dealings with customers. The more powerful the customer, the less dominant is the firm, and consequently the less able is it to impose narrow codes of behaviour to which the customer is expected to adhere. As DuPuy (1999, p. 56) puts it, 'the customer who has to give in to the producer is also the one who has to . . . follow a complex process of rules and procedures, running from one place to the next, all because the system was not designed for the customer's convenience, but for the bureaucrats who have certain tasks to do'. Zeithaml and Bitner (1996, p. 318) state that 'many organisations have discovered that to be truly responsive to customer needs, front-line providers need to be empowered to accommodate customer requests and to recover on the spot when things go wrong.' While there are some differences between the new service management writers over exactly what empowerment of the front-line means, two examples of empowerment in action in US service firms give an overall indicator of the concept. A central aspect of empowerment concerns the increasing discretion given to front-line workers. Zemke and Schaaf (1989, pp. 91–2) describe how American Airlines solicited a range of suggestions from their workforce which involved pushing greater responsibility out to the front-line... Flight attendants and passenger service agents now receive training in 'on the spot' problem-solving and many are empowered to make adjustments of up to several hundred dollars for American's passengers.

A corollary of this is the demise of extensive formal procedural rules and regulations: 'thus, one of the hallmarks of an empowering organisation is a relatively thin employee rule book' (Zeithaml and Bitner, 1996, p. 319). The classic example of this, quoted extensively in the new service management literature, is of Nordstrom, an up-market retail firm. The Nordstrom rule book reads: 'Rule #1: Use your good judgement in all situations. There will be no additional rules.'

Teamwork

DuPuy (1999) argues that while the production line, or bureaucratic, service firm was built on structured coordination with no meaningful lateral or vertical cooperation, the new service firm must have cooperation built into it. The greater variability of customers that is experienced at the front line has knock-on effects for the rest of the firm. The workers in the back office, that is, where there is no direct customer contact, and those in the front line can no longer interact purely on the basis of structured rules and procedures. Rather, there must be active cooperation around the shared need to deliver quality service to the customer. For some service firms this has meant breaking down old functional divisions which put front line and back-office workers separate in order to create teams of service workers dedicated to serving particular types of customers. Zeithaml and Bitner suggest that

> the effective promotion of teamwork may require restructuring around market-based groupings rather than along traditional functional lines. This means that people who impact the customer (or a particular customer segment) will work together as a team to coordinate their efforts, regardless of their functional affiliations.

Appropriate measurement, rewards and recognition

Appropriate measurement here means measurement of front-line workers' performance according to *customer*-based standards. The contrast is made between these and the internal company-based standards that should belong to the production line approach to services of the past. Customer-based standards are 'operational goals and measures based on pivotal customer-requirements that are visible and measured by customers. They are operations standards set to correspond to customer expectations and priorities rather than to company concerns such as productivity or efficiency' (Zeithaml and Bitner 1996, p. 209). New service management writers emphasise that front-line workers' performance should be measured on a range of hard and soft customer-based standards. For Heskett *et al.* (1997) this is the service version of the 'balanced scorecard' approach to performance management (Kaplan and Norton, 1993). Rewards should also be related to performance against customer-based standards. There is a debate, however, on how rewards should be linked to performance. There are strong advocates for directly linking pay to performance (Zemke and Schaaf, 1989, p. 70; Zeithaml and Bitner, 1996, p. 327), while other writers argue that a key reward should be the intrinsically satisfying nature of the job itself (Schneider and Bowen, 1995). Consensus is re-established, however, regarding the need for other frequent forms of recognition for good performance. As Zemke and Schaaf (1989, p. 75) put it,

> recognition and celebration . . . are a way of reaffirming to people, in highly human terms, that they are an important part of something that matters. They can be significant motivators for people in any organisation, but especially so in a service organisation, where pride of product is essentially pride in personal performance.

Development of a service culture

It is often 'more difficult for management to control employees in service firms' (Schneider and Bowen, 1995, p. 236). Hence, the argument that, 'if you are planning to lead a company where all members of your staff are customer-focused, you need their commitment, not their obedience' (Canning, 1999, p. 68). For the new service management writers this commitment needs to be underpinned by a service culture. For Gronroos (1990, p. 244), a service culture entails 'a culture where an appreciation for good service exists, and where giving good service to internal as well as ultimate, external customers is considered a natural way of life and one of the most important norms by everyone'. Schneider (1986) and Schneider *et al.* (1992) have conducted research into a 'passion for service' that they regard as an essential part of a service culture in a firm. The research focused on what other elements of worklife went hand in hand with a passion for service. From research in three financial service firms they found that a passion for service among the workforce was strongly linked to a positive view of the service delivery process, and to a positive view of a range of HRM practices.

In other words, the HRM and related practices within the cycle of capability from this viewpoint appear to be self-reinforcing. Well-designed support systems allied with favourable HRM practices lead to a passion for service which will lead to behaviours giving customers positive views of overall service quality. This in turn leads to higher job satisfaction for the front-line workers. And so the virtuous cycle of capability is perpetuated. A win : win : win scenario is created in the service triangle. Customers win because service firms become more responsive and adept at delivering quality service. Front-line workers win because they are provided with the support systems to do what they primarily want to do – give satisfaction to customers – and the supportive HRM practices that can underpin job satisfaction. Finally, management wins because it is able to generate further revenue from the customers whose consumption decisions are positively influenced by the experience of the encounters with the firm's front-line workers. More customers stay loyal to the firm, and the loyal customers are the most profitable stream of revenue generation.

The above summary of the new service management approach to HRM implicitly suggests that there is a universal 'one best way' to manage human resources in contemporary front-line work. There is, however, another sub-stream in the literature which advocates a contingency approach to HRM in front-line work. The idea is that different sorts of front-line work merit different sorts of HRM approaches. Bowen and Lawler (1992 and 1995) have applied the contingent HRM approach to service work specifically focusing on the empowerment dimension of HRM.[1] They argue that while the production line approach to services, with minimal empowerment, is increasingly outmoded, in certain circumstances it can still make business sense to pursue it. They argue that a production line approach makes business sense when:

- the business strategy centres on low cost and high volume production in a predictable stable market;
- the tie to the customer is transactional in nature, involving only a short-period of interaction;
- the technology is routine and simple.

The type of people best suited to successfully pursuing a production line approach are taken to be staff who have low interpersonal skills and low development aims and managers who follow 'theory X', favouring centralised and hierarchical direction and control. In other circumstances (which are becoming more and more prevalent), the empowerment approach is more appropriate. The appropriate circumstances for the empowerment approach are when:

- the business strategy centres on differentiation and personalisation in unstable, unpredictable markets;
- the tie to the customer is relational in nature, involving a long period of inter-action;
- the technology is non-routine and complex.

Bowen and Lawler argue that this empowerment approach is best suited to staff with high interpersonal skills and high development aims and managers who follow 'theory Y', favouring an approach which seeks to align and integrate the goals of the organisation and the individual. If it is the case that competition is making the production line approach less appropriate, and the empowerment approach more appropriate, then both the contingency writers and the new service management writers who stress 'one best way' would broadly agree on the form of HRM practices that should be adopted in the majority of front-line work.

Finally in this section, I turn to the connections between the new service management school and a wider management literature – notably, the work of Peters and Waterman, and of authors behind perhaps the two most important business restructuring innovations of the late twentieth century, total quality management (TQM) and business process re-engineering (BPR).

There are a number of clear overlaps between Peters and Waterman's *In Search of Excellence* (1982) approach and that of the new service management school. Both have an emphasis on the creation of shared customer-oriented cultures and values in companies, and HRM aspects advocated by service management writers echo Peter and Waterman's 'people-focus' policies. The closest overlaps, though, come when Peters and Waterman advocate that companies be 'close to the customer'. Here they parallel the new service management school by suggesting that weak companies remain locked into a bureaucratic approach of treating the customer like a 'bloody nuisance whose unpredictable behavior damages carefully made strategic plans' (p. 156). The way forward, exemplified by the chosen excellent companies, is to be 'customer-oriented', to ensure that 'customers intrude into every nook and cranny of the business' (p. 156). An important further parallel is that implicit in Peters and Waterman's argument is a win:win:win scenario. Customers win because the proximity of firms to them results in high-quality service, management win because they are able to use the information gleaned by being so close to customers in order to innovate ahead of their competitors, and workers win because greater autonomy and the opportunity to give high-quality service to customers rescue meaning for the bureaucratic 'man waiting for motivation' (p. 55).

While Peters and Waterman are traditionally seen as emphasising the soft, cultural side of management, total quality management (TQM) has been seen as encompassing a soft and a hard side, a cultural focus combined with a technical, operational side (Wilkinson *et al.*, 1998). Although the precise definition of TQM is contested, three core aspects can be drawn out – namely customer orientation, process orientation and continuous improvement – which are implemented through appropriate improvement tools, measurement systems and management and organisational processes (Hill and Wilkinson, 1995). While TQM aims to speak to management in all organisations, again there are specific parallels with the new service management school. First, there is the shared stress on customer orientation, such that within TQM it is axiomatic that quality is defined in terms of meeting customer requirements. Just as with service management writers, there is an emphasis that performance measurement must be related to customer-defined, and customer-focused, issues rather than to internal (bureaucratic) ones. Second, there is a similar (and similarly ambiguous) emphasis on 'soft' HRM practices such as empowerment and teamwork within both the TQM literature and the service management writing. Finally, there is the TQM concept of organising production as a process chain from the external customer ever inwards within the organisation. Within this process chain, every member of the organisation is linked ultimately to the final customer via a series of 'internal customers'. This casts each organisational member as equivalent to a front-line worker, for each worker is placed in a direct relationship with customers, whether external or internal.

BPR is regarded by Sennett (1998) as central to the 'new capitalism' of western, particularly Anglo-Saxon, economies. BPR is primarily associated with the work of Hammer and Champy (1995). They argue that organisations of all kinds have become trapped within bureaucratic structures which do little to meet the increasing demands of customers. Too often, they state, organisations structure work to meet their own outdated ideas of internal efficiency such that 'no one looks outward toward the customer' (1995, p. 28). To challenge this, however, comes the rise of the customer in the context of increased competition between firms.

The key implication of this for BPR advocates is the need to break down the functional departmental structures of producer-dominant bureaucracies. Work should be restructured around 'business processes', which are 'a collection of activities that takes some or more kinds of input and creates an output that is of value to the customer' (1995, p. 35). Common themes from such re-engineering include several jobs being combined into one, greater empowerment of workers, a change in work units from functional departments to process teams, jobs change from simple tasks to multi-dimensional work, and values change towards customer orientation. Again, striking parallels with the new service management school are apparent. Hammer and Champy's triumphant cry of the death of strict bureaucratic, or production line, organisation through the rise of the customer, could have been taken straight out of any number of pieces by service management writers. There are echoes too of the satisfaction mirror concept, with Hammer and Champy arguing that 'after re-engineering, work becomes more satisfying, since workers achieve a greater sense of completion, closure and accomplishment from their jobs ... They are focused on customers whose satisfaction is their aim' (1995, p. 69). The importance of customer-oriented values is present in both the BPR literature and the service management one, as is the call for the empowerment of workers. Further, the BPR emphasis on fundamental re-organisation of work around customer-focused processes clearly echoes

TQM's process and customer orientation, and can be seen as a more radical statement of the emphasis on cross-functional teamwork advocated within the new service management school.

Overall, therefore, there is a good deal of overlap between the new service management school and wider management literatures. The new service management school is a close cousin to these other management approaches, which themselves often seem to slip into each other (Wilkinson *et al.* 1998, p. 185). What is distinctive about the service writers is that they systematically seek to bring out distinctive implications (because of the direct presence of the customer) for HRM practice within front-line work.

Critical evaluation of the new service management school

This section offers a critical evaluation of the arguments outlined above. So far the new service management literature has largely escaped critical scrutiny from other writers. This section, therefore, is informed primarily by my own observations. First, I examine the *empirical* basis of the new service management school before highlighting important *conceptual* problems in its arguments.

Examining the empirical basis of the new service management school

There is an important problem in constructing an empirical critique of a prescriptive literature such as the new service management one. Because this literature points to what HRM practices should be like, it means that its proponents can argue that it is irrelevant to point to evidence showing that its HRM model is not put into widespread practice in front-line settings. They can argue that it misses the point to concentrate on outlining research into the general nature of front-line work – research which shows that:

- typically the front-line worker in the USA has been the lowest-paid and least-trained member of the organisation (Barbee and Bott, 1991);
- service firms in the USA tend to lag behind manufacturing firms in the use of involvement practices (Bowen and Lawler, 1995, p. 292);
- the recent introduction of a national minimum wage in the UK has had a major effect largely in service industries (Metcalf, 1999);
- front-line workers in the USA tend to be trapped in jobs with very few career opportunities (Herzenberg *et al.*, 1998);

- in the UK, service 'operations experience very high levels of labour turnover among lower [front-line] grades' (Willman, 1989, p. 216);
- service workers in the UK and USA often do not have a real ability to voice their interests collectively because trade union organisation is very weak in many service industries, and alternative voice mechanisms are rare (Towers, 1997; Freeman and Rogers, 1999).

The new service management writers can just sit and nod, and say that this may all be true, but it does nothing to counter our arguments. They can reply that the generally poor conditions for service workers reflect the continued production line approach which will gradually dissipate once the logic of their arguments becomes clear to service managers through education and market forces.

Despite this counter-argument, empirical evaluation is still useful in two senses. First, it is possible to examine the empirical evidence underpinning some of these writers' key concepts. Notably, the front-line-worker-satisfaction–customer-satisfaction mirror is a concept presented as having empirical research validation. It is useful to examine how robust this empirical research validation is. Second, the new service management writers call on a range of examples of 'exemplary' HRM practices in 'leading-edge' service firms. This section will examine some of their own examples to see whether they do in fact support the arguments being made.

The idea of a 'satisfaction mirror' between front-line workers and customers is an important part of the new service management arguments. First I will lay out some statements made by new service management writers regarding the research support for the concept. Then I will detail the actual evidence provided to support the concept. This will allow me then to judge whether the statements quoted are tenable.

Some very strong and important claims are made by leading service management academics regarding research support for the satisfaction mirror. Zeithaml and Bitner (1996, p. 304) state unequivocally that 'there is concrete evidence that satisfied employees make for satisfied customers'. Schlesinger and Heskett (1991b) are confident enough about the relationship to entitle an article in the influential *Harvard Business Review*, 'Employee satisfaction is rooted in customer satisfaction.' Bowen (1996, p. 34) also suggests a clear relationship between worker job satisfaction and customer satisfaction:

The spillover effect from employee attitudes to customer satisfaction invites a fresh look at the employee job satisfaction–job performance relationship (Bowen, 1990). As is well-known, meta-analyses of this relationship have established it as minimal to modest (for example, Iaffaldano and Muchinsky, 1985). However, if customer satisfaction is the measure of employee performance, its relationship to employee satisfaction tends to be stronger (see Schneider, 1991, and Schneider and Bowen, 1993, for reviews).[2]

Table 2.1 Research into relationships between customers' view of service quality and workers' perceptions of job satisfaction, related attitudes, service climate and HRM practices.

Study (all are primarily studies of correlations except Schneider et al., 1998)	Findings re relationship between customers' views of service quality and job satisfaction	Findings re relationship between customers' views of service quality and other relevant worker attitudes	Findings re relationship between customers' views of service quality and workers' views of service climate	Findings re relationship between customers' views of service quality and workers' views of some management practices (only sig findings summarised)
Parkington and Schneider (1979)	–	Workers' frustration (non-sig) Turnover intention (non-sig) Organisational satisfaction (sig–mild)	Sig–strong	–
Schneider et al. (1980) – same data set as above study[4]	Non-significant	Organisational satisfaction (non-sig with individual facets of service quality)	–	(Workers' views of) Personnel support (strong) Equipment support (strong)
Schneider and Bowen (1985)	–	Turnover intention (sig–weak, negative)	Sig–strong	Systems support (strong) Supervision, work facilitation (both mild) Career, socialisation (both weak)
Schneider and Bowen (1993)	–	–	Sig–strong	Systems support (strong) Supervision, work facilitation (both mild) Career, socialisation (both weak)

Schmidt and Alscheid (1995)	—	—	Sig–strong	Service support (weak) Monetary support (mild)
Johnson (1996)	—	—	Sig–mild	Service systems (mild) Training (mild) Reward and recognition (mild)
Ryan et al. (1996)[5]	Sig–weak (re job/company satisfaction)	Stress (sig–mild, positive)	—	Training (weak) Teamwork (weak)
Schneider et al. (1998)	—	—	'Findings support a relationship of reciprocal causality' (p.158)	Support for a model in which 'foundation issues [including work facilitation] yielded a climate for service, and climate for service in turn led to customer perceptions of service quality' (p.150)

Note: 'Sig' stands for statistically significant, that is, the finding reported would occur only by chance one in twenty or one hundred times.

This claim is echoed by Schneider (1991, p. 154):

> employee and customer perceptions are positively correlated in a wide variety of settings and industries . . . These positive relationships exist across a broad spectrum of measures taken on employees (perception of service emphasis, of HR practices, of *job satisfaction*, and of employee turnover) and measures taken on customers (customer perceptions of service quality and customer satisfaction). (Emphasis added)

There are also a number of statements made regarding correlations between customer views of quality and 'a climate for employee well-being'. Schneider and Bowen (1993) argue that their research supports the existence of a relationship between these two factors. Zeithaml and Bitner (1996, pp. 304–5) summarise the study: 'through their research . . . Benjamin Schneider and David Bowen have shown that both a climate for service and a climate for employee well-being are highly correlated with overall customer perceptions of service quality'.

These are important claims because if they are true they go some way to upholding the win : win : win potential of service work. It is vital, therefore, that the evidence on the satisfaction mirror is subject to detailed scrutiny. Table 2.1 summarises the relevant findings from the studies cited in support of the satisfaction mirror argument. There are eight main studies examining the relationship between customer perceptions and the attitudes of front-line staff.[3] The summaries highlight first any evidence reported regarding workers' job satisfaction, and then detail other relevant findings. Note that for evidence to be considered convincing, relationships should be reported consistently as statistically significant and strong.

The central point to emerge from this summary is that *the studies offer virtually no support for the argument that customers' views of service quality are positively correlated with front-line workers' job satisfaction.* Two studies report data on job satisfaction. The finding of Schneider *et al.* (1980) is that there is no significant correlation between job satisfaction and either customer views of service quality or customer views of individual facets of service quality. The absence of any report in Schneider's other studies is revealing, given the considerable emphasis in the later studies on the importance of replicating earlier studies. It is safe to assume that the absence of findings regarding job satisfaction in Schneider's later studies reflects one of two things. Either job satisfaction was measured in the studies but no findings were reported on it because there were no significant correlation findings, or Schneider and colleagues were in the position to measure job satisfaction but declined to do so because they assumed that there would be no significant findings regarding it. Neither case offers any succour to the satisfaction mirror argument. Ryan *et al.* (1996) is the only study to offer a glimmer of support for the satisfaction mirror argument. Unfortunately, the very weak correlations (0.20) found here are rather overshadowed by the stronger correlations (0.41 and 0.30) found between workers' *stress levels* and customer satisfaction. On balance, even this study offers evidence in line more with a customer satisfaction/worker stress relationship than with a satisfaction mirror.

What then about evidence in support of the argument that a climate for 'employee well-being' is positively correlated with customers' views of service quality? The Schneider and Bowen (1993) study is where this claim first originated. What do the authors mean by this concept of 'a climate for employee well-being', and how do they measure it in their study? Unfortunately, the authors fail to give a meaningful definition of the concept. Their measurement of it, however, is clear. They measure a 'climate for employee well-being' by measuring worker perception of the following HRM practices: work facilitation, supervision, organisational career facilitation, organisational status, new employee socialisation, and overall quality of HRM practices. Some of these might constitute elements of a climate for well-being, but there are some major omissions. Absent are many factors that others would place as central to a definition of a climate for worker well-being. Not least, there is no mention of pay levels, of the actual nature of the work or of job security. Without consideration of these factors any discussion of a climate for worker well-being must be invalid. Otherwise, workers could be dissatisfied with their pay levels, they could feel that their work was dehumanising and degrading, and they could feel very insecure in their work, and yet they could still potentially report a highly positive climate for well-being.[6] It is also worth noting that the data on the relationship between worker perceptions of a narrow range of HRM practices and customers' view of service quality are rather mixed. The most consistent data on this relationship relate to workers' perceptions of work facilitation, where four studies report mild or weak correlations. Heskett *et al.* try to cling to this and draw back in the idea of the satisfaction mirror. In summarising Schneider and Bowen (1993) they add their own interpretative comment in the brackets: 'Schneider and Bowen concluded that "the degree to which employees believe their work is facilitated [an expression of satisfaction] yields the most consistent information about customer satisfaction".' In making this addition in the brackets they are arguing that a worker's statement that 'I have the ability and tools to do the job' is akin to 'I am satisfied in my job'. This is plainly inadequate.

Yet without these increasingly desperate redefinitions, the new service management school is left with only the most banal of conclusions from their statistical studies. They can point out that the data support the view that workers' view of the climate for service is consistently, strongly and, perhaps, reciprocally related to customers' view of service quality. In other words, where workers perceive the firm to have a good service approach, customers tends to perceive higher service quality. This is a long way from the satisfaction mirror idea and the statements quoted earlier. Schneider *et al.* implicitly admit the distance travelled from the search for a holy grail linking workforce satisfaction and welfare with customer perceptions of service quality. They state that (1998, p. 159) :'the key to positive customer perceptions of service quality, then, may be listening to customers and creating conditions that will meet those customers' expectation and needs'. We are left with the banal insight that to achieve high service quality management should ensure work systems are geared toward that. *The implications of such work systems for the workforce are left hanging, however.*

Hand in hand with their development of a prescriptive HRM model, new service management writers also draw extensively on a range of examples from firms that are portrayed as 'leading-edge'. The earlier part of this chapter made uncritical reference to a few of these examples. Here I will turn a critical gaze on some of these examples to see how far they do support the arguments of the new service management school.

The provision of high-quality training is one of the central elements of the prescriptive HRM model. But what exactly do the new service management writers mean by 'high-quality' training? Zeithaml and Bitner (1996, p. 317) are particularly enthusiastic about the training given at Target Stores, a major US retailing firm:

> Since 1989 Target Stores . . . has used training to enhance the service orientation of its contact employees. Every time the company opens a new store, it sets up a portable 'Target University' to train new employees. One of the first things employees learn is to refer to shoppers as 'guests'. Employees also go through four hours of role playing to learn how to deal with different types of difficult customers. They learn how to 'schmooze with your guests, and compliment them on their clothing. If they're buying pet food, talk to them about their dog.'

While the title of 'Target University' may sound impressive, the details given of its curriculum suggest its practices are rather less than impressive. Readers are expected to think of high-quality training as involving a few hours of role play on awkward customers, and the development of schmoozing. Indeed, it seems that for Zeithaml and Bitner, teaching workers to ingratiate themselves with customers is a central part of high-quality training. Training at the Imperial Hotel in Tokyo, which they praise unconditionally and offer as exemplary practice, involves 'service manners training' in which workers are taught the etiquette and importance of appropriate bowing. As Zeithaml and Bitner (1996, p. 318) put it,

> because the bow is used regardless of the national origin of the guest, considerable time is spent on the intricacies of proper bowing. A bow of welcome involves a 15–degree angle, a bow of gratitude is 30 degrees, and a bow of apology is a full 45 degrees from the normal straight standing position.

Workers are taught the importance of this through training in 'guest psychology' which imparts the axiom that 'guests wish to experience an appropriate feeling of prestige or superiority, purely by virtue of their using what is commonly evaluated as a deluxe enterprise'. Given the need to make customers feel superior it is perhaps surprising that the 'straight standing position' for workers is described as 'normal'.

Zemke and Schaaf (1989) offer examples of '101 companies that profit from customer care'. In discussing the importance of imparting high-quality training to the front-line workforce they use the following example (p. 61):

> many of the companies we studied simply refuse to turn new employees loose on unsuspecting customers until a requisite amount of training has been successfully accomplished. At Land's End and L.L. Bean, two of the bright stars in catalog retailing, new customer service reps aren't allowed near a telephone until they have spent a week or more in training.

Here, we find out that the authors think that it is impressive that front-line workers receive as much as one week's training. Most observers would interpret this level of training as being very low. Further, the opening clause of the quoted two sentences informs the reader that it is only 'many' of the leading service firms that even give this derisory amount of training.

A critical reading of some of the main examples used to demonstrate high-quality training in practice leads to a questioning of whether the rhetoric used by the new service management writers actually serves to hide a very different reality even in their exemplar firms. In a moment of disarming candour, Zemke and Schaaf (1989, p. 63) confirm this impression. They state that

> fortunately, in many customer contact roles, the actual level of technical skill required to deliver satisfying service is not terribly high. The primary needs of most front-line people can be met with some very basic 'here's how we do it here' training.

In other words, high-quality training can effectively mean minimal training.

If many of the examples of high-quality training are unable to stand up to scrutiny, how far does the management writers' description of certain firms as exemplars square with other research undertaken in those same firms? Zemke and Schaaf (1989) and Zeithaml and Bitner (1996) cite Disney as a model, in a number of senses, of exemplary service management in action. Yet through participant observation research which involved considerable contact with the front-line workers, Van Maanen and Kunda (1989) and Van Maanen (1991) were able to uncover an important dark side to the Disney 'smile factory'. This dark side is important in that it appears to be a necessary and central aspect to the overall Disney approach to managing the workforce. For instance, Van Maanen (1991, p. 60) states that:

> To get a job in Disneyland and keep it means conforming to a rather exacting set of appearance rules . . . facial hair or long hair is banned for men as are aviator glasses

and earrings and women must not tease their hair, wear fancy jewelry, or apply more than a modest dab of makeup. Both men and women are to look neat and prim, keep their uniforms fresh, polish their shoes, and maintain an upbeat countenance.

Further, little discretion or empowerment is given to the workers: 'in the rare event sustained interaction with customers might be required, employees are taught to deflect potential exchanges to area supervisors or security' (p. 60). In this context, the workers at Disneyland come to describe their roles as akin to being 'line signs', 'pretty props', 'shepherds' and 'talking statues'. The troubling nature of the work as suggested by these terms informs efforts by the workforce to increase the number of rests they can have in a day:

> self-monitoring teams ... can sometimes manage a shift comprised of 15 minutes on and 45 minutes off each hour. They are envied by others and rides that have such a potential are eyed hungrily by others who feel trapped by their more rigid (and observed) circumstances. (1991, p. 63)

The newly hired workers are seen as questioning (among themselves) some of the training in customer service skills that they are given but as unable to openly raise these questions with management. Job security is low, and the public and demeaning sacking of workers for relatively trivial transgressions of rules is not uncommon. Indeed, Van Maanen (1991, p. 76) himself was a victim of such a process:

> The specific violation ... involved hair growing over my ears, an offense I had been warned about more than once before the final cut was made ... Dismissal began by being pulled off the ride after my work shift had begun by an area supervisor in full view of my cohorts. A forced march to the administration building followed where my employee card was turned over and a short statement read to me by a personnel officer as to the formal cause of termination. Security officers then walked me to the employee locker room where my work uniforms and equipment were collected ... As now an ex-ride operator, I was escorted to the parking lot where two security officers scraped off the employee parking sticker attached to my car. All these little steps of status degradation in the magic Kingdom were quite public.

Van Maanen's is not a universally negative picture of worklife at Disneyland, for he emphasises the considerable pleasure that comes from the camaraderie with fellow workers both during work hours and after. The key point is that the dark side is important and quite obvious given the appropriate research approach, but it is a dark side that does not find its way into the new service management literature, where Disney is given unreserved praise.

The case of Taco Bell, a US-based Mexican-style restaurant chain, also suggests the need to be wary of taking examples within the management literature at face value. Schlesinger and Heskett (1992) are particularly keen to offer Taco Bell as an example of the 'new model for the service firm' which makes a decisive break from the industrial approach of the past. They contrast it to the old approach typified by McDonald's, stressing how Taco Bell management has adopted sophisticated recruitment based on life themes, how they created self-directed work teams in which there is multi-skilling, and considerable discretion given to front-line staff to resolve customer problems. Bowen and Lawler (1995), however, cast doubt on the validity of this rosy picture. These authors use Taco Bell as an *exemplar of the production line approach* to service work which is contrasted with the empowerment approach. This gives us directly contrasting interpretations of the same firm offered by writers from within the new service management school. The counter interpretation offered by Bowen and Lawler cannot be shrugged off as being informed by a critical sociologist's agenda.

The possibility arises that new service management literature may be informed by a tendency to put a positive spin on examples when this is convenient. The way in which Zemke and Schaaf (1989) praise the HRM systems of Club Med strengthens this suspicion. Club Med, the holiday resort company, is praised for its recruitment processes, which are able to pick out suitably young, enthusiastic and out-going candidates. The authors praise its training and the way in which front-line workers are kept informed of customer comments and of their resort's financial situation. They even praise it for the low wages that it offers and the fact that there is high turnover of front-line staff. This is perplexing, for according to one of the axioms of the new service management school the perpetuation of systematically high turnover is a central aspect of the old 'cycle of failure'. However, Zemke and Schaaf still manage to interpret the situation positively because, 'Club Med...sees advantages in a system where front-line people pull out instead of burn out: there's a constant influx of fresh energy and a camaraderie born of people sharing a job they like to do' (p. 102). In effect, therefore, the reader is presented with a case in which wages are low, the nature of the work is likely to generate burnout, and turnover is high, but which is still presented in a positive light.

Conceptual problems

The core problem with much that is written within the new service management school is that it is underpinned by unitarist assumptions. A unitarist perspective of the workplace assumes a coincidence and harmony of interests between parties. There is no real place for or understanding of workplace conflict in this perspective and it is assumed that there is just one undisputed source of loyalty in an organisation (Fox 1966). Any perspective which suggests that there will be systematic sources of conflict at work necessarily stands at odds with unitarism. For instance, a pluralist or radical perspective would suggest that there are likely to be key potential sources of conflict between management and the workforce. This is not to say that there will be conflict over everything but it does imply that an adequate perspective must be able to consider and conceptualise sources of conflict (Edwards, 1995).

The new service management school is essentially unitarist in the way it downplays the issue of conflict, explaining away any conflict in terms of miscommunication rather than in terms of a clash of interests. The satisfaction mirror can also be analysed as an essentially unitarist concept which attempts to describe and create a situation in which there are shared interests between all three parties in front-line work – customers, workers and management.

It may appear that sustaining a unitarist perspective on front-line work should be more difficult than holding such a perspective for work on information or materials. This is because in the latter context those holding a unitarist perspective have to make a case for the natural harmony of interests between only two parties – management and workforce. In front-line work, unitarism implies the confluence of interests of three parties – management, workers and customers (Heery, 1993). Hence the need for more sophisticated unitarist devices, such as the satisfaction mirror concept, which erect a smoke-screen so that observers are meant to see only a harmony of interests. Within the satisfaction mirror concept, given the prevailing market imperatives of service quality, antagonism and conflict between any of the three parties arises essentially through miscommunication, rather than through a clash of interests. There will be tension and frustration for both customers and workers when the workers are unable to deliver high-quality service. Indeed, Heskett *et al.* see this as the number one source of frustration for front-line workers. Customers will be frustrated and antagonised, acting on their discontent through either voice (complaints direct to workers, or to management) or exit (moving their custom to another firm). But this tension essentially comes about because the firm's management is failing to properly 'listen to the customer' (Zemke and Schaaf 1989; Zeithaml and Bitner 1996; Heskett *et al.* 1997). It is a failure of miscommunication. And it is a failure that can be rectified with the appropriate management tools of customer focus groups and surveys to see what sort of service customers really want. Further note that, here, the market (signalled through customers exiting) creates a self-correcting system. Through customers exiting, management realises that it needs to listen more to the customer. It acts on this improved communication by redesigning their services and service delivery mechanisms in ways which allow front-line workers to be able to give high-quality service to customers. This leads to satisfied customers, workers and management. Conflicts and tension are solved entirely through appropriate communication prompted by signals sent by the market. In addition, front-line workers can aid this system of communication by channelling back to management voices of discontent that they pick up from their direct interactions with customers. Hence, in the new service management literature there are repeated exhortations regarding the need for management to listen to the voice of the front-line worker. As will be explored in more detail in Chapter 7, this is not an elevation of the voice of front-line workers *per se* within the organisation. Rather, it is an elevation of a proxy of the customers' voice.

The natural, self-correcting position implied by the satisfaction mirror concept, then, is one of win : win : win, a confluence of interests of the three parties. The *surface* brilliance of the satisfaction mirror concept is that it interprets the presence of the third party, the customer, not as an extra level of complexity in forging a harmony of interests. Rather, *the customer becomes the focus around which the interests of management and workers naturally coalesce.* Management and customer interests are equated, because if customers are satisfied they will tend to be loyal to the firm, and loyal customers tend to generate the most profitable revenue streams. The rather more difficult aspect comes in creating an artifice through which worker and customer interests are equated. The satisfaction mirror is just such an artifice. Here, if the customer is satisfied the worker will tend to be satisfied. As long as management is able to apply sophisticated recruitment techniques in selecting workers with the appropriate service attitudes, this should flow naturally. Those with high customer empathy and customer service attitudes will feel more satisfied in their jobs if they are able to deliver high-quality service to customers. As noted above, however, the research data show no support for a relationship between workers' job satisfaction and customers' satisfaction with service quality.

It is not difficult to understand this finding. The satisfaction mirror is conceptually weak because it implicitly assumes that the predominant interest of the (appropriately selected) front-line worker is to satisfy customers. This is a fundamentally inadequate assumption. It may be reasonable to argue that one of the important interests of workers, presocialised in customer empathy, would be to satisfy customers, but it is not reasonable to state, as Schlesinger and Heskett (1991b) do, that 'employee satisfaction is rooted in customer satisfaction'. While it is difficult to talk abstractly about the interests of workers, a body of various social theories and research suggests that workers' satisfaction is often informed by the nature of the work (whether it is skilled and challenging, and allows autonomy in decision-making), by economic factors such as pay levels and job security, and by the nature of the social relations at work (how workers relate with their fellow workers and with customers, for instance). The relative importance of these factors will vary according to specific contexts of the worker, such as the labour market, and family positions. The nature of the interests will also vary according to the institutions which allow their articulation. But what is clear is that conceptually they are factors that have to be taken into account when making broad statements about worker satisfaction. They are factors which are not taken into account within the idea that satisfied customers will lead to satisfied front-line workers.

Conclusion

The first part of this chapter summarised the main arguments of the new service management school. This literature stresses that contemporary HRM in front-line work should depart from the production line approach of the past. Underpinning the suggested HRM approach is the concept of the satisfaction mirror between customers and front-line workers. Front-line workers are more satisfied in their jobs when they are able to satisfy customers, and customers are more likely to receive high-quality service if the front-line workers are satisfied in their jobs. The new service management writers advocate the adoption of a set of HRM-related activities to inform a 'cycle of capability': careful selection, high-quality training, well-designed support systems, empowerment, teamwork, appropriate measurement and rewards, and the overall development of a service culture.

This new service management literature is an important one. There is good reason to believe that it informs service managers' actions and attitudes. It is, therefore, vital to have a critical evaluation of it. In a number of ways the new service management literature has been found wanting. Empirically, attention was paid to research which is presented as providing 'concrete evidence' of and 'confirming' the key concept of the satisfaction mirror. In fact, research evidence offers virtually no support for the concept. Because their arguments are prescriptive, new service management writers can effectively claim immunity from the mountain of evidence which shows systematic low wages, low training, restricted career paths and high turnover in many service industries. However, the chapter was able to scrutinise their use of examples from their self-designated exemplary firms. A number of important examples were shown to be unable to stand up to close scrutiny. Conceptually, the new service management school was shown to be underpinned by a unitarist perspective, with all its associated weaknesses. The relationship between customers, workers and management is portrayed as harmonious and self-correcting. Short-term problems may arise, but only through problems of communication rather than through clashes of interests between the parties. In the satisfaction mirror concept the customer becomes the focus around which the interests of front-line workers and management coalesce. The satisfaction mirror was shown to be fundamentally conceptually flawed, however.

Notes

1   See also Willman (1989) and Lashley (1997) for a contingency approach to HRM in service work.

2   Important claims are made for the secondary review of evidence in Schneider (1991) and Schneider and Bowen (1993) – claims that the articles are unable to uphold. Neither article provides the 'review' on links between job satisfaction and customer satisfaction to which Bowen refers.

3   Only studies which have passed through rigorous academic refereeing are reported. Thus, for instance, the studies of a less rigorous nature contained within a special issue of *Human Resource Planning* (Ulrich *et al.*, 1991; Tornow and Wiley, 1991; Wiley, 1991; Paradise-Tornow, 1991; Schlesinger and Zornitsky, 1991) are excluded from consideration. This matches the approach adopted within the rigorous studies discussed in the text.

4   Because the same data set is used for both of these studies, findings are only reported once in the table.

5   In this study the relevant customer variable is 'customer satisfaction' rather than customer perception of service quality.

6   Indeed, rather shooting themselves in the feet, Schneider et al. (1980) suggest that job satisfaction may be relatively unaffected by the sort of HRM practices that Schneider and Bowen include in their studies. In seeking to explain how workers' job satisfaction is not correlated with customers' perceptions of service quality, they write that 'the lack of significant correlations between employee feelings of satisfaction and customer perceptions of service suggests that employees were able to distinguish meaningfully their descriptions of branch practices and pro-cedures from their feelings of satisfaction. Internal analyses of the employee scale intercorrelations revealed this separation for job satisfaction, clearly showing its general independence from the more descriptive perceptions' (p. 265). That is to say, there was little connection between job satisfaction and the HRM factors included in the Schneider *et al.* (1980) study.

CHAPTER 3

Critical perspectives on service work

The new service management school's analysis of service work may have fallen down under scrutiny, but can the critical literature on service work offer a more illuminating conceptual approach to chime with existing research evidence? In this chapter I am concerned with examining recent contributions which offer a critical, distinct and broad overview of the management and experience of contemporary service work, especially of front-line work.[1] I examine, in turn, George Ritzer's McDonaldisation thesis, du Gay's work on consumption and identity at work, and feminist analyses which emphasise the gender-based servility in contemporary service work.

Ritzer and the McDonaldisation thesis

George Ritzer's McDonaldisation thesis (1996, 1998, 1999b; Ritzer and Stillman, 2001) updates the work of the famous German sociologist, Max Weber (1921/1978) on the rise of rationality and the bureaucratic organisation in western societies. While in everyday parlance the term bureaucracy is often used in a pejorative sense to denote the existence of 'red tape', Weber used the term in a different, analytical sense. For instance, Levitt's (1972) call for the production line approach to services could be seen as a call for the bureaucratisation of service work. Weber argued that a bureaucracy was an organisation underpinned by the logic of *formal rationality*. Formal rationality involves a prioritisation of creating the most efficient means to achieve an end. Ritzer argues that the increasing pervasiveness of formal rationality, or the process of *rationalisation*, can best be conceptualised in terms of McDonaldisation. He sees McDonald's as a clear and easily recognisable manifestation of how far rationalisation has gone in contemporary societies. McDonald's epitomises the process of McDonaldisation, but this process applies to many spheres of life other than just a particular fast food chain.

For Ritzer, McDonaldisation involves four main dimensions – efficiency, calculability, predictability and control. Efficiency is understood in terms of 'the optimum method of getting from one point to another' (1996, p. 9). Ritzer often stresses that calculability means an emphasis on the quantitative aspect of work and products, so that 'quantity has become equivalent to quality' (1996, p. 9). While this may be one manifestation of calculability, the wider concept applies to an emphasis on counting, calculating and measuring phenomena (1996, p. 59). The idea is that only if an organisation can measure something can it increase efficiency. For the third dimension, Ritzer argues that 'rationalization involves the increasing effort to ensure predictability from one time or place to another. A rationalized society therefore emphasizes such things as discipline, order, systematization, formalization, routine, consistency and methodical operation' (1996, p. 79). If something is to be done efficiently and repeatedly, the process involved must be predictable. The final dimension of McDonaldisation is control. Although Ritzer never explicitly defines what he means by the concept, implicitly it involves the ability of one party to determine an overall process. Here, he also stresses the importance of control achieved through the substitution of non-human technology for human technology. Whereas 'a human technology (a screwdriver, for example) is controlled by people, a non-human technology (the assembly line, for instance) controls people' (1996, p. 11).

Ritzer argues that there is a general McDonaldisation of society. His is not an argument restricted to service work, which is the key focus of this book. However, given that his paradigmatic case, McDonald's, 'to which the argument continually returns' (Smart, 1999, p. 8), is a service firm it seems fair to assume that his arguments should have particular resonance within service work. Indeed, Ritzer (1998, p. 60) argues that 'the process of McDonaldization is leading to the creation of more and more McJobs. The service sector, especially at its lower end, is producing an enormous number of jobs, most of them requiring little or no skill'. He also notes that the 'service worker...has come to dominate McDonaldized systems' (1998, p. 63). In the general sphere of work, Ritzer argues that McDonaldisation leads to the worker becoming akin to 'a mechanical nut' (1996, p. 139), and a 'human robot' (1998, p. 60). There are also distinctive aspects to the control of service workers in McDonaldised jobs. Not only are front-line workers' actions controlled, but also their words are controlled through the imposition of scripts to which they are expected to adhere when interacting with customers. Ritzer argues that 'the scripting of interaction leads to new depths in the deskilling of workers. Not only have employee actions been deskilled; employees' ability to speak and interact with customers is now being limited and controlled' (1998, p. 64). Ritzer also calls on Hochschild's (1983) arguments concerning management control of emotional labour from service workers to assert that 'what we have here is a series of unprecedented efforts to control employees. It is not simply what people do and say on the job that many organizations now seek to control, but also how they view themselves and how they feel' (1998, p. 64). In McDonaldised jobs the emphasis on efficiency means that workers tend to be treated as robots to be controlled and as costs to be minimised. In the paradigmatic case of Ritzer's thesis, McDonald's has systematically paid low wages, given little training or job security and gone to great lengths to avoid the unionisation of its staff (Vidal, 1998; Royle, 2000). Ritzer argues that although these McDonaldised jobs are highly dehumanising the rebellion or resistance of workers against them tends to be low, because 'if most of one's life is spent in McDonaldized systems, then there is little or no basis for rebellion against one's McDonaldized job since one lacks a standard against which to compare and judge, such a job' (1998, p. 67).

Ritzer's work has been widely read, leading to some of the highest sales for a sociology book ever achieved. Given this and his wide-ranging arguments, there can be little surprise that it has received considerable attention in the academic literature. Some writers seek to extend and apply his ideas (Bryman, 1995) while others are more critical of his approach (Alfino *et al.*, 1998; Wood 1998; Smart, 1999). I will weave criticisms particularly relevant to service work within my own critical discussion of his arguments with specific reference to service work. Following the pattern set in the previous chapter's evaluation of the new service management school, it is useful to consider empirical and conceptual criticisms.

Before constructing an empirical, evidence-based critique of an argument it is important to be clear on the type of empirical claims made within the argument. On this point, there is a good degree of ambiguity in Ritzer's work. As is suggested in the title of his major book, his thesis suggests the encroaching McDonaldisation of society as a whole. The front cover of the book depicts the globe as a squashed filling within a McDonald's bread bun. The message is clear: the world is becoming a McWorld. Within this book the reader is frequently confronted with sentences suggesting that McDonaldisation is a pervasive force in contemporary societies. For instance, he writes, 'much of the world has been McDonaldized' (1996, p. 15). However, in his subsequent (1998) writing which focuses specifically on the McDonaldisation of service work, Ritzer tempers down his claims considerably. Here Ritzer begins entering large caveats to his earlier arguments. He writes that 'the McDonaldization of a significant portion of the labor force does not mean that all, or even most, of the labor force is undergoing this process' (1998, p. 68). So, overall in his work, Ritzer puts forward rather different empirical claims – from the extreme claim of a global McDonaldisation of society to a more tempered claim that McDonaldised jobs comprise a 'significant portion' of the labour force which may or may not equate to a majority of the labour force. In empirically assessing his arguments I will take the more tempered claim as his position.

The first point to note is that Ritzer fails to cite wider evidence to back up his assertion that a significant portion of the labour force hold McDonaldised jobs. In the introductory chapter to his 1998 book extending his McDonaldisation ideas, Ritzer offers the following as a justification for such a gap:

> what is clearly missing to even the most casual observer is a series of citations of social scientific research on the topics dealt with in these pages. That is not because I bear some animus in relation to such work, but rather because there is little or no 'scientific' research into the topics being dealt with here (1998, p. 13).

To put it bluntly, this justification is inadequate. There *is* a great deal of research data on the nature of jobs in societies. This book, for instance, contains multiple references to books and papers pertaining to the nature of service work. The best recent source of directly relevant evidence on the nature of service jobs in the USA is provided by Herzenberg *et al.* (1998). They undertook a two-stage approach to compiling an overview of the nature of service jobs. Firstly, they carried out or commissioned a range of case-studies of particularly common types of service work. This allowed them to create a taxonomy, or a map, of what they saw as the four main types of service work. One of the categories of service work, which they call the *tightly constrained work system*, encompasses the very dimensions of McDonaldised jobs that Ritzer writes about. In the tightly constrained work system, jobs are narrowly defined, there are low skills and production is paced by technology or customers. Typical jobs here are phone operators, fast-food workers and cheque proofers. They work in organisations which operate in high-volume, low-cost markets, where quality is standardised. The second stage of Herzenberg *et al.*'s research was to go through comprehensive job lists for US service industries and to allocate the entire labour force to one of the four categories they identified. From this process they concluded that around 4 per cent of service jobs in the USA could be legitimately characterised as operating within a tightly constrained work system. In other words, only 4 per cent of service jobs share the characteristics of what Ritzer regards as McDonaldised jobs. McDonaldised jobs do not comprise a 'significant portion' of the service labour force.

This leads the discussion on to an examination of the conceptual problems in Ritzer's thesis regarding service work. A key problem, as Smart (1999) notes, is that it is unclear what forces drive rationalisation. Although Ritzer (1998, ch. 5) later attempted to clarify this by stressing the key role of capitalists' pursuit of profit in McDonaldisation, the problem remains regarding his understanding of how capitalists pursue profit. As has been widely rehearsed in discussions of Fordism and post-Fordism in manufacturing industries, rationalisation and Taylorism are *not* the sole necessary outcomes of capitalists pursuing profits (Piore and Sabel, 1984; Berggren, 1993). Analysis must take into account the specific competitive terrain in which the firms are operating. Chapter one laid out contemporary evidence from a range of service industries showing that service firms compete not only by price and/or cost but also by service quality. Unfortunately, the key service quality dynamic of contemporary service work is completely ignored by Ritzer. Ritzer is as unsatisfactorily one-eyed in his focus on the bureaucratic logic that flows from price competition as the new service management school is in its focus on the logic of the customer and service quality. Perhaps the most important sleight of hand in the construction of the McDonaldisation thesis is Ritzer's discussion of the dimension of calculability, in which he states that 'quantity has become equivalent to quality' (1996, p. 9). This statement is brazenly not true. It may be that (and it is, as the next chapter shows) management is very concerned with measuring service quality, often trying to quantify it, but this is to say that *quantification is part of management measuring quality*. This is very different from saying that quantity and quality are *equivalents*.

Ritzer's perverse logic is seen in practice when, discussing calculability, he argues that

> the performance of fast-food restaurants is also assessed quantitatively, *not qualitatively*. At McDonald's, for example, central management judges the performance of each restaurant 'by the numbers: by sales per crew person, profits, turnover, and QSC [*Quality*, *Service*, *Cleanliness*] ratings' (1996, p. 64) (emphasis added, square brackets in original).[2]

So, despite Ritzer's prefacing sentence, the reader sees that, even at McDonald's, the most McDonaldised of service firms, service and quality are important factors for management. Just because central management wants a quantification of these factors does not mean that somehow quantity and quality have become equivalents. A more accurate statement is that performance at McDonald's is measured quantitatively *and* qualitatively, albeit, in the specific case of McDonald's, with a greater emphasis on the quantitative aspect. Rather than assuming away service quality, analysis needs to take into account the implications of its important role in the competitive terrain.

Another important weakness of Ritzer's thesis is the tendency within it to reduce both workers and customers to mere automatons in the face of the structural dynamic of McDonaldisation. As Wood (1998) notes, this criticism is exactly the central criticism made of Braverman's (1974) all-embracing thesis of the deskilling dynamic of monopoly capitalism (Friedman, 1977; Burawoy, 1979; Thompson, 1984). The analogy between workers in McDonaldised jobs and robots is made more than once by Ritzer (1996, p. 25; 1998, p. 60), and Ritzer cites approvingly Shelton's (no date) argument that

McDonald's has in effect 'succeeded in automating the customer' (1996, p. 154). It seems that this language, which implies negligible space for the will and/or agency of individuals, is not accidental, for Ritzer (1998, p. 67) explicitly states that he sees little desire for resistance from workers in McJobs:

> There is little or no basis for rebellion against one's McDonaldized job ... To Braverman (and Marx), there is a creative core (Marx's species being, for instance) lying just below the surface that is ever-ready to protest, or rebel against, the rationalized and exploitative character of work. However, can the creative core survive intact, or even at all, in the face of growing up in a McDonaldized world, being bombarded by media messages from McDonaldized systems, and being socialized by and educated in McDonaldized schools?

This Orwellian vision of the total dominance of McDonaldisation is deeply flawed. Even within Ritzer's own logic, how far can it be true to state that people grow up 'in a McDonaldized world' when, by his own (incorrect) admission perhaps less than a half of jobs are McDonaldised? Even within his own flawed logic and flawed empirical estimates, then, there are substantial alternative spheres of social life in which at least an implicit contestation of the principles of McDonaldisation can lurk. But in reality the reader need look no further than Ritzer's paradigmatic case, McDonald's, to see very clear evidence of substantial resistance of service workers. Ritzer himself notes that at McDonald's, 'there is a high turnover rate: only slightly more than half the employees remain on the job for a year or more' (1998, p. 59). While there can be many causes of individual cases of turnover, when year in, year out, workers systematically leave a firm within a few months, only someone with an assumption of the totalising power of McDonaldisation can fail to interpret such turnover as a form of substantial resistance to McDonald's (and hence McDonaldised) jobs.[3]

These empirical and conceptual criticisms of Ritzer's arguments strike at the most fundamental aspects of his thesis. Despite its weaknesses, however, Ritzer's work can also be read as an important reminder of the potential continuities with the bureaucratic, production line approach to service work. The criticisms of Ritzer have not suggested that the bureaucratic logic is not still a very important one in large sections of service work – rather, they have taken issue with Ritzer's one-eyed focus on this bureaucratic logic. A more adequate understanding of the management and experience of service work must be informed not only by analysis of this bureaucratic logic but also by an analysis of the logic of service quality and the customer highlighted by the new service management school. I seek to develop such an understanding in the following chapter's discussion of the customer-oriented bureaucracy. Before this, however, I will consider other important critical approaches to contemporary service work.

Du Gay – consumption and identity at work

Du Gay has constructed an argument that the 'cult(ure) of the customer' (du Gay and Salaman, 1992) is invading the organisation of much of contemporary work. In this sense, du Gay is actually making an argument concerning the nature of all work, not just service work. He is suggesting that 'the language of the sovereign customer is increasingly embedded in a wide-ranging series of organisational structures, practices and technologies' (du Gay and Salaman, 1992, p. 622). Quoting Peters (1987) and Peters and Waterman (1982), he argues that the customer is increasingly being used as a key source of legitimacy within organisations. Management actions are justified in terms of following the dictates of the sovereign consumer, and the restructuring of work is justified as necessary to give service to customers. This spells the end for bureaucratic work organisation, with its emphasis on stable organisations with members following standard policies and procedures. Within total quality management and just-in-time production systems, increasingly, internal relations within firms are reconceptualised as customer relations. A colleague in another department becomes an internal customer.

Having elsewhere constructed this argument as applicable to all forms of work, in his book *Consumption and Identity at Work* (1996) du Gay implicitly argues (p. 5) that these factors will be more keenly felt and observed in service work. He follows Urry's (1990) argument that the blurring of production and consumption in service work means that in this context there is a greater possibility for an emergence of a new form of identity at work. He argues that it is necessary to move away from ideas that work identity stems from roles within work. Rather *it is necessary to see the connections between consumption and production for identity at work*. He sees this connection as lying in the concept of the 'enterprising self' which has come to be pervasive in the spheres of both consumption and production. The service worker is called on to be enterprising in meeting changing customers' demands, and the customers themselves are seen as enterprising. Within the dominant ideology of the enterprising self, 'the employee, just as much as the sovereign consumer, is represented as an individual in search of meaning and fulfilment, looking to "add value" in every sphere of existence' (du Gay and Salaman, 1992, p. 627). Thus the identity of the customer and the worker come to resemble each other because both are based on the enterprising self. In his book du Gay attempts to show these factors at work in the UK retail sector, suggesting that there has been a breakdown in the previous bureaucratic ways of organising retail work, and a rise in identities at work based on the idea of the enterprising self underpinned by the concept of consumer sovereignty.

Du Gay offers some potentially important insights into the structure and experience of service work. He suggests that the customer increasingly becomes a key source of legitimacy in service organisations – it becomes increasingly difficult to even find the language to contest an action which is justified in terms of it helping to serve the customer. This point is explored more fully in the discussion of the customer-oriented bureaucracy in Chapter 4. It is also a considerable strength that du Gay opens up the debate on work identities to allow a consideration of how people's identities as consumers and producers may be linked. However, there are important problems in the specific way that he attempts to link them. He quotes Bauman approvingly to the effect that in a market economy people's identities will be constructed primarily in terms of consumption (1996, p. 76), but does not follow through this logic to suggest how management could seek to use service workers' identities as consumers in the reorganisation of service work. This is a more useful avenue to go down in exploring the links between production and consumption identities, but one which is spurned by du Gay.

Rather, he prefers to see the link enacted through both consumption and production being colonised by the concept of the enterprising self. Unfortunately, this concept of the enterprising self is unhelpful in a number of senses. Crucially, it is a concept with little empirical underpinning. In his study of identity in the UK retailing industry, du Gay calls on data from only nine interviews with front-line workers (and rather more with managers). Even within this small sample he is unable to paint a convincing picture of the enterprising self colonising people's identity both as consumer and workers. Second, he uses the enterprising self concept in such elastic ways that it tends to lose any analytical purchase.[4] By contrast, Legge (1995), calling on Keat (1991) and Fairlcough (1991), provides a much more accomplished and precise analysis of the rise of the discourse of enterprise in the UK. She argues that enterprise has two key meanings. It can convey the meaning of a noun – 'the commercial enterprise' – as well as that of a verb – to be 'enterprising' by taking risks and showing initiative. The simple point she makes is that 'in the UK in the 1980s, the government attempted to equate these meanings' (p. 81) particularly in terms of how people should think about their work, and the identity they should forge at work. Legge makes no attempt to relate the concept of the enterprising self to consumption. This is because the discourse of the enterprising self is one that resides primarily in the sphere of production. In the sense of everyday understandings the language of enterprise is understood only in production. If a manager asks workers to be more enterprising in the future, the worker would understand that they are being asked to be more proactive, agile, even bold and risk-taking. If consumers are asked to be more enterprising this is likely to simply cause confusion. What does it mean for a consumer to be enterprising?[5] No help is offered by du Gay to answer this question. Even within Gabriel and Lang's (1995) masterful overview of consumption and its interpretations the imagery of the enterprising consumer is conspicuous by its absence. The concept of the enterprising self does not speak to the experience of consumption and customers. Therefore, although du Gay professes to be strongly opposed to the assumption that identities are formed primarily within the sphere of production, his argument repeats this same mistake. Identities, in both consumption and production, are framed around the enterprising self, but enterprise is a production-based concept. It is no accident that du Gay is unable to call on empirical evidence of consumers thinking of themselves in enterprising terms.

A final important weakness in du Gay's approach is that his focus on the issues of enterprise and the enterprising self leads him at times to suggest that bureaucratic structures of work have been resolutely swept away. Appearing to take Peters and Waterman at their anti-bureaucratic word, he mirrors the new service management school's assumptions that the rationalising approach to service work has had its day. Unlike the new service management school, however, he sees bureaucracy being replaced, not by new HRM and management practices, but by market relations. For instance, he argues that 'a fundamental aspect of managerial attempts to achieve this reconstruction involves the re-imagination of the organisation. Frequently this means *the supplanting of bureaucratic principles by market relations*' (du Gay and Salaman, 1992, p. 616) (emphasis added). Du Gay is inaccurate on two counts here. First, the terrain of price competition means that the rationalising imperative in the organisation of service work has not disappeared. Second, the reorganisation that has occurred in service work has not been one based on the imposition of market relations within organisations. Service workers continue to work, mostly, for large firms in direct, hierarchical employment relationships that are *not* analogous to market relations.[6] It is to the terrain of competition around service quality that we must look to see what is new in service work.

Feminist analyses – service or servility?

Unlike the other critical perspectives reviewed in this chapter the feminist analysis of service work does not have one dominant writer advancing the perspective. However, by drawing on a number of writers it is possible to construct a relatively coherent body of feminist and related work which offers some important and distinctive insights into the management and experience of front-line work. A key contribution of wider feminist analyses of work is the way in which apparently gender-neutral terms and practices at work have been deconstructed to show the existence of important hidden gender-based subtexts (Cockburn, 1985; Phillips and Taylor, 1986; Steinberg, 1990; Witz, 1992).

Of particular relevance to the debates concerning contemporary front-line work has been the argument that bureaucratic organisations although appearing gender-neutral are centrally informed by gendered sub-texts in which women are systematically placed at a disadvantage (Ferguson, 1984; Pringle, 1989; Acker, 1990; Savage and Witz, 1992; Putnam and Mumby, 1993; Halford *et al.*, 1997). For instance, Acker argues that it is no accident that bureaucratic structures and values are much closer to men's lives and assumptions made about men (for example, men as rational, with a primary commitment in the sphere of work) than they are to women's lives and assumptions made about women (for example, women as emotional, with a primary commitment to the domestic sphere). A central emerging conclusion taken from the literature on service work examined so far has been that the logic of the customer has come to join the bureaucratic logic as a key principle in the organisation of service work. To the extent that the bureaucratic logic is no longer predominant in front-line work, it may therefore suggest the potential for the position of women in front-line work to be improved. Whether this potential will be fulfilled is put into question, however, by writers who argue that the stratification of the service workforce by gender and race is particularly prevalent *because of* the interface with the customer. For instance, Mac-Donald and Sirianni (1996, p. 13) argue that:

> Women, youth, and minorities comprise the bulk of the part-time and contingent work force in the service sector. For example, Karen Brodkin Sacks (1990) has noted that the health care industry is 'so stratified by race and gender that the uniforms worn to distinguish the jobs and statuses of health care workers are largely redundant ' (p. 188). Patients respond to the signals implicitly transmitted via gender and race and act accordingly, offering deference to some workers and expecting it from others.

Here, the attitudes and behaviours of the patients do not just reflect but also reinforce the disadvantage of women and ethnic minorities in front-line work. Indeed, a stronger argument has been put forward that attitudes and behaviour of customers (or at least management's interpretation of these) can be seen as a primary enforcer, rather than just reinforcer, of women's disadvantage in front-line work. This is certainly suggested by the actions of the airline PanAmerican in the 1970s as described by Nielsen (1982). Up until the 1970s airlines in the USA were able to systematically discriminate against flight attendants, 'on the bases of sex, marital status, and age' (p. 81). ' "Use them till their smiles wear out; then get a new bunch" was the policy that had been put into effect by the airlines' (p. 81). However, in the 1970s unions claimed that these practices were illegal. PanAmerican in turn fought against this. They argued their discriminatory practices were legitimate because the overall performance of females in the job of flight attendant was superior to that of males. To back this up they submitted a survey which they claim indicated that there was a clear 'passenger preference' for stewardesses, and they offered testimony from a psychiatrist and psychologists to support their arguments.[7] The psychiatrist argued that male passengers (who made up the majority of passengers) 'would generally feel more masculine and thus more at ease in the presence of a young female attendant' (Nielsen, 1982, p. 97).

A more subtle form of enforcement of female disadvantage in front-line work due to customer attitudes and behaviour was reported by Filby (1992) who undertook observational research in three betting shops in the UK. Filby found that the upskilling of the female front-line workers through training in product knowledge foundered because in part product (betting) knowledge was seen by male customers as a foreign domain for the female staff (also see Lawson, 1996). Male customers preferred to interact with female front-line staff in a way in which female submissive sexuality was frequently brought into play. If the women possessed superior technical, product knowledge this would undermine male customers' use of submissive female sexuality. Filby argues that such a process is likely to be common in many front-line settings: 'it seems likely that the development of services, particularly focused around leisure as well as the established areas of sales, catering, clubs and pubs (Hey, 1986) offers scope for working environments in which sexuality plays a prominent part . . . In many services . . . gender constructions are part of the total package which constitutes the product' (p. 37). In other words, for certain types of service work expectations of submissiveness and deference from female front-line staff systematically inform customer perceptions of service quality (Paules, 1991; Wood, 1992).

Indeed, PanAmerican's argument that male passengers feel more masculine and therefore more at ease in the presence of a female flight attendant is a clear example of a gendered definition of service quality. Further, management is likely to take a gendered definition of service quality as given and will adopt HRM practices with the aim of achieving high service quality. Thus, management will tend to hire women staff into low-status front-line jobs in which customers expect deference as part of service quality. Further, training may be significantly gendered, with the content of customer service skills training sessions likely to differ subtly but significantly according to the gender composition of the group to be trained. The overall gendered process becomes pervasive and circular. MacDonald and Sirianni (1996, p. 15) argue that service 'occupations are so stratified that worker characteristics such as race and gender determine not only who is considered desirable or even eligible to fill certain jobs, but also who will want to fill certain jobs and how the job itself is performed'. In addition, how a front-line job is experienced will be centrally informed by gender (Benson, 1986). Whyte (1946) found that male front-line workers in jobs of low status were more likely to experience stress than were female staff who had experienced greater socialisation into accepting roles of deference and low status (also see Shamir, 1980). Hochschild (1983) for flight attendants, Cockburn (1985) for radiologists, Williams (1989) for nurses, LaPointe (1992) for restaurant workers, and Spradley and Mann (1975) for cocktail-serving all argue that the nature and experience of front-line work is very different for a woman than for a man.

Individually, these are important points and are developed sympathetically in the systematic examination of gendered segregation and disadvantage in front-line work in Chapter 9. However, added together, these points may be interpreted as suggesting that the service society should be deconstructed as *the servile society* (MacDonald and Sirianni, 1996; Guerrier and Adib, 1999), in which women may be less dominated by a masculine bureaucracy only to assume front-line roles demanding servility and deference, in which this servility is deeply gendered.[8] For instance, Hall (1993) argues that restaurants which promote a gendered-waitressing (as opposed to waitering) way of working in effect promote and legitimate a 'gendered image of a deferential servant' (p. 456). This has particular disadvantages for women restaurant workers who must 'learn to "humble" themselves each time they approach a table of customers' (Elder and Rolens, 1985, quoted in Hall, 1993, p. 456). *While there are significant merits in many of the individual points derived from feminist analysis, this overarching characterisation of service work as servile work is misplaced.* The most fundamental problem goes to the heart of the limitations of feminist analyses of work. The key strength of feminist analysis lies in its ability to deconstruct apparently gender-neutral concepts and practices. However, on its own it is unable to provide an adequate understanding of the political economy of capitalism in the context of contemporary front-line work. A characterisation of the service society as the servile society betrays a weak wider political economic understanding because it in effect ignores the continuing importance of the bureaucratic logic in service work. The key point is that it is frequently inefficient for management to order front-line workers to be servile to customers. The servile worker lets the customer dictate the pace and the nature of the service interaction. Each service interaction becomes time-consuming and management has to hire extra staff to deal with the customers. There appears to be a significant dilemma for management: How to achieve both efficient production and high service quality (by meeting implicit customer expectations of deference)? The way out of this dilemma is for management to structure the service interaction such that front-line workers control the interaction while giving the appearance to customers that the control lies in their own hands. This point also lies well with other feminist analyses which have shown that the apparently deferential female service worker does not systematically experience servility, but rather takes refuge and pride in the way that she is able to control and manipulate the customer (Paules, 1991). Rather than seeing this as a form of misguided false-consciousness, or simply as a form of resistance (Hall, 1993), it should be seen as informed to an important degree by the material demands made by management.

Conclusion

Overall, the last two chapters have reviewed four main perspectives on front-line work – the new service management school, Ritzer's McDonaldisation thesis, du Gay's focus on the discourse of the enterprising self, and feminist analyses. Each perspective has direct implications for the content of HRM policies, for the interpretation of these policies, and for front-line workers' subjective experience of their work. Table 3.1 summarises these implications. For the new service management school, HRM policies are structured around the creation of a cycle of capability. In this unitarist perspective, HRM policies are interpreted as underlying a unity of interests among customers, workers and management. Front-line workers achieve high satisfaction partly through the satisfaction mirror and partly as a direct result of HRM policies.

The most widespread critical perspective on service work is Ritzer's thesis concerning McDonaldisation. Although his analysis does not directly concern itself with HRM policies, clear inferences can be drawn. HRM policies are likely to involve a strong emphasis on treating labour as a cost to be minimised because of the imperative for efficiency. In these terms HRM is to be viewed as part of the overall, and largely inevitable, dehumanisation process that is McDonaldisation. Workers become dehumanised at work, often taking on a robot-like status.

Du Gay argues that the 1980s and 1990s have seen the rise of central dominant discourse of the enterprising self. Although he tends not to explicitly consider the implications of this for HRM policies, clear inferences can be drawn. From the way he tends to contrast the enterprising discourse against bureaucracy, HRM policies involve a movement away from bureaucratic policies towards an imposition of market relations within organisations. Although he argues there is space for resistance to this discourse of the enterprising self (du Gay, 2000a), the implications of his approach is that workers tend to come to conceive of themselves in enterprising terms.

Finally, feminist analyses have been presented. This perspective suggests that apparently gender-neutral HRM policies should be deconstructed and examined for a hidden gendered subtext. In this way, HRM policies in contemporary front-line work can be seen as designed to achieve customers' (often) gendered expectations of service quality. Individual HRM policies that flow from this aim can also be shown to be frequently implicitly gendered in a way that leads to disadvantage to women. There is an ambiguity in this analysis as to how far the structures of servility will be reflected in front-line workers' subjective experience of the work.

The last two chapters have also put forward critiques of each of these perspectives in turn. Here, I will briefly outline two common themes in these critiques as a prelude to the following chapter's presentation of my own customer-oriented bureaucracy perspective. A key theme pursued has

Table 3.1 Implications for HRM of perspectives on service work

Perspective on the nature of service work	Implications for content of HRM policies	Implications for interpreting HRM policies and their effect on service workforce
New service management school	Policies to achieve cycle of capability	HRM practices develop win : win : win scenario. Highly satisfied and motivated workforce created.
Ritzer – McDonaldisation	Cost-minimising and bureaucratic policies	HRM as part of an overall process of dehumanisation. Workers increasingly become robot-like.
Du Gay	Imposition of market relations; development of enterprising culture	HRM as part of wider totalising discourse of the enterprising self. Workers increasingly conceive of themselves in enterprising terms.
Feminist analyses	HRM policies to achieve customer's (gendered) expectations of service quality	HRM policies as gendered. Workforce increasingly subject to gender-based servility.

been that analysis of the experience of front-line work must step outside the focus on the management–worker dyad to consider the role of the customer. Further, it should do this in a way that can conceptualise the customer as a source of potential pleasure and pain. Ritzer can be criticised for all but ignoring the role of the customer in the experience of front-line work. The proponents of the new service management school can be praised for the extent that they bring the customer into the analysis, but were criticised for the way in which the customer was used in their analysis as a focus for the coalescing of management and worker interests. A strength of feminist analyses is that they alert us to potential ways in which customers can systematically be a discomforting presence in the service labour process. All this suggests the need for a more sustained analysis of customers in their own right. The following chapter's discussion of the customer-oriented bureaucracy concept includes an analysis of the nature of customers in contemporary front-line settings. We cannot know what it means to be customer-oriented unless we have an adequate understanding of the customer. Second, I have argued consistently against a tendency for analysts to have a mono-focus on a single key imperative driving the nature of front-line work. In the cases of the new service management school, du Gay and feminist characterisation of the servile society, the criticism concerned the tendency for the perspective to lose sight of the continuing importance of the bureaucratic imperative of efficiency in front-line work. In their own way, each analysis has been swept up in a focus on the new (the rising importance of service quality, the rise of the discourse of the enterprising self, or an assertion of gendered servility), and has lost sight of key continuities with the bureaucratic organisation of front-line work. In the case of Ritzer, by direct contrast, the criticism of mono-focus relates to his inability to see beyond the bureaucratic logic. An adequate understanding of front-line work must be based on an ability to see the importance of both the bureaucratic logic and the logic of the customer arriving through the growing importance of service quality.

Notes

1   Hochschild (1983) effectively offers a single-issue contribution focusing on emotional labour, which is considered at length in Chapter 8.
2   See also Bryman (1995), who finds difficulty in applying Ritzer's concept of calculability to Disney theme parks.
3   Klein (2000) appears to share Ritzer's assumption that service jobs are becoming predominantly 'McJobs': 'low skill, low pay, high stress, exhausting and unstable' (p. 237). Klein, however, shares none of Ritzer's assumptions concerning the lack of resistance to this dehumanising work. This treatment by service firms 'breeds disloyalty – what goes around, comes around' (ch. 11).
4   In du Gay and Salaman's (1992) piece, enterprise/enterprising is used in the following senses: as relating to the qualities of being self-reliant, self-actualising and empowered (p. 622, 626, 628); as being 'synonymous with the politico-ethical project of Thatcherism' (p. 627); as a series of techniques for restructuring the internal world of the organisation along 'market' lines (p. 624); as 'more than a political rationality, it also takes a technological form: it is inscribed into a variety of often simple mechanisms...through which various authorities seek to shape...the conduct of persons' (p. 629); as a discourse 'of which the culture of the customer constitutes a key element' (p. 615); and as the application of 'entrepreneurial principle' (p. 628).
5   Note that in the debate between Fournier and Grey (1999) and du Gay (2000) there is continued reference in both sides of the debate to the presence of enterprise in the sphere of production, but not in the sphere of consumption.
6   See Chapter 6 for a discussion of a 'contracted-out' model of work organisation that is applicable to some specific forms of sales work. This is the type of front-line work closest to market prinicples.
7   PanAmerican neglected to consider how far 'passenger preferences' were in part informed by the common use of sexuality in advertising. As Nielsen notes, the

companies continued to market their sky girls in hard-hitting campaigns...Continental Airlines in newspapers and on radio, claimed, 'We really move our tail for you.' On Continental...the management had used Playboy bunnies as stewardesses for one week in 1975 (1982, p. 117).

8 Also see Rothman (1998, p. 134) for a characterisation of service work as servility without recourse to gender.

CHAPTER 4

Service work: the customer-oriented bureaucracy

Chapter 1 highlighted that service organisations operate in terrains in which there are *dual* imperatives of minimising cost and delivering customer-oriented service quality. Chapters 2 and 3 criticised existing literatures on service work for failing to take into account these dual pressures. This chapter outlines the concept of the customer-oriented bureaucracy as a way forward. This interpretation of the organisation of service work has important implications both for HRM and for workers' experience of service work. Through the lens of the customer-oriented bureaucracy HRM is interpreted as functioning primarily as a means to create and maintain a fragile social order out of the contradictory pressures underlying service work. Front-line workers' experience is also contradictory. The dual pressures structuring their work mean that there are both more tensions and potentially more spaces for these workers. The chapter is structured as follows. First, the nature of the customer in front-line work is investigated – specifically regarding service quality. We cannot expect to understand customer service work without first understanding the customer. Next, the chapter outlines important dimensions of the customer-oriented bureaucracy, with an extended examination of the implications for HRM. This then allows a consideration of how workers experience service work.

The customer and service quality

It is easy to become lost among the myriad images of the customer contained in literatures spanning marketing, economics, HRM, sociology, political economy and cultural studies. The reader is confronted with contrasting images:

the sovereign, rational customer of mainstream (neo-classical/marginalist) economics (Frenzen *et al.*, 1994), or the customer as manipulated, irrational pawn (Packard, 1957; Ewen, 1988); the customer as autonomous, hedonist (Bell, 1976; Campbell, 1987), or the customer as formally rational and robot-like, controlled by dominant producing organisations (Ritzer, 1996; Marcuse, 1964); the customer as a celebrated, active figure in the creation of advertising-based culture (Twitchell, 1997), or customers as slaves to impulses out of their control (Veblen, 1925; Schor, 1998). Overviews of the many literatures on the nature of the customer highlight the multiple images of the contemporary customer that exist in these literatures (Agnew, 1993; Gabriel and Lang, 1995; Edwards, 2000; Rosenthal *et al.*, 2001), but rarely go further than this.

There are two key steps to take to make sense out of these debates. First, it is crucial to consider the level of analysis at which the customer is being discussed. An image of the powerful customer might make sense in examining how a small firm reacts to an increasingly informed body of customers, but it will make less sense in considering the position of an individual customer confronted by large multinational corporations. Second, in order to take analysis further it is useful to identify the key dimensions around which debates on the customer take place. There are two dimensions central to the debates. *The first dimension concerns whether customers' behaviour is informed primarily by their own agency or is determined by the structures of producing organisations.* As Edwards (2000, p. 6) puts it, 'consumption taps into a wider question of structure and action'. *The second dimension concerns the degree to which customers are formally rational or formally irrational.* As noted in the previous chapter, formal rationality refers to a prioritisation of finding an efficient means to achieve an end, and to an emphasis on predictability and calculability.

Although there is a tendency in much of the literature to place customers on one side or the other within these dimensions, a more appropriate view is one which sees *dualism* within customers. *Customers are simultaneously constituted by both producing organisations and their own will or agency.* Here, it is necessary to differentiate whether it is the individual or collective aspect of producing organisations and of customers that is being considered. The focus in this book is upon the implications of the customer for the nature of work in producing organisations. The focus therefore is on the implications for the individual producing organisation in relation to a collectivity of customers. Except in a situation of monopoly, the individual producing organisation cannot be assumed to have unambiguous determinative power over customer behaviour. Rather, the individual producing organisation is in a position of *competitive appeal and enchantment regarding customers*. This concept allows space for a consideration of the way in which individual production organisations still seek to structure customers' behaviour, albeit in a context in which they compete with other producing organisations. That firms seek to appeal to, and enchant, customers also suggests customer agency. An appeal or an attempted enchantment is something that calls for action from the customer. Enchantment, moreover, contains the idea that customers are active participants in the creation of meaning. The storyteller can enchant the audience only if the audience members invest part of themselves in the experience. The brand or the logo is a clear contemporary manifestation of competitive enchantment by the individual producing organisation. Even Klein, a vehement critic of the dynamic of logo-centred capitalism, concedes that consumers play an active role in this process of enchantment (2000, pp. 141, 143, 149). Finally, it should be noted that the concept of competitive appeal and enchantment is also useful because the concepts of appeal and enchantment connect, respectively, to the formally rational and formally irrational aspects of the customer.

Just as customers are simultaneously constituted by producing organisations and their own agency, so *customers are simultaneously both formally rational and formally irrational*. Campbell's (1987) analysis is notable here. He delivers a lacerating attack on the view of mainstream economists for their emphasis on customers' rational, utilitarian approach to satisfaction. He argues that this focus upon utility and satisfaction of needs means that there is a complete neglect of customers pursuing pleasure, driven by desire (ch. 4). The distinction between need/satisfaction on the one hand and desire/pleasure on the other is an important one for Campbell. He argues that these two principles relate to very different kinds of activity (p. 60):

> [Need/satisfaction] relates to a state of being and its disturbance, followed by action to restore the original equilibrium. Hence a state of need is a state of deprivation, in which one lacks something necessary to maintain a given condition of existence, and realisation of this leads to exploratory activity in the environment in order to find whatever is capable of remedying this lack. The paradigm for this model is food-seeking arising from an awareness of hunger. By contrast, pleasure is not a state of being so much as a quality of experience. Not properly in itself a type of sensation, pleasure is a term used to identify our favourable reaction to certain patterns of sensation. Desire is the term used to refer to a motivational disposition to experience such patterns... The paradigm for this model is the initiation of sexual activity following an encounter with a potential mate.

The existence of these two forms of behaviour within consumers, the former of which is formally rational and the latter of which is formally irrational, means that views of consumers which ignore one or the other are inadequate. Unfortunately, Campbell fails to follow this logic through. Having made the case that the economists' neglect of desire/pleasure is unsupportable, he then makes a mirror image of their error by ignoring utility and the satisfaction of needs in his creation of 'a theory of consumer behaviour which is predicated upon a hedonistic rather than a utilitarian framework of thought' (p. 60). What is clearly needed is a view that encompasses both the formally rational *and* formally irrational aspects of the customer.

The view of both aspects of customers' behaviour is actually present in much of contemporary advertising, one strand of which appeals to the formally rational customer through an emphasis on price and utility, and another strand of which seeks to enchant the formally irrational customer through an emphasis on the symbolic meaning of products. As Fine (1995, p. 151) points out, although the sociological/cultural studies literature on advertising 'focuses on the more fanciful advertising associated with branded products', the other strand of advertising emphasising 'lower prices' remains significant. Goods elicit or contain not just symbolic meaning, known as 'sign-value' (Baudrillard, 1971/1988) or 'identity value' (Warde, 1991), but also utility or use-value. Advertising both reflects and reproduces this duality. For instance, a typical car advert will outline the use-value of the customer by detailing the car's efficiency and value for money. It will also suggest a sign-value that comes from ownership of such a car, such as sexiness or ruggedness. The coexistence of formally rational and formally irrational aspects of the customer is also reflected in the dual languages that exist in the management literature on customers. Writers who prioritise the formally rational aspect of the customer speak of the imperative of 'satisfying the customer' (Heskett *et al.*, 1997). Writers who prioritise the formally irrational aspect of the customer, however, speak of the imperative of 'delighting the customer' (Peters and Waterman, 1982). The language of satisfaction is congruent with a formally rational model of the customer, while the language of delight and pleasure is congruent with a view of the customer as irrational.

So far the discussion of the nature of the customer has been at a general level. The discussion now turns to focus upon the customer *within the specific context of front-line service work*. Although this form of consumption has been all but ignored in the wider sociological literature, the service management literature contains an important research stream which explicitly focuses on the customer interacting with the service organisation. Pioneered by Parasuraman *et al.* (1988, 1991), this has focused on creating a generic model, and measurement tool, of the customer's perception of quality in the service interaction. The five-factor model developed from systematic studies of customer perceptions of service interactions is called SERVQUAL and is shown in Table 4.1. Although it is not discussed in these terms, the SERVQUAL model can be seen to reflect the formally rational and irrational dualism of the customer. Two factors, reliability and responsiveness, pertain directly to the formal rationality of customers, to their desire for efficient service. Two other factors, empathy and assurance, however, pertain more to the formal irrationality of the customer, to their desire to be treated in a social and emotional manner as important figures.

When moving from a consideration of the customer at the general level to a consideration of the customer within front-line service work an important distinction must be made regarding the individual/collective level of analysis. It is still the individual producing organisation that is the focus, but,

Table 4.1 Parasuraman *et al.*'s SERVQUAL model of service quality

Dimension	Definition
Reliability	The ability to perform the promised service dependably and accurately
Responsiveness	The willingness to help customers and provide prompt service
Tangibles	The appearance of physical facilities, equipment, personnel and communication materials
Assurance	The knowledge and courtesy of employees and their ability to convey trust and confidence
Empathy	The caring, individualised attention provided to the customer

regarding the customer, both the collective and the individual level must be considered. It remains the case that the producing organisation must be configured to deal with customer behaviour at a collective level. The concept of competitive appeal and enchantment holds good here, therefore. What is different for front-line work is that the organisation must also deal directly with individual customers. In the situation of an individual customer interacting directly with an individual service organisation the power shifts strongly to the producing organisation. Service organisations are in a strong position to directly determine customers' behaviour in service interactions. This power, however, is limited by two key factors. One is the dynamic created by the continuing context of competition with other producing organisations. Service organisations can compete with each other on the basis of the degree to which customer behaviour is directly determined by the organisation. When one service organisation starts attracting customers on the basis that 'customers are our number one priority', that 'here the customer is the king' then other service organisations are also pushed in that direction. As Zeithaml and Bitner (1996, p. 75) note, there has been a 'rapid escalation of customer expectations' within service industries, and these expectations have been fuelled by fierce competition and advertising. Ritzer (1999a, p. 75) similarly notes that 'once one setting has been reenchanted, competitors must follow suit or risk the permanent loss of business'. The second factor is the incongruity that would be experienced by the customer. They would move from being appealed to and enchanted, to being suddenly dictated to. Service organisations seek to reconcile this by subtly attempting to direct customer behaviour while also attempting to ensure that the customer feels that they are in charge.[1] The trick for front-line workers, then, is to be 'both deferential and authoritative' (Benson, 1986, p. 159), to direct behaviour but to convey the impression that the customer is in charge. As Leidner (1993, p. 139) puts it, when managers try to manipulate customers, they must 'finesse' their actions so that it appears that the customer is still in charge.

This feeling of being in charge is the key sign-value consumed in contemporary service interactions, and can be termed the enchanting myth of customer sovereignty.[2] The idea is present in Wolf's (1999, p. 70) description of a customer's experience of a superstore: 'the lights, the music, the furniture, *the cast of clerks* create a feeling not unlike a play in which you, the shopper, are given a leading role'(emphasis added). This in turn echoes Williams's analysis of the first French department stores as arenas of enchantment and seduction where customers were invited to live out fantasies. In these 'palaces' of consumption the customer, addressed as 'Sir' or 'Madam', becomes, mythically, the sovereign. In addition, both the SERVQUAL and the critical incidents approaches to customer perceptions of quality allude to the enchanting myth of sovereignty in service work. 'The waiter treated me like royalty. He really showed he cared about me' is one revealing example of a positive critical incident reported by a customer to Bitner *et al.* (1990). Within the SERVQUAL model, the 'assurance' and 'tangibles' factors relate to the customer considering whether it appears that they will be treated as the centrally important figure. The 'empathy' dimension can be interpreted as the customer considering whether the front-line staff have come round to look at the interaction from the (mythically) sovereign customer's viewpoint. The process of enchantment suspends disbelief – a process that a number of writers see as central to (formally irrational) customer behaviour. Lynch argues that 'any action which increases the *self-esteem* of the customer will raise the level of satisfaction' (1992, p. 128). Although individual customers, at some level, may know that notions of their sovereignty are mythical the fact they still go along with this myth reflects the 'distinctively modern faculty, the ability to create an illusion which is known to be false but felt to be true' (Campbell, 1987, p. 78). It is a pleasurable illusion after all.[3]

The renaming of service recipients as 'customers' in a range of settings such as railways (from 'passengers'), health care (from 'patients'), university business schools (from 'students') and state housing bodies (from 'tenants') is partly informed by management using language to propound the enchanting myth of sovereignty in service interactions. Whereas the 'customer' is the sovereign a priori of mainstream economics, the 'passenger' exists only as a secondary actor in relation to the pre-existing railway. The language of the 'customer', therefore, is more likely to perpetuate the enchanting myth of sovereignty.

Consumption, however, is a fragile process (Edwards, 2000). *Enchantment may easily turn to disillusionment in the moments when the individual customer's lack of sovereignty becomes starkly apparent.* Think of the customer enchanted by an advertising message and by the behaviour of front-line workers. Think of this same consumer seduced into spending beyond his or her means then faced with a menacing debt collection agency acting on behalf of the firm. Consider also Bitner *et al.*'s (1990) critical incidents approach to service quality in this light. To take one example, Bitner *et al.* identify customer displeasure as occurring when 'the waitress refused to move me from a window table on a hot day because there was nothing left in her section'. Bitner *et al.*'s negative 'critical incidents' in service delivery effectively centre on the customer slipping from enchantment into disillusionment. As Ritzer (1999a) suggests, customer disillusionment may occur precisely because the continuing rationalising, bureaucratic imperative of production becomes apparent. Think, for instance, of the crack of disillusionment that would occur if visitors to Disneyland's enchanted kingdom witnessed the routinised procedures for the summary dismissal of workers so vividly described by Van Maanen (see Chapter 2). Relatedly, Leidner (1993, p. 131) notes discourtesy expressed by customers to front-line workers as occurring when the bureaucratic 'inflexible routines' of the production organisation intrude upon the service interaction.

Implications for work organisation and HRM

The investigation of the nature of the customer in front-line service work shows that claims of the 'authoritative customer' (Abercrombie, 1991; Miller, 1995; du Gay, 1996) fail to adequately capture the complexities and contradictions of the situation. As such, it is inappropriate to simply put forward a model of a customer-oriented organisation to illuminate front-line service work. A hybrid model, or ideal type, of a customer-oriented bureaucracy is a more appropriate way to capture the mutually constituted nature of the customer, and the significant power that continues to reside with the individual producing organisation. *This concept of the customer-oriented bureaucracy captures the requirement for the organisation to be both formally rational, to respond to competitive pressures to appeal to customers' wishes for efficiency, and to be formally irrational, to enchant, responding to the customers' desire for pleasure, particularly through the perpetuation of the enchanting myth of customer sovereignty.*[4] In the language of the service management literature, the service organisation must deliver satisfaction but also pleasure; it must deliver efficiency, reliability and responsiveness, but also empathy, tangibles and assurance.[5] This is the key tension of contemporary service work – a tension that even faces McDonald's, that most bureaucratised of service firms. For instance, Leidner's study of McDonald's notes (1993, p. 217) that when she asked one of the trainers about McDonald's goals for customer service, 'he told me quite sincerely, "We want to treat each customer as an individual in sixty seconds or less" '. Simply seeing McDonald's as a routinsed, bureaucratic structure misses a key tension at the heart of the firm.

Table 4.2 shows key dimensions of work organisation in the customer-oriented bureaucracy. The table shows that in addition to the usual bureaucratic characteristics such as dividing labour (or jobs) in order to maximise

Table 4.2 Features of the customer-oriented bureaucracy

Dimension	Customer-oriented bureaucracy
Key management role	Fashioning a fragile social order[6]
HRM	Important as engendering dual-focused, efficient and customer-oriented worker behaviour, and as seeking to cope with ensuing tensions
Labour process	Quantity *and* quality focus
Basis of division of labour	Efficient task completion *and* customer relationship
Basis of authority	Rational-legal rules *and* customer
Form of control	Imperfect bureaucratic measurement *and* customer-related norms
Affect	Rationalised emotional labour
Flexibility	Maintaining internal stability *and* adapting to customer variability

task efficiency, and basing control upon work measurement, there is an imperative to structure service work by different principles, such as dividing labour to ensure a customer relationship, and using customer-related norms in control. The concept and the table leave open the question of *how* management may seek to resolve the tensions arising from the dual logics at play in the organisation of front-line service work. The discussion of each dimension in turn below, however, does indicate some ways in which management has approached these dilemmas in practice in a range of service settings.

Key management role/HRM

The model of the customer-oriented bureaucracy contains within it the dual logics of rationalisation and orientation to the formally irrational aspects of customers. There is an imperative for work to be organised to be competitively efficient, to appeal to the utilitarian sense of the customer. In addition, work has to be organised to enchant the sensibility of the customer, particularly through the enchanting myth of sovereignty. There are dual organisational principles infusing the concept of the customer-oriented bureaucracy. Whereas a bureaucracy is dominated by the principle of rationalisation, within the customer-oriented bureaucracy this principle is joined with customer orientation. Taylorism is coupled with 'Tailorism'. The routinising logic of standardising procedures is married to the logic of dealing with variable and unpredictable customers. The need to improve efficiency by cutting costs is joined as an organisational imperative by the need to deliver high-quality service. Thus Zeithaml and Bitner (1996, p. 324) discuss the reorganisation of front-line work as driven by the need to 'cut costs and simultaneously improve customer service'. Note also what they say regarding the multiple uses to which technology has been put in service firms:

> technology is used in service business to lower costs, increase productivity, improve the way service is delivered... personalize the service, collect data on customer needs, add value for the customer, differentiate the service, and build relationships with customers (p. 35).

In other words, management uses technology as an instrument both to rationalise production (lower costs, increase productivity) and to make the firm more customer-oriented (improve the service, personalise it, collect data on customers, add value for them and build relationships with them). The model of the customer-oriented bureaucracy, therefore, points to an essential tension at the heart of contemporary service work. It also points to the consequent imperative for management to attempt to fashion a social order out of these dual logics. Management must ensure the creation of profit through the orderly running of the organisation. Any social order so fashioned should be seen as fragile, with tensions latent rather than dissipated because contradictions and tensions are there ready to surface at any time.

In the production line or bureaucratic approach to service work, HRM may have a relatively peripheral role. There is a strong, largely mono-, focus on efficiency, with front-line workers expected merely to comply to the standardised procedures enshrined in technology and rules. By contrast, the model of the customer-oriented bureaucracy suggests that HRM will assume a central role in service management because it can operate at two levels. First, it can be used to *promote* the dual-focused, efficient, committed and customer-oriented worker behaviour that is required. At the second level, it can offer a range of approaches to *cope* with the inevitable ensuing tensions. Although, in practice, individual HRM policies might operate at both these levels, the distinction between the levels is a useful analytical one. The distinction offers a fuller anatomy of HRM and its aims than are put forward by the new service management or suggested by the critical perspectives reviewed in the previous chapter. The following discussion of HRM will focus on the two levels identified.

A central part of many definitions of HRM is that it involves a systematic attempt to link employment policies with business strategy (Legge, 1995).[7] As such, distinctions have been made between 'hard', cost-minimising HRM policies (for example, short-term employment contracts) to match price-competitive product markets and 'soft', resource-maximising HRM polices (for example, emphasising staff development) to match quality-sensitive product markets (Sisson, 1994). The model of the customer-oriented bureaucracy highlights that there is an imperative for employment policies to be simultaneously both hard and soft because the competitive terrain faced by service firms increasingly demands both efficiency and service quality. If HRM involves systematically linking employment policies to business strategy, for many service firms this will lead to systematically created, but internally contradictory, employment policies. This internal contradiction can be seen in the policies prescribed by many of the new service management writers. Zemke and Schaaf (1989), for instance, entitle one section of their book, 'controlling for diversity'. There is the bureaucratic need for control, and there is the customer orientation need to cater for customer diversity. Similarly, Zeithaml and Bitner on one page present the end-of-bureaucracy story, by arguing that if management wants 'customer satisfaction in every service encounter' they must 'encourage spontaneity' (1996, p. 126), but on another page present the bureaucratic logic par excellence, by stating that management must translate customer expectations into 'behaviours and actions that are definable, *repeatable*, actionable' (p. 205). Controlled diversity, repeated spontaneity – these are the phrases of internally contradictory policies that seek to promote efficiency and to cater to the formally irrational aspect of the customer.

Another way in which HRM can assist in promoting dual-focused behaviour is through its use of rhetoric. Indeed, a number of commentators suggest that HRM's importance lies in its rhetorical and symbolic roles (Keenoy, 1990; Legge, 1995). The point made is that the power of HRM lies not so much in its substantive content, in terms of, for instance, actual training and hiring practices, but rather in the language and symbols it uses and the effect these have on the workforce. If management devises mission statements which stress commitment to the workforce, to their development, training and career, and if management continually reinforces this through forums such as team meetings and performance appraisals, then this may have an effect on engendering a level of workforce commitment – regardless, to a degree, of whether this rhetoric is actually matched by concrete practices. A key rhetorical aspect of HRM is the creation of a language which suggests shared interests between management and workforce. Thus training is discussed in terms of the mutual benefits that it brings to the organisation and to the individual worker. The language of teamwork is stressed, since this suggests working together towards a shared goal. In the context of front-line work, management can also present customer orientation as a shared value. Skilful management may be able to use language to delegitimise a sphere of separate workforce interests by so emphasising the confluence of worker and customer interests that the former become subsumed into the latter.[8]

Management can use the win : win : win HRM rhetoric to fashion a level of discourse in which tensions can be redefined away. Within the labour process, the tensions of maintaining a dual quality and quantity focus (discussed below) can be made less visible by redefining the issue as one of 'balance'. Hence the popularity of managing through the *balanced* scorecard (Kaplan and Norton, 1993). A crucial job of lower management and supervisors becomes the creation of individual points of 'balance' with individual workers – often through the forum of the performance appraisal. A fragile social order, in which a dual focus is maintained, is more likely to be held together if management can tailor specific quality and quantity performance targets to individual workers – to take into account differing points at which 'balance' becomes manifest tension and conflict.

The focus now turns to the second, coping function of HRM. The idea here is brought out well in a moment of rare candour by Zeithaml and Bitner (1996), writers firmly within the new service management school. They highlight the contradictory demands made of front-line workers and place the need for HRM within this contradictory context (pp. 310–11):

> Front-line service workers are asked to be both effective and efficient: they are expected to deliver satisfying service to customers and at the same time to be cost effective and productive in what they do. A physician ... for example, is expected to deliver caring, quality, individualised service to her patients but a the same time to serve a certain number of patients within a specified time frame. A checker at a grocery store is expected to know his customers and to be polite and courteous, yet also to process the groceries accurately and move people through the line quickly ... These essential trade-offs between quality and quantity and between maximum effectiveness and efficiency place real-time demands and pressures on service employees ... Given the demands, conflicts, and pressures of service jobs, how can organisations ensure efficiency and effectiveness and maintain a service-oriented work force?

The answer they give is that management must adopt HRM practices.

At this second level, HRM can contribute to the maintenance of the fragile social order in the front-line workplace by carefully controlling and limiting the (inevitable) manifestations of tensions. Thus in a book on *Best Practices in Customer Service* (Zemke and Woods, 1999), authors present ideas on allowing 'steam blowers' in the service workplace. Barlow and Maul write (1999, p. 168):

> Let's face it. Everyone needs to vent from time to time, to blow off some steam. Allow your staff the opportunity to talk about their frustrations, their stress, and the reasons for it. The key to managing steam blowers is to keep the negativity enclosed, within limits. If everyone is constantly venting, no work will ever get done and staff can easily talk themselves into a negative mood ... If you manage the negativity, it will be less likely to spread during work hours into the hallways and the lunch room.

Note that the authors are not concerned with ameliorating the factors which might lead to 'everyone constantly venting'. Rather, they are concerned with the management, the enclosing, of the venting, which is the manifestation of tension through informal spoken communication. Similarly, Zemke and

Schaaf (1989, p. 65) argue that the high-quality training that management offer to front-line staff should include training in 'stress management and emotional self-defense strategies'. Again there is an emphasis on the management and limiting of the manifestations of tensions. Ideally, in this approach the tensions are 'managed' within individual workers. Counselling should be offered on a one-to-one basis. A failure to cope with tensions then becomes a failure of the individual worker rather than the outcome of a particular contradictory social situation.

Another management approach to coping with tensions involves the generation of a surface-level, 'fun' atmosphere in the service workplace. Bowen (1996, p. 44) proposes that 'mood at work' (George and Brief, 1992), which is concerned with 'affect *at* work', rather than the more deep-seated 'affect *about* work', may be particularly important in the service workplace. It may 'spill over' onto customers, and it creates a means of coping. Although rarely discussed in research findings, this call for action for management and HRM to focus on the surface mood at work is likely to be frequently mirrored in management action seeking to create a 'fun' and 'positive' level of social reality above deep-seated organisational tensions. Thus, a manager at McDonald's is observed going round telling his staff that when he asks them how they feel, they should reply with a resounding 'outstanding'. 'Don't you feel better after that?' he asks them (personal video). A systematic adoption of this approach within a call centre is reported by Kinnie *et al.* (1998). The title, 'Fun and Surveillance: The Paradox of High Commitment Management in Call Centres', captures the point well.

Labour process

The model of the customer-oriented bureaucracy highlights that management asks that service workers have both a qualitative and a quantitative focus in the work that they do. They must maintain the enchanting myth of customer sovereignty but they must do this efficiently and as quickly as possible. A number of writers have highlighted these qualitative and quantitative demands made of workers in the labour process and interpreted them as specific manifestations of a wider fundamental contradiction of work within capitalism discussed in the labour process literature (Knights and McCabe, 1997; Knights *et al.*, 1999). The building blocks of this literature are simple but have profound implications for understanding work and societies. First, if workers do not own the tools they work with or the products or services they create then they are necessarily alienated from their work. Second, there is a necessary indeterminacy of labour within the employment relationship. When managers hire workers they are hiring the potential to labour, or the labour power, while it is actual labour that they want delivered. There is indeterminacy in the translation of labour power into actual labour. In seeking to address this, management attempts to treat workers as if their labour was not alienated. Revealingly, in front-line work, in coaxing workers to deliver high-quality service, management often stresses that workers should take 'ownership' of customer interactions (Frenkel *et al.*, 1999). But front-line workers own nothing but their labour power. Ownership is an artifice that can crumble when management also asks workers to deliver high productivity in terms of the quantity of customers served. The concept of the customer-oriented bureaucracy captures this view of contradiction within the labour process but broadens the analysis to see contradictions systematically present in other aspects of work organisation.

Division of labour

A key aspect of a bureaucracy is its complex division of labour based on the aim of maximising the efficiency of task completion. Adam Smith's (1776) description of the minute division of tasks and jobs in a pin factory is perhaps the most famous example of this basis of division of labour in practice. Frederick Taylor's 'scientific management' principles for job design applied, for instance, in Ford's assembly line production, is another manifestation of this principle. Within the customer-oriented bureaucracy, however, the division of labour is also structured around the need to cater to the formally irrational nature of the customer. Specifically, in front-line work, the enchanting myth of customer sovereignty must be maintained. The enchanting myth of sovereignty is unlikely to be achieved if the customer is passed around the organisation on an (opaque) assembly line journey. This much is suggested by DuPuy's description of a customer journey in a bureaucracy (1999, p. 56):

> The customer . . . has to follow a complex process of rules and procedures, running from one place to the next, all because the system was not designed for the customer's convenience, but for the bureaucrats who have certain tasks to do . . . The key symbolic word in the Kafkaesque world of bureaucracies might well be 'file': 'I have your file' . . . 'Your file is incomplete'; 'Your file was not sent over to me' and so on.

The enchanting myth of sovereignty is more likely to be achieved if the maintenance of customer relationship is a guiding principle for the division of labour. Such a division of labour also allows for an easier communication between the (partly) irrational customer and the organisation. The irrational customer is likely to communicate in emotional and social modes that are difficult to capture in the written word, or file, that is the axiomatic mode of communication in the bureaucracy. If there is a relationship between the front-line worker and the customer, however, such irrational aspects to the communication are less likely to be marginalised. The bureaucratic division of labour is likely to lead to customers interacting with different front-line workers in a series of encounters, while the need to cater for the irrational aspect of the customer is likely to lead to customers interacting with the same front-line worker over a period of time.

Gutek (1995) summarises the encounter/relationship difference, pointing out that in encounters each service interaction is complete in itself, and front-line workers are, in the eyes of both the customers and the workers, inter-changeable. Relationships, by contrast, happen in the context of an ongoing series of transactions in which a particular front-line worker and particular customer become known to each other and expect continued interaction in the future. Gutek's concept of a 'pseudo-relationship' also captures a way in which management may typically attempt to create a fragile social order out of the potentially contradictory approaches to the division of labour. As also described by Winslow and Bramer (1994), management is able to use expert systems to allow front-line workers to instantly call up a range and depth of information on customers to allow them to 'make encounters feel more personal', and to allow a 'simulation' of a relationship. Indeed, in front-line work, business process re-engineering (BPR) can be seen as exactly suited to creation of pseudo-relationships. As described by Hammer and Champy (1995), BPR tends to involve the creation of a limited number of front-line workers – so as to prevent the bureaucratic shunting of customers and their files around the organisation – supported by expert systems that can rational-ise jobs, and store a range of customer information to better allow the front-line worker to simulate a relationship with the customer. While pseudo-relationships may create a form of social order between the two logics, this is likely to be a fragile one. The line between a simulation of a relationship and an encounter may be a thin one, easily crossed over in service interactions.

Basis of authority

For Weber (1921/1978), in a bureaucracy the basis of authority is rational-legal authority – the idea that power, as formalised in rules and procedures, is legitimised because those rules are seen as encapsulating formal rationality. In the customer-oriented bureaucracy, authority also derives from the customer. Power can become legitimate if it is seen as acting for the customer. The dual bases of authority underlie the common perception of 'two bosses' in many service settings (Mars *et al.*, 1979; Shamir, 1980). TQM attempts to draw these two, potentially contradictory, bases of authority symbiotically together. As Legge (1995, p. 219) notes, at the heart of TQM is a managerial prioritisation of quality in which quality is defined, at least rhetorically, as 'conformance to the requirements of the *customer*' (emphasis added). In addition, TQM contains 'hard' rational techniques to achieve efficiency within production. It contains not just an assertion of customer authority, but also an assertion of rational authority, based on the hard principles held by management. The great sleight of hand in this sophisticated attempt to create a fragile social order out of the dual logics is that the 'customer' whom management is holding up as the figure of authority is defined in such a way as to prioritise his or her formally rational nature. TQM rests upon an image of a customer whose behaviour and attitudes can be measured, predicted and managed. TQM and BPR rest uneasily with the customer as the emotional, rebellious hedonist, who may be swayed by sudden and inexplicable psychological processes.

Form of control

Management control can be thought of as 'the ability of ... managers to obtain desired work behaviour from workers' (Edwards, 1979, p. 17). In a bureaucracy, control rests primarily upon measurement of outputs and of process behaviours, particularly regarding adherence to hierarchically imposed procedures and rules (Edwards, 1979; Ouchi, 1979). To cater for the formally irrational aspect of the customer, the organisation must accept that front-line workers, in particular, may have to go beyond predesigned procedures. Further, the sign-value of the enchanting myth of customer sovereignty is very vulnerable to disruption from the appearance of the producing organisation's bureaucratic procedures (Ritzer, 1999a). Moreover, as this sign-value of the enchanting myth becomes an important part of the 'product' emanating from the service interaction, the clear bureaucratic measurement of work outputs becomes much more problematic. Hence the customer-oriented bureaucracy points to the supplementing of the bureaucratic form of control through the operation of customer-related norms. Mills (1986, p. 125) notes that 'although output and process controls may be implemented to control performance in service operations, self-control [based on customer-related norms] will also be pervasive'. Sturdy (1998) concurs. In his review of customer orientation training programs for customer service work, he argues that these programs tend to *supplement* the traditional direct and bureaucratic control.

In many customer service organisations, control through customer-related norms begins with recruitment decisions. A wide set of literature points to the considerable emphasis that customer service management places on pro-customer attitudes and values among candidates when making recruitment decisions (Zeithaml and Bitner, 1996; Stanback, 1990; Sturdy *et al.*, 2001). Management then seeks to refine the internalisation of these customer-related norms through socialisation, formal training programs and performance appraisals (Korczynski *et al.*, 2000), aiming to develop an overall service culture in the organisation. The contradictions inherent in the dual existence of these forms of control are examined in Chapter 7.

Affect

Within the bureaucracy, emotional expression is generally discouraged and devalued as irrational. Within the model of the customer-oriented bureaucracy, however, the bureaucratic code of impersonality is replaced by the requirement to deliver rationalised emotional labour. Martin *et al.* (1998) and Putnam and Mumby (1993) highlight the *rationalised* nature of emotional labour in many contemporary service settings by contrasting it with the qualities of the expression of emotions in 'feminist' non-rationalised organisations. Management desires positive emotions expressed to the customers, especially empathy to allow an easy consumption of the enchanting myth of sovereignty. But management also needs these emotions delivered *efficiently*. In Hochschild's (1983) seminal study the management desire for rationalised emotional labour comes through most clearly in her discussion of the emotions required of flight attendants during the competition-inspired 'speed-up' of the 1970s and 1980s. She writes (p. 126) that, 'before the speed-up, most workers sustained the cheerful good will that food service requires. They did so for the most part proudly'. It was only after the speed-up and the prioritisation of efficiency, 'when asked to make personal human cost at an inhuman speed', that the tensions of emotional labour became significant. Rationalised emotional labour is examined in more depth in Chapter 8.

Flexibility

The bureaucratic, production line approach involves a blinkering from the external environment and an emphasis on establishing internal stability to maximise efficient production. In the customer-oriented bureaucracy there is, in addition, a focus on the external environment of the customer. The 'un-manageable' aspect of the customer (Gabriel and Lang, 1995) means that the organisation must seek to be flexible to cope with this unpredictable environment. There are two levels to the unpredictability and variability of the customer. At the level of the individual customer, variability exists in idiosyncratic behaviour and expectations within a specific service encounter. This has been noted above. At the level of customers as a whole, unpredictability and variability exist in the overall level and timing of demand. The lack of a temporal buffer between production and consumption in customer service organisations, or perishability, means that these organisations are very vulnerable to the consequences of overall customer unpredictability and variability. As Zeithaml and Bitner put it (1996, p. 389), 'the fundamental issue underlying supply and demand management in services is the lack of inventory capability. Unlike manufacturing firms, service firms cannot build up inventories during periods of slow demand to use later when demand increases.'

An organisation unconcerned with efficiency may be able to cope with such variability through running excess capacity. The concept of the customer-oriented bureaucracy, however, highlights that again management is faced with a dilemma. In practice, there seem to be two main ways for management to attempt to construct a fragile social order in the context of these tensions. One is to seek to reduce the uncertainty by increasing the predictability of changes in customer demand. Hence there has been a huge growth in the production of software programs that are marketed to the rational manager with promises of finding predictable patterns within apparent random fluctuations in customer demand (Cleveland and Mayben, 1997; McLaughlin, 1998; Klein, 2000). Zeithaml and Bitner (1996, p. 395) argue that 'sometimes the patterns of demand appear to be random . . . yet even in this case, causes can often be identified. For example, day-to-day changes in the weather may affect use of recreational, shopping, or entertainment facilities'. In these cases service managers are left with the chaos theorists who seek to identify the proverbial butterfly in the clouds whose gently flapping wings are seen as underlying the unpredictable nature of short-term weather patterns (Gleick, 1987). There is inevitably at least partial failure in this approach.

The second main way in which management is likely to seek to cope with the tensions is to turn to the labour force for flexibility. Two very different types of labour force flexibility have been identified – numerical flexibility and functional flexibility (O'Reilly, 1994). Numerical flexibility refers to the ability of management to adjust workforce numbers in line with fluctuations in demand. Functional flexibility refers to the ability of the workforce to undertake differing tasks in line with fluctuations in customer demand. Here, there must be a degree of multiskilling to allow workers to move quickly from one type of job to another when necessary. The model of the 'flexible firm' has been proposed as a way of combining these very different approaches (Atkinson, 1985). Here the workforce is segmented, with the 'core' staff delivering functional flexibility and staff in the 'periphery' delivering numerical flexibility. In a range of service industries, the expanded use of numerical flexibility appears to be one of the key ways in which management seeks to create a fragile social order out of the context of constraining tensions (Walsh, 1990). Even if service firms adopted the flexible firm approach, such an approach is subject to its own distinct tensions and dysfunctions (Geary, 1992). Given these tensions and given that management must tend to be ignorant of the likely length of an unexpected increase in customer demand, another important form of flexibility is that of *labour-stretching*. As Zeithaml and Bitner (1996, p. 399) put it, 'in many service organisations, employees are asked to work longer and harder during periods of peak demand'. Such (systematic) incidents of labour-stretching may trigger a breakdown in the fragile social order of the service workplace. Regardless of HRM policies to shore up a social order, systematic labour-stretching may lead to increased turnover, to increasing dissent to customers and to managers, and may even inform collective trade union action.

Implications for the experience of front-line work

In examining what this model of the customer-oriented bureaucracy implies for the experience of front-line work, it is important again to consider at what level of analysis the customer is being discussed. For front-line workers seeking meaning in their work, customers may be regarded as 'socially embedded'. This relates to Granovetter's (1985) wider concept that economic actors and economic exchanges are socially embedded. When two people undertake an economic exchange they are also necessarily taking part in a social relationship – a social relationship which can have meaning or displeasure quite distinct from the economic exchange taking place. Granovetter's is a simple idea yet it is one of the most important critiques of the (neo-classical) economists' guiding concept of the rational, atomistic economic agent. The idea of embeddedness can readily be used in an analysis of the customer – particularly in the context of interacting with front-line workers. The customer as well as being an economic actor is a social one. The service interaction between a front-line worker and a customer is an economic and a social interaction. It is noteworthy that the word 'customer' derives from the word 'custom', one meaning of which refers to established ways of behaving. A way of behaving can only be 'established' by a social and historical process. Studs Terkel captures the ideal of socially embedded worker–customer interactions well. In his collection of conversations with American people in *American Dreams: Lost and Found* (1999), he describes Gaynell Begley:

> She is behind the counter at the store. There is a steady stream of customers; small children, old people, husky young men off the road repair gang...She addresses each by name. There are constant soft, jocular exchanges. 'A transaction here is not entirely economic. It's a matter of friendship and socializin' for a minute. That's as important to me as gettin' that quarter.'

As will be discussed below, the socially embedded customer has important implications for the experience of front-line work.

What then, about the implications of the chapter's preceding analysis for the experience of front-line work? The analysis implies that the experience of front-line work is best conceptualised in terms of *tensions*, *spaces* and *fine lines*. If the organisation of front-line work is underpinned by essential contradictions then it becomes obvious that the front-line worker is positioned in a potentially *tension*-ridden situation. Most starkly, the worker may be caught between conflicting demands of management and the customer. As one store worker interviewed by Weatherly and Tansik (1992, p. 5) put it:

> I'm damned if I do; damned if I don't. You just can't win. Either [the boss] is mad at me, or the customer is. If I don't get my work done, [the boss] is going to yell at me. But if I don't help the customers, they get pissed at me.

It is worth dwelling on the apparently commonplace final sentence in this quotation, and considering it in light of the concept of the enchanted and disillusioned customer. The customers become 'pissed' at the worker precisely at the point when enchantment turns to disillusionment. Enchanted by the general idea of the sovereign customer, reinforced perhaps by specific advertising relating to this store, the customer enters the store expecting service to match this concept of sovereignty. But this concept of sovereignty is a myth, especially so in the context of the front-line workplace, which is informed by a bureaucratic logic as a well as a customer-oriented one. The enchanting myth slips to disillusionment as the customer is confronted by front-line workers who are undertaking bureaucratic tasks related to the internal functioning of the firm and who thus do not treat him or her as a sovereign. The sting of powerlessness is sharp when set against the initial sense of sovereignty. And this may give rise to anger, abuse and aggression. To what or whom will this anger be directed? In the sharp pain of the moment it is less likely to be directed at the structural contradictions of the situation than at the front-line worker immediately present before the customer and on the surface at least immediately responsible for the painful journey from enchantment to disillusionment. In this very important sense the irate customer should be seen as a *systematic* part of the social relations of the front-line workplace.

The irate customer, systematically present, is an important figure in the experience of front-line work. Irate customers are likely to cause considerable pain to front-line workers (Korczysnki, 2001). This is because these workers are hired on the basis of, and further socialised into, holding strong pro-customer attitudes, particularly customer empathy. When a party to whom you are empathetic and favourably disposed turns against you in an irate manner this is likely to cause sharp pain. In this way, the irate customer should be seen as another key catalyst in the breakdown of the carefully forged, but necessarily fragile, social order of the front-line workplace. The pain they cause arises out of the structural tensions of the situation and makes meaningless management rhetoric of balance and shared interests. This pain may also be a key factor informing 'burnout' among front-line workers – a factor examined in more depth in Chapters 5 and 8.

If customers can be a source of pain for front-line workers, they can also be an important source of pleasure and satisfaction. Front-line workers who are empathetic to customers, who are able to help customers, who solve customer problems and who receive thanks in return are likely to see that as an intrinsically satisfying part of their job (Tolich, 1993). In research with which I was involved in call centres in Australia, Japan and the USA, we interviewed call centre workers and asked them what they liked best about the job. A very clear pattern emerged of workers volunteering that they enjoyed the job best when they could 'help people' (Frenkel *et al.*, 1999; Korczynski *et al.*, 2000). Hodson and Sullivan (1995, p. 282) also stress the importance to service workers 'of experiencing the satisfactions of assisting others'. This idea of relations with customers as a key source of satisfaction can also be linked with the concept of the socially embedded customer and the idea of *spaces* in front-line work. It is highly relevant that when asked in their own words about the satisfaction from helping customers, workers tend to use the language of helping people, mothers, kids, rather than *customers*. Williams (1987, p. 106) reports a survey of Australian flight attendants which shows that the most important reasons for becoming a flight attendant was 'working with people'. She notes that

> this was emphasised again in interviews as a positive aspect of the job. 'I enjoy flying because I meet people – caring for people – to do something for someone. Doing extra if someone is ill gives me satisfaction'. 'Helping mothers with a baby and the "thank you" means more to you than the travel.' Another said: 'Little kids travelling on their own, you get pleasure out of doing that sort of thing'.

When asked for particular examples of satisfying incidents, front-line workers tend to talk of 'this old man', or 'this nice woman'. In other words, they are relating to the service recipient primarily as socially embedded people, rather than as customers.[9] Even at Ritzer's least favourite fast-food restaurant, there can be a not insignificant degree of social embeddedness in the service encounter. Leidner (1993, p. 230) writes on the basis of her ethnographic study of two service firms: 'many of the encounters between workers and customers at McDonald's and between agents and prospects of Combined Insurance were experienced by both parties as real social exchanges'. Further, a key satisfaction for workers from customers comes from having 'regulars' with whom it is enjoyable to interact (Tolich, 1993). As Hodson and Sullivan (1995, p. 280) put it:

> Many service workers prize their regular customers because they have the opportunity to build a personal relationship with the customer. In this case, a genuine relationship may replace the struggle to control the relationship.

Front-line work may frequently provide the spaces for such socially embedded pleasures – despite the bureaucratic structures and emphasis on efficiency in the large organisations that predominate in many service industries.

The idea of the customer-oriented bureaucracy suggests that management will frequently be caught in a position of considerable ambiguity. This ambiguity implies the potential for workers to actively create spaces in which their organisational life can become more meaningful and enjoyable. To return to Weatherly and Tansik's (1993) study of store workers, they found that frequently workers reacted to being caught between conflicting demands from customers and management by creating spaces – by negotiating with management, by pre-empting conflicting demands by repositioning themselves (physically, and metaphorically), and also by simply avoiding conflicting demands through the creative reinterpretation of such demands. In this context, the authors suggest that front-line workers may welcome role ambiguity, and they offer some statistical findings to support this. Blau (1974) suggests that a key contingency in this is the degree to which the immediate supervisor is wedded strongly to either the bureaucratic logic or the customer-oriented one. More generally, the dual legitimate logics of the customer-oriented bureaucracy provide workers with a language to justify the spaces they have created. If confronted by irate customers, for instance, workers can seek to protect themselves by prioritising bureaucratic rules and procedures (Leidner, 1993). Conversely, workers can to a degree legitimately justify spending extra time solving 'that nice old man's problem' because in so doing they are being 'customer-oriented'. They can legitimately justify the non-work-related chats they have with 'regulars' in terms of helping to keep customers loyal. Miller's (1981) historical study of the development of French department stores provides an interesting example of consumers and front-line work involved in socially embedded gendered spaces. In the stores both the customers and the staff were very predominantly female. Department stores in many countries became an important public female space, an 'Adamless Eden' in the memorable phrase of Reekie (1992). Although Miller and Reekie are predominantly interested in drawing out the ambiguous advantages this brought women customers, it is also possible to see potentially important benefits from such female spaces for female staff. Despite being subject to considerable constraints in their work roles (Benson, 1986), they could still derive real pleasure from being able to interact with other women (rather than just 'customers') in a public sphere. Laermans (1993, p. 89) notes that 'for more and more women, the stores became equivalents of male downtown clubs and cafes...a number of stores even provided free meeting rooms for women's organisations'. In this sense, Corrigan (1997, p. 62) is correct to suggest that 'department stores played a role in emancipating women'.

Examining front-line workers' experience of customers in terms of tensions and spaces has shown how customers can constitute important and *simultaneous* sources of both pain and pleasure in their work (Benner and Wrubel, 1989; Blau, 1974). Tolich's (1993, p. 368) ethnographic study of a supermarket concludes that 'grocery clerks simultaneously viewed their customers as sources of stress and satisfaction'. Williams (1987, pp. 106–7) reports that a survey of Australian flight attendants showed that while 'working with people' was the dominant reason for taking on the job, 'passenger attitude' was the second most important source of job dissatisfaction. A contribution of the customer-oriented bureaucracy model is to offer systematic reasons why this is likely to be the case in many front-line workplaces. Tensions and spaces are part of the front-line workplace which is underpinned by essential contradictions. Benson (1986, p. 6) shows in her study of a US department store that

> when managers and customers exerted unified pressure on the saleswoman, her life could be difficult indeed; but [that] when she could play one off against the other she could create new space for herself on the job.

There are systematic reasons that the customer appears to front-line workers as 'our friend, the enemy', in the memorable phrase of the department store workers studied by Benson.

There is another important way in which front-line workers may be caught between the demands of the customer and those of management. Above all, workers must ensure that the seductive and enchanting myth of customer sovereignty is perpetuated in the service encounter. As Campbell (1987) argues, to derive pleasure from goods and services consumers must see consumption as an 'autonomous field of action' in which they are in control (Hewer and Campbell, 1997, p. 190). Thus workers must give the appearance to the customer that it is the customer who is in control of the interaction. At the same time, however, they have the bureaucratic imperative of dealing with the customer efficiently in as short a time as possible. Thus, management charges them with the necessity to take control of the interaction in order to complete it efficiently. Taken together, these two points mean that front-line workers must seek to efficiently structure and control an interaction while giving to the customer the impression that it is the customer who is in control. front-line workers, therefore, as much as management, have to walk a *fine line* in maintaining the fragile social order of service work. In Tisdale's (1986) discussion of nursing, this fine line is expressed as a 'narrow path', on which 'it is easy to slip'.

Conclusion

To understand service work it is necessary to understand the customer. The first section of this chapter argued that the customer should be seen as both rational and irrational. In service encounters, the service quality that customers seek embraces both efficiency and the (formally irrational) enchanting myth of sovereignty. Goods and services elicit both use-values and sign-values. In service interactions, the use-value consumed is the speedy and reliable performance of a service, for instance the serving of food in a café, while the key sign-value consumed is the impression that the customer is important and in charge – the enchanting myth of sovereignty. With this established, the chapter turned to examine the implications of this understanding for work organisation and HRM. The model of the customer-oriented bureaucracy was put forward as a way of capturing the dual imperatives in the organisation of service work – the need to be customer-oriented, to create the enchanting myth of customer sovereignty and to be efficient at the same time. The model puts forward the implications of these logics across a range of dimensions of work organisation, highlighting the dilemmas for management in each area. Management must somehow create a fragile social order that promotes sufficient efficient and customer-oriented behaviour from the front-line workforce to ensure the creation of a profit. HRM plays a key role here, both in promoting the appropriate worker behaviour and in seeking to diffuse the inevitable tensions that arise. Finally, the chapter turned to examine the implications for the experience of front-line work. While a negative interpretation of the customer-oriented bureaucracy might focus solely on the tensions created for the workforce by the existence of the dual logics underlying their work, my argument was that as well as tensions, the structures of the customer-oriented bureaucracy also bring spaces and fine lines. The analysis in this chapter has been theoretical, but it has been grounded theory with empirical research called on from a range of service settings. The following chapter pushes the empirical aspect to the forefront with an analysis of how the model of customer-oriented bureaucracy can illuminate three important types of front-line work.

Notes

1   There are parallels between this point and Offe's (1985) argument that a key social function of service work is that it involves the maintenance of 'normal conditions' by reproducing the wider social structure.
2   The enchanting myth of customer sovereignty involves both 'empowerment and entrapment' for the customer (Sturdy *et al.*, 2001). There is empowerment in the sense that the service interaction must be structured to give the appearance of customer control, and in the sense that customers can potentially use the myth to their advantage by challenging service organisations to live up to their (mythical) promises. There is entrapment in the sense that the emphasis is upon the *appearance* of control, and in the sense that management tends to structure the service interaction with this dominant sign-value in mind. Individual customers who do

not seek to consume the enchanting myth of sovereignty thus often find themselves trapped, against their will, in a series of (mythically) empowering relationships with front-line workers.

3   Although customer sovereignty is a myth, it is an enchanting one that connects with widespread societal norms. As Edwards (2000) and McDonald and Sirianni (1996) note, the norm of 'the customer as king' is widespread. There are two important material bases for this norm. One is the stream of messages put forward by producing organisations compelled to competitively appeal and enchant. The other is the strength of the marginalist economics school whose message supports and is propounded by powerful interests. Miller (1995) argues that although there remains a 'wide discrepancy between economic theory and the world', marginalist economics has increasingly colonised aspects of economy and society as an ideology, informing people's perceptions and images of the world.

4   Another way in which to think of the duality captured in the concept of the customer-oriented bureaucracy is suggested by Bryman's concept of 'Disneyisation' (1999). Bryman contrasts Disneyisation against Ritzer's concept of McDonaldisation by arguing that Dinseyisation is a process aligned with post-modernity and consumer culture studies (which stress the irrational nature of the consumer), while McDonaldisation is aligned with modernity and Weberian analysis emphasising the dominance of rationality. The concept of the customer-oriented bureaucracy posits the presence of both of these aspects and places them in the specific context of front-line work.

5   In Offe's (1985, pp. 105–6) terms, within service labour,

> On the one hand, the particularity, individuality, contingency and variability (of the situations and needs of clients ...) must be preserved ... On the other hand, service labour must ultimately bring about a state of affairs which conforms to certain general rules. The definition of service labour ... draws attention to processes of individuation and differentiation on the one hand and coordination and standardization requirements on the other. Service labour can be deemed successful if it effects a balance between these two aspects.

6   Not discussed in this model centring on work organisation is another important way in which management may seek to create a social order out of contradictory tensions. Management can take the need to preserve the myth of sovereignty and combine it with the bureaucratic need to use the organisation's resources efficiently by designing the service interaction such that the customer, apparently autonomously, undertakes part of the service labour. The genius of this device is that it reinforces the enchanting myth of sovereignty because customers feel more in charge if they are active co-producers, and it saves the organisation labour resources. Writers have discussed it in various terms: the rise of the self-service society (Gershuny and Miles, 1983; Glazer, 1983), the rise of unpaid labour (Glazer, 1993; Ritzer, 1996) or the rise of customers as co-producers (Lachman, 2000). Not surprisingly, management writers have also been keen to stress the

benefits of 'look[ing] to consumers to increase productivity' (Lovelock and Young, 1979; Normann, 1984). This literature clearly brings out how widespread an element this has become. Ritzer provides relatively trivial examples – of customers now using cash machines to withdraw money from banks, and of McDonald's customers being trained to clear the table after them. Both examples entail customers using their own labour in a service transaction in which previously a front-line worker's labour would have been expended. In this sense, he argues that customers are more exploited than workers, for at least workers are paid some money. In this, he misses an important point that the reward to the customer is the greater sense of control over consumption, and the perpetuation of the comforting and seductive myth of sovereignty. Glazer's (1993) account is more wide-ranging, arguing that the use of customer labour in the US health and retail sectors has in effect meant proportionately greater use of unpaid female labour. She also argues that the increasing use of customer labour tends to lead to the deskilling of the remaining front-line jobs. Although her evidence on this point needs to be considerably strengthened, her thesis remains a provocative one. She stresses that the move to customer labour occurred not because customers were clamouring for it but because service organisations needed to increase efficiency by lowering their costs. In part, she links this bureaucratic imperative to the sovereignty myth, writing that 'any service work could be transferred to customers with the disingenuous offer of freedom' (1993, p. 219).

7   Although not uncontested, the basic idea that employment policies will be strongly influenced by the competitive terrain in which firms act is difficult to argue against. The idea has a long lineage in pre-HRM analyses of work. For instance, a key insight of labour process analysis is that the 'frontier of control' in the workplace between management and labour is heavily influenced by the nature of competition within firms' product markets (Braverman, 1974; Friedman, 1977; Edwards, 1979). Certainly, qualifications must be made regarding over-deterministic views of the relationship between a firm's product market competition and its employment policies. One of the most important of these is Child's (1972) concept of strategic choice (echoed by Kochan *et al.*, 1986), which posits that management behaviour is not solely environmentally determined and that there is scope for a degree of strategic choice for management in decision-making, not least within employment relations. Another qualification is that the link between product market competition and employment policies should not be seen simply in terms of a rational, linear decision-making process by management. However, once the qualifications are made, the basic insight still stands. HRM, in part, represents simply an attempt to systematise the link between employment policies and business strategy and/or product market competition.

8   Indeed, this is precisely the way in which the satisfaction mirror concept is used in the new service management school. Recall the critique in Chapter 2 that showed how the climate for employee well-being was a spectacular misnomer. The point developed here is that not only is this a misnomer, but that the elements within the 'climate for employee well-being' are defined as such only because they are the

factors that could be found to correlate (to a degree) with customer evaluation of service quality. In other words, workers have legitimate interests only in so far as they inform customer interests.

9 The idea of socially embedded spaces within the structures of worker–customer interactions has clear parallels with Goffman's (1983) concept of a loose coupling of a specific interaction with the macro structural arrangement in which it is situated.

CHAPTER 5

Analysing distinctive types of front-line work

As noted in Chapter 1, this book has two main aims – it should illuminate the general nature of front-line work, and it should be able to shed light on specific types of service work. The previous chapter presented the customer-oriented bureaucracy model as a way in to understanding contemporary front-line work generally. This chapter uses the concept to examine features of important, distinctive types of front-line work. It is, thus, directed at the second main aim of the book. The concept of the customer-oriented bureaucracy highlights dual pressures informing the structuring of service work; it leaves open the issue of how management seeks to resolve these dilemmas in practice. This chapter shows that in relation to hospitality work, call centre work and health care work, the way in which management seeks to create a (fragile) social order out of the dual logics can have some important differences in different service settings. I have chosen to focus on these three types of service work in part because they are numerically important areas of employment. In addition, they represent important aspects of employment in the service economy. Hospitality work is a long-established area of service work and is associated with consumption as leisure. Call centre work, by contrast, is a new arena of employment, which is associated mostly with financially related consumption, and highlights the importance of the role of technology in service work. Health care work, undertaken by nurses, nurse aides and health care assistants, is generally more highly skilled than hospitality and call centre work. It is associated with consumption related to welfare and stands as the form of front-line work in which there is the deepest attachment between front-line worker and service recipient. The chapter examines each of the types of work in turn, examining the dual pressures underlying the work, how management has sought to resolve the dilemmas highlighted in the concept of the customer-oriented bureaucracy, and how this has affected the way the work is experienced by the front-line staff.

Hospitality work

This section focuses on front-line hospitality work, that is work in restaurants, hotels, cafes, bars and clubs. Approximately 10 per cent of the UK workforce is employed in the sector (Boella, 1996, p. 24). Front-line hospitality work is best examined through the lens of the customer-oriented bureaucracy. Indeed, a number of perceptive studies have already highlighted the dual and often contradictory logics underlying the management and experience of hospitality work. Jones *et al.* (1997, p. 552), for instance, in their study of a large American-owned hotel chain operating in the USA, Austria, Britain and Poland, conclude that 'international hotel companies, like Americo, are caught between the apparently contradictory impulses of standardisation and customisation but are unable to abandon either'. This is an important study, for it goes beneath the surface of a hospitality company that is systematic in its pursuit of the sort of HRM policies advocated by the new service management school. In this hotel chain, empowerment was high on the management agenda, while a great deal of attention was given both to hiring according to criteria of customer service attitudes and to widespread communication. Systematic training was given in customer service skills, and there was a strong focus on the generation of an overall service culture in the organisation. As Jones *et al.* show, all these elements were informed by the customer-oriented strategy of the firm. However, these factors joined but did not supplant the bureaucratic emphasis on increasing efficiency through measurement. This meant that although the hotel staff were empowered in the sense of being able to make more decisions on the basis of their own customer service values, they were still subject to systematic and pervasive performance measurement.

Shamir (1978), in a widely quoted study, also refers to key dual logics underpinning the structure of the UK hotels that he studied. He argues that, 'we can summarise our description by saying that... the hotels [are presented] with two major demands – a demand for flexibility on the one hand and demand for a high degree of control and coordination on the other.' The demand for flexibility stems from the variability of customers, while the demand for control stems from a bureaucratic rationale tied to the need for cost control. Shamir's study is an important one because he directly criticises the contingency approach to organisational analysis. A key aspect of the contingency approach is that there is an optimum 'fit' between an organisation and its environment, for example, its customers. Contingency approaches suggest that organisations should and will be more standardised if their customers' requests are standardised and will be more loose and flexible if their customers' demands are more variable and idiosyncratic. This is a banal insight that in fact serves to obscure the continued tensions between rationalisation and customer orientation in service organisations. Rather than suggesting that organisations' policies 'fit' their environment, analysis should highlight that there are different ways in which management seeks to create a social order – some firms (for example, the Americo hotel chain) will have more explicitly customer-oriented structures and policies, while others (for example, McDonald's) will have more bureaucratic procedures. The point is that both logics are likely to be present to a significant degree in service organisations and that management must seek to create a social order (that is necessarily fragile) out of these potentially contradictory logics. This key insight is lost with the concept of 'fit'.

This is exactly the argument that Shamir makes with regard to contingency approaches to management structures and policies in hotels. He reviews the contingency approaches of Burns and Stalker (1961), Woodward (1965) and Thompson (1967) – all of which still have a considerable degree of prominence in organisational behaviour literature – and draws out a number of propositions from their analysis. He argues that these approaches fail to capture the fundamentally dualistic nature of management structures and policies. For instance, Burns and Stalker's approach would suggest that the hotels Shamir studies should be able to be located along a continuum *between* mechanistic organisations and organic ones. However, he finds that the hotels are *both* mechanistic and organic. He concludes by arguing that

> the traditional hotel structure can be seen as resolving the conflict between the demands of bureaucracy and those of hospitality [that is, customer orientation], by employing some mechanistic means of control and giving the appearance of a mechanistic organisation on one hand, but preserving the ability to adjust to hospitality requirements on the other. (p. 301)

Management policies in front-line work will often wax and wane between customer orientation and rationalisation in the endless search for the 'balance' between the two. This facet is well brought out in the hospitality context by Sosteric's (1996) study of a nightclub. In the club studied, the relaxed, non-standardised, customer-oriented policies were not reaping high enough profit levels and so new managers were brought in to instigate policies emphasising efficiency, standardisation and hierarchical control. This in turn led to considerable resistance and discontent from staff and signs of dissatisfaction from the regular customers. In turn this led to the return of the original management team. These dynamics are common to many service workplaces. Another aspect of hospitality work commonly noted by studies, that of conflict between types of staff, can be usefully illuminated by reference to the concept of the customer-oriented bureaucracy. The most common form of inter-staff conflict in hospitality is 'the conflict between "front of house" department and "back of house" departments' (Shamir, 1978, p. 288). A well-known example of this is the conflict between waiters and kitchen staff (Whyte, 1948). This conflict, apparently endemic to hospitality work (Bowey, 1976; Dann and

Hornsley, 1986; Wood, 1992), stems from the 'back of house' production being run along more bureaucratic lines with an emphasis on efficiency in production, with the 'front of house' positions being subject to more direct pressures to be customer-oriented.[1] When the waiter's customer-oriented demands for a particular, idiosyncratic, form of meal preparation clashes with the kitchen staff's bureaucratic imperative of efficient meal preparation, then the conflict becomes expressed in shouts of personal insults. Often the chefs are male and the waiting staff female, and so the conflict is also played out in gender terms (for instance see Spradley and Mann, 1975; Snow, 1981). This conflict, often manifest in interpersonal tensions, may be an important aspect of hospitality work, for Snow's study suggests that many hospitality workers left their jobs because of interpersonal disputes, both between and within departments. Significantly, these interpersonal disputes had a structural basis in that they were based primarily on differences over how work should be performed.

The previous chapter discussed how the dual logics of contemporary service work increasingly push management into attempting to make the organisation not only flexible in order to meet variable customer demand but also sufficiently stable to maximise efficiency of production. It was suggested that one way in which managers in service firms seek to create a fragile social order out of these pressures is to adopt the practices of 'the flexible firm' (Atkinson, 1985), with a stable core and numerically flexible periphery. Walsh (1990) shows that in the UK hotel and retail firms that he studied the use of casual and seasonal employment to cover unpredictable and seasonal variations in demand was a common strategy. Further, he suggests that numerically flexible employment was central to the nature of employment structures in much hospitality work (also see NEDO, 1986; Wood, 1992; Guerrier, 1999, pp. 169–70). In part this reflects the greater variability in the overall level and timing of customer demand in this sector than in other service sectors (Lockwood and Guerrier, 1989).

Another distinctive aspect in the structure and experience of some types of hospitality work is tipping. This can be usefully examined in terms of its role in authority and control and in the nature of the worker–customer relationship. Notably, Mars *et al.* (1979, pp. 84–5) argue that the effect of tipping is that 'instead of working for one boss the employee is working for two ... Tipping both expresses and supports a split in managerial authority'. Similarly, Paules (1991, p. 54) notes that, 'in transferring control over the worker's income to the public, the tipping system divests management of a traditional source and symbol of managerial authority and detracts from the employee's sense of obligation to the company'. In other words, in hospitality work, tipping informs a clear manifestation of the dual sources of authority central to the concept of the customer-oriented bureaucracy. The customer's unique role, in tipping, of furnishing of monetary rewards also has important and distinctive implications for the nature of the relationship between the worker and the customer. As with the introduction of direct payment in all social relations (Titmuss, 1970), it tends to lead to a greater instrumentality in the relationship. A number of studies of waiting staff show that workers often relate to customers instrumentally, seeing customers less in the socially embedded terms common to other types of front-line work and more in terms of their tipping potential (Bowey, 1976; Spradley and Mann, 1975; Mars and Nicod, 1984). Tipping promotes the view of customers as a means to an end (that is, monetary reward). Paules's rich ethnographic study of waitressing in a New Jersey restaurant brings this out starkly: 'she [the waitress] adopts a detached, calculating attitude towards her parties, viewing them foremost in terms of their tipping potential' (1991, p. 12). Further, Paules notes that, 'if the customer is perceived as material that is processed, the goal of this processing is the production or extraction of a finished product: the tip' (p. 34). The considerably more dehumanised relationship between worker and customer is apparent in labels given by waiting staff to customers. Mars and Nicod, for instance, note the following terms used by waiting staff with regard to customers: 'bastards', 'bitches', 'prostitutes', 'peasants', 'snobs', and 'pigs'.

While these are important *effects* of tipping in hospitality work, an important question concerns why tipping exists. In part it is a socially embedded historical legacy of the hospitality industry. As Wood (1992, p. 17) notes, a number of authors have argued that the industry has its origins in the class of domestic servants who maintained the homes of the ruling classes in the latter half of the nineteenth century and first half of the twentieth (Saunders, 1981; Riley, 1985). According to Saunders, the decline in the number of domestic servants in the first part of the twentieth century coincided with the first significant growth in hotel employment. From this angle, tipping can be seen as a historical legacy of the relations of servility and deference between domestic servant and wealthy employer. In addition, tipping can also be seen as a key managerial mechanism for constructing a fragile social order in the context of the way in which the dual logics of the customer orientation and rationalisation are played out in the specific circumstances of hospitality work.[2] First, it is clearly a mechanism that perpetuates the enchanting myth of customer sovereignty. For instance, Paules (1991) sees tipping as being central to the symbolism of restaurant work in which 'the customer accepts the imagery of...master' (p. 131). In addition, it allows management to address the problems of control in front-line work – which, as Chapter 7 shows, relate to the issues of observability, variability and output measurement. Tipping in hospitality work occurs in those jobs where these problems are heightened. So for waiting staff, for instance, management cannot easily observe the waiting work being undertaken (observability), it cannot easily set rigid rules and procedures for waiting staff to follow because customers in cafes and restaurants may be highly variable (variability) and nor can it easily measure the output in terms of the customer's view of the service quality (output measurement). In this context, hospitality employers have seized on the historical legacy of tipping as an apparently easy solution to these problems. Further, another attraction for employers is that tipping helps to construct a fragile social order by effectively making waiting staff internalise both customer-oriented and bureaucratic imperatives. Tipping encourages staff not only to act in customer-oriented ways but also to be conscious of the need to deal with customers speedily and efficiently. As Paules (1991) points out, waiting staff can increase their tips by acting in customer-oriented ways, but it is also the case that 'an employee can increase her tip income by controlling the number as well as the size of tips she receives' (p. 26). Tipping becomes a mechanism whereby it is left to individual workers to construct their own point of 'balance' within the dual logics. It is also a mechanism which forces female waiting staff to internalise their use of sexuality in service interactions (Spradley and Mann, 1975).

This all means that tipping is likely to be a key factor informing the high labour turnover in the hospitality industry. Not only does it lead to a greater internalisation of tensions by staff, but it often represents a virtual abdication of other HRM practices by management – practices which in other front-line settings have a role in constructing and maintaining a fragile social order. Lucas (1995) points out that a body of literature has developed characterising the hospitality sector in terms of ad hoc management. Mars *et al.* (1979, p. 83) argue that tipping underlies what can be called 'a managerial vacuum, that is, a tendency for managers to isolate themselves from their staff, to know little of what goes on in their organisations and to avoid overall responsibility for their employees'. Herein lies a key contradiction in the experience of hospitality work. While tipping increases the internalisation of tensions for staff it also frequently leads to the creation of important spaces for them – spaces partly provided by the accompanying 'managerial vacuum'. As Paules (1991, p. 78) notes, regardless of paper procedures and rules from head office, the waiting staff in the restaurant she studied 'enjoyed considerable autonomy, or freedom from external constraint in their work lives'. Another important space for meaning and satisfaction in hospitality work exists in the possibility for pleasurable socially embedded relations with customers. Although tipping tends to instrumentalise relations, the growth in hospitality firms orienting towards specific niches of customer types provides a greater possibility for the identification of the front-line worker with the customer. Both Marshall (1986) and Crang (1993) explore this in detail. Marshall's study of a restaurant found that most staff did not experience their work as *work* because relations between workers and customers were so pleasurable and socially embedded. Much of the job of waiting involved socialising with customers who not infrequently were friends from outside the work environment. Crang notes the pleasures to be gleaned in a niche, 'lifestyle' restaurant where to be chosen for employment implicitly affords one membership of a cultural community, with membership having considerable kudos.

There is evidence that while much of hospitality work may have been undertaken traditionally within a managerial vacuum, within larger organisations this is no longer the case. Butler and Skipper's (1981) study showed that in larger restaurants management increased surveillance of the work, rather than just relying on the functioning of tipping system. This, in turn, led to greater resentment of surveillance, with restaurant workers interpreting station inspection, daily inspection of tables and equipment as indicative of distrust. Enter HRM with its systematic language of balance and mutuality to mask social situations of conflict and contradiction. Hoque (2000), for instance, argues persuasively that for many large hotel firms, systematic HRM polices are now common. At the same time, his data point to the dual imperatives of efficiency and service quality underlying the structuring of hotel work. HRM rises not only as the size of organisations rises but also as the need for the creation of a (fragile) social order within the contradictory demands of hotel work rises.

The constraints of space prevent a further examination of the tensions, spaces and fine lines in the experience of hospitality work. One further point is worth making, however. While many of the studies discussed in this section have been based in the UK, it is important to note Wood's (1992, p. 156) argument that many of the characteristics of UK hospitality work are mirrored in other countries, particularly the USA and Australia.

Call centre work

Call centre employment is growing dramatically in many advanced economies. Estimates suggest that 1.3 per cent of the working population in Europe will be employed in call centres in the early years of this century (Datamonitor, 1998). Call centres now employ 160000 people in Australia (ASU, 2000). The literature on call centres parallels the literature on the general nature of service work, with strong positive images put forward by management writers, and equally strong negative images emanating from writers who take a critical perspective. Management writers suggest that increasingly call centres feature highly skilled and well-trained employees who are empowered, and committed to the job of delivering high-quality customer service (Cleveland and Mayben, 1997; Hook, 1998; Durr, 1996; Menday, 1996). Against this cheerleading approach to call centre work a number of authors have painted an overwhelmingly negative picture of it. Call centres have been labelled 'the new sweatshops' (*Guardian*, 2 June 1998), and 'bright satanic offices' (Baldry *et al.*, 1998). Many echo Taylor and Bain's (1999a, p. 115) summary of the experience of call centre work in which there is little space for satisfaction in the job:

in all probability, work consists of an uninterrupted and endless sequence of similar conversations with customers she never meets ... The pressure is intense because she knows her work is being measured, her speech monitored, and it often leaves her mentally, physically and emotionally exhausted.

The case for an overwhelmingly negative picture of call centre work is strongest in the one in four cases where the work involves outbound sales (NTO Tele.com, 1999) – not least because of different implications for control systems in structured outbound sales work. The implications and distinctiveness of *sales* work are examined in the following chapter. The discussion of call centre work in this section, however, concentrates on call centre service work rather than sales work.

While the critical studies of call centres are a welcome antidote to the saccharine analysis offered by management writers, both approaches are flawed in their own way. Management writers can construct a harmonious picture of call centres only by suggesting a coalescing of interests around the customer and the goal of customer orientation, while critical writers tend to stress the increased rationalisation and Taylorism in call centre work. It is the familiar picture of both approaches being too one-eyed and hence failing to capture the full, deep-seated contradictions of call centre work – contradictions of pleasures and pains in the experience of the work, and contradictions in the management of such work centring on the attempted creation of a (necessarily fragile) social order out of the potentially contradictory logics of customer orientation and rationalisation. Call centres have been most commonly created following BPR initiatives in organisations (Knights and McCabe, 1997). As Chapter 2 suggested, BPR initiatives are informed not simply by rationalising, efficiency aims, but also by a desire to reconfigure the work process in a more customer-oriented manner. As a report has noted, call centres are attractive to organisations for two main reasons (Datamonitor, 1998). First, they allow a dramatic reduction in costs per customer transaction compared with face-to-face transactions. This is the logic of efficiency pushing the development of call centres. Second, they also enable organisations to deliver what they consider to be higher and more consistent levels of customer service, for instance, through allowing customers to make transactions outside normal business hours, and through the creation of a 'one-stop shop' to deal with a range of queries. This is the logic of customer orientation pushing the development of call centres. It is clearly necessary to be aware that call centres will vary according to different emphases on rationalisation and customer orientation (Lankshear *et al.*, 2000; Batt, 2000). However, it is clear that *both* logics have been important overall.

These dual origins of call centres systematically inform the management and experience of call centre work. Elsewhere, I have shown how the concept of the customer-oriented bureaucracy helps to illuminate work in five call centres in Australia, Japan and the USA that colleagues and I studied (Frenkel *et al.*, 1998; Frenkel *et al.* 1999; Korczynski, 2001). Here I will summarise some of the key themes in that analysis, and connect it to other research on call centres. As Arzbacher *et al.* (2000, p. 1) suggest, call centres lie between 'neo-taylorism and customer orientation'. As a study by URCOT (2000), a union research centre in Australia concludes, there are elements of *both* 'modern sweatshops' and 'positive modern workplaces' in many call centres. The dual dominating logics of call centre work came through most clearly in the management emphasis on both quantitative and qualitative measures of work performance. This dual emphasis on what Taylor and Tyler (2000) call 'hard' and 'soft' measures has been picked out by a range of researchers who have studied call centres (Knights *et al.*, 1999; Belt *et al.*, 1999). In one of the call centres I studied, the management aim of creating a fragile social order out of these competing focuses came through in the way managers noted that they were constantly switching emphasis between one and other, trying to estab-lish a form of equilibrium that they never quite reached. One team leader noted that 'it's exasperating to the reps [centre workers] but also to manage-ment. It's almost as if we have double standards.' This is a quintessential refrain of management operating in organisations infused with dual logics. As the focus on one waxes, the focus on the other wanes (see also Alferoff and Knights, 2000), and so over time reflective managers come to see their stand-ards as being double. Tensions between managers were also informed by dual logics of customer orientation and rationalisation. For instance, in one Australian firm, senior management attempted to use a classic Taylorist time-and-motion study technique entitled 'clerical work measurement'. However, another manager had vetoed this, because, he argued, 'cutting talk time cuts service'. One manager champions rationalisation, while the other champions service quality emanating from customer orientation.

The dual bases of the division of labour were also clearly present in the five centres. Management sought the development of pseudo-relationships with customers – combining both the aim to develop a relationship with a customer with the bureaucratic aim of efficient task completion. Workers were in-structed to give out their first names to customers, and were able to draw up a wide range of information on the customer almost instantaneously. However, workers were instructed not to direct customers to return calls to specific workers but to encourage customers to call back the centre as a whole. Management was opposed to the development of relationships between spe-cific workers and specific customers, because this worked against manage-ment aims of efficient call-handling. If customers waited for a specific worker to be available, rather than the next available call centre agent, the customer would necessarily have to wait longer in the queue. For management, cus-tomers waiting a long time in the queue were synonymous with inefficiency in their operations.

The nature of control in call centres has been a particular focus for writers from a critical perspective (Callaghan and Thompson, 2000; Mulholland, 2000;

Rose, 2000). These studies do well to bring out the pervasive system of measurement and monitoring, present in many call centres, that is facilitated by the information relayed by the information technology that call centre agents work on. This is a heightened form of traditional bureaucratic methods of control. What was also notable about control in the call centres that I helped to study was that this bureaucratic control was supplemented by the use and development of customer-related norms (Korczynski *et al.*, 2000). So the system of control could be best analysed through the lens of the customer-oriented bureaucracy. Managers wanted to hire people only if they held customer-oriented values. These values were further developed in training and performance appraisal sessions in which workers were constantly asked to put themselves 'in the customer's shoes'. In many cases, customer-related values also informed attitudes and behaviour on the job (also Lankshear *et al.*, 2000). Thus, HRM practices sought to establish and maintain a customer-oriented culture. Another important aspect of HRM in the call centres studied was the conduct of individual performance appraisals. Here the emphasis was on managers 'negotiating' individual points of 'balance' with individual workers regarding targets and standards for the qualitative, customer-oriented aspect of the work, and for the quantitative, bureaucratic aspect of the work. Taylor (1998) notes a similar phenomenon of appraisals leading to differing targets for individual workers in the call centre he studied. Indeed, Taylor and Tyler (2000) suggest that the way differing targets were set may have been gendered in the sense that female workers' targets tended to prioritise the 'soft', qualitative side while male workers' targets seemed to focus on the 'hard', quantitative side. Although the data they present to support this argument are suggestive rather than compelling, the concept of the alignment of female with the customer orientation logic and male with the bureaucratic logic is one that finds echoes in many other studies of differing types of service work. In addition, research has uncovered the importance of management rhetoric in attempting to fashion a (fragile) social order in the call centre workplace. Notably, Alferoff and Knights (2000) demonstrate that a call centre manager tried to fuse together a vision of balance and shared interests through a vision of a 'beautiful call' which would bring customer satisfaction (and, implicitly, worker and management satisfaction).

If the concept of the customer-oriented bureaucracy helps to illuminate the management structuring of call centre work, can it also help our understanding of the experience of call centre work? Taking the analytical approach of focusing on tensions, spaces and fine lines as suggested in the previous chapter, research into call centres suggests some very acute tensions, and some significant limitations on the spaces available. Key to these heightened tensions and circumvented spaces is the role of technology. For instance, technology immediately routes the next call to a call centre agent as soon as she or he has finished dealing with one customer. This means that call centres involve a high intensity of labour. Latent tensions are likely to lead to considerable experiences of stress when call centre agents' exposure to the contradictions of the work is intensified. The high levels of turnover in call centres (IDS, 1999; Bain and Taylor, 2000; Wallace *et al.*, 2000) are likely to be centrally informed by this. The intensification of labour means that the fragile social order of call centre work is frequently and systematically broken down.

Further, some authors have suggested that the pervasive gaze of technology, and the amount of information on worker behaviour it relays to management, effectively denies workers any space. For instance, Fernie and Metcalf (1997, p. 3, p. 10) argue that:

> The possibilities for monitoring behaviour and measuring output are amazing to behold – the 'tyranny of the assembly line' is but a Sunday school picnic compared with the control that management can exercise in computer telephony...In call centres the agents are constantly visible and the supervisor's power has indeed been 'rendered perfect' – via the computer monitoring screen – and therefore its actual use unnecessary.

Taylor and Bain (1999a) have rightly criticised this argument by showing the continued possibilities for resistance in call centres. But this criticism does not go far enough, and the lens of the customer-oriented bureaucracy allows us to see this. Conceptually, Fernie and Metcalf echo Ritzer's arguments of the service worker as automaton and robot, completely controlled by technology and management. As Chapter 3 showed, Ritzer could construct this argument on only the sands of denying the importance of service quality by equating quality with quantity. Similarly, Fernie and Metcalf can construct their argument of the perfection of management control in call centres only by ignoring implicitly the importance of service quality. Note that they argue that 'the possibilities for...measuring *output* are amazing to behold' (emphasis added). However, technology measures output only in bureaucratic, quantitative terms, such as the number of calls processed and the average length of calls. It does nothing to measure output in terms of the service quality delivered to individual customers. The true measure of this lies with the customers and hence is extremely difficult for management to measure directly, however well endowed with technology it may be. So, even in call centres with their often heightened tensions, there are spaces not only for resistance but also for finding pleasure and meaning in the work.

Research into the pleasures of call centre work is much more sparse than research highlighting monitoring and stress. This reflects not only the heavily critical perspective that has informed much of research on call centres, but also the traditional focus of research upon the worker–management dyad. The research reported in Frenkel *at al.* (1999) and Korczynski (2001) shows that the key main pleasure from the work in the five centres in Australia, Japan and the USA related to the socially embedded interaction with customers. In interviews, researchers asked call centre workers what they regarded as the best aspect of their jobs. Time and again, those interviewed replied that the best part of the job lay in 'helping people', in 'sorting out somebody's problem and getting a thank you'. This was a significant source of satisfaction in the job (and one that is invisible to researchers with an exclusive focus on the worker–management dyad). It meant that although 69 per cent of our (approximately 610) survey respondents from the call centres reported a degree of stress, 73 per cent of respondents still reported satisfaction with the job. Such are the contradictory experiences of call centre work.

An even more piquant contradiction in the experience of call centre work is that customers, as well as being the key source of satisfaction in the job, are often a key source of pain and stress (Lankshear *et al.*, 2000). This can be understood by reference to the multiple aspects of the customer outlined in the previous chapter. The socially embedded customer necessarily offers space for pleasure and satisfaction, but the dark side of the customer, drawn into view by the movement from enchantment to disillusionment, may lead to pain. The potential for pain from abusive customers in call centres is actually intensified compared with other forms of front-line work because of the distinctively technologically mediated, and hence partially disembedded, nature of customer–worker relations. To an important degree call centres disembed the customer–worker interaction, replacing what would previously have been a face-to-face interaction with one conducted on the telephone, creating a greater social distance between the two parties. As Milgram (1974) and Bauman (1989) have shown, the greater the social distance and technological mediation between two people, the greater the likelihood that the social basis and humanity of the interaction is stripped away. In front-line work, this simply means that the enchanted then disillusioned customer is more likely to become abusive to front-line workers if the interaction is over the phone rather than face to face. One call centre consultant notes that 'we are not dealing with face-to-face transactions. People feel free to rant and rage at a disembodied voice' (quoted in the *Guardian*, 2 June 1998). The issue is far from a trivial one. Another report in the *Guardian* notes (14 June 1999):

> According to research by the Industrial Society, more phone calls, fewer staff and higher expectations are just some of the growing trends contributing to the dramatic increase of 'phone rage'. 'It's obvious that the problem is widespread,' says...a training consultant for the society...Phone rage can be very costly in terms of lost customers, stressed out employees and low morale.

These quotations make reference to classic conditions for a breakdown of the fragile social order of the customer-oriented bureaucracy – the enchanting myth of sovereignty ('rising expectations') being undermined by the bureaucratic logic of production ('fewer staff'), with disillusionment turning to abuse because it is only a 'disembodied voice' against which customers rage.

Sensitive research has also highlighted how call centre work necessitates a fine line to be negotiated by the staff. Arzbacher *et al.* (2000, p. 11) put it that call centre workers need to be able 'to move between tight regimentation and flexibility, matter-of-factness and friendliness, subordination and responsibility'.

Health care work

This discussion is concerned with the heavily populated occupations of nurses and nursing aides, and with other types of health care occupations that rank lower than doctors in organisational power and status. Health care in many advanced economies has been undergoing considerable restructuring during the last two decades. In many cases, these changes can best be conceptualised as movements away from the domination of health care organisations by professionals and professional knowledge (Friedson, 1970) through a simultaneous increase in 'customer' orientation and in rationalisation – the key dual logics highlighted by the concept of the customer-oriented bureaucracy. The *Guardian* (5 June 2000) reported that the UK prime minister, Tony Blair, had attacked the culture that the 'consultant [a highly specialised and highly qualified doctor] is king'. This attack on the dominance of medical professionals was partially supported by a spokesperson for the Royal College of Nursing (the UK union-cum-professional body representing the majority of nurses), who employed a stark rhetoric of customer orientation in arguing that, 'the idea that the consumer is king, rather than the consultant, is absolutely key'. This language of customer orientation is no accident, for it echoes key government and management initiatives of the last two decades in the UK (Harrison and Pollitt, 1994; Elston, 1995). From the White Paper of 1987 (DoH, 1987) onwards, a major objective of successive governments has been to develop practices and rhetorics associated with consumerism in the public sector National Health Service. Increasingly, patients have been relabelled and reinvented as consumers of health. This customer-oriented market approach of UK governments is part of a pattern common to many advanced economies. Flowing from this, management has adopted a host of related practices in health care workplaces. Nurses, for instances, find themselves being put through service quality training courses (Bolton, 2000). Management regards the regular customer satisfaction surveys as of 'fundamental importance' (Morgan and Murgatroyd, 1994).

Equal in significance to these 'customer'-orientation policies have been systematic pressures in many economies to rationalise health care production, increasing efficiency and cutting costs. Glazer (1993) and Olesen and Bone (1998) have highlighted the restructuring of health care provision in the USA, which led to health care insurers exerting strong and systematic pressures on the providers of health care to rationalise production. Pratschke (2000) argues that the approach adopted in the USA, with its rationalising consequences, has been researched and supported by major international bodies such as the Organisation for Economic Cooperation and Development, the Council for Europe, the European Union and the World Health Organisation. In short, there have been simultaneous pressures of customer orientation and rational-isation driving the reorganisation of health care work. Indeed, Bolton (2000, p. 2) suggests that the aim of the UK government has been that the two should inform each other: 'central government identified consumerism as a means of increasing efficiency'. The full contradictions of health care work, therefore, are best captured through the lens of the customer-oriented bureaucracy and its focus on both key logics at play.

If we focus first on the management approach to structuring health care work, the dual logics are apparent in what Pratschke acutely sees as the key management task in contemporary health care (in Ireland and Italy): 'the ability of managers to pare down staffing levels to a minimum without sacrificing "quality of care"' (2000, p. 27; also see Ackroyd and Bolton, 1999). This in itself suggests an enormous pressure on management to some-how establish a (fragile) social order in these conditions. This is the cue for the entry of HRM and its associated rhetorics in the health care sector. A new cadre of managers with no medical background has introduced many of the HRM practices and phrases that are so common in other types of front-line work. Individual performance appraisals are increasingly practised for nurs-ing staff and are used to help find individual points of 'balance' between efficiency and patient-focus. Target-setting has also been introduced and formally monitored in some hospitals. As is discussed below, the central tension of nursing work involves being caught between the need to be effi-cient and a strong desire to give meaningful care to embodied patients. The HRM palliative to maintain the fragile social order in this context is to run 'time management' training courses for nurses, so that tensions are internal-ised by nurses rather than expressed in conflictual behaviour and demands (Wicks, 1998, p. 113).

The basis of the division of labour in health care work is also informed by dual logics. Some writers have focused on the introduction of increasingly rigid medical procedures, known as protocols, as evidence of deskilling and Taylorism (Walby *et al.*, 1994; Flynn, 1992) while others have pointed to 'skill dilution' (Thornley, 1996). Here, implicitly, the division of labour is config-ured around efficient task completion, the classic bureaucratic approach. However, as Bolton (2000) and Ackroyd and Bolton (1999) point out, the nursing labour process does not lend itself easily to the simple application of Taylorism, with the core medical skills difficult to translate into simple procedures to be followed. Here is a key difference from call centre work where, to a significant degree, the technical aspect of the work has often been taken over by expert computer systems. Further, Bolton points out that these rationalising techniques are joined by a different logic in the changing division of nursing labour. A key development in many countries has been the advent of what is known as 'primary care'. As Wicks puts it, 'primary nursing is patient-centred rather than task-centred and is characterised by each patient having a single, identified, qualified nurse who is responsible for their care during the entire period of their hospital stay' (1998, p. 186). In other words, here the basis of the division of labour is centred around establishing a 'customer' relationship. BPR initiatives in health care have contained dual elements in the division of labour. For instance, while Vogelius and Hagedorn-Rasmussen (2000) stress how BPR applied in a Danish social work setting has emphasised technical rationality and quantitative efficiency, Leverment *et al.* (1999) have outlined a BPR initiative in a UK hospital which has sought to break down narrow occupational specialisms to configure a range of health care occupations in teams centred around establishing a 'customer' relationship. These initiatives are in part a reaction to the view that the 'hyperspecialised' organisation of hospitals 'dissected patients as if they were automobiles on the assembly line or in for repair' (DuPuy, 1999, p. 68). The bureaucratic hyperspecialisation of health care informed an increasingly dominant imagery, as held by the health care specialist and experienced by the patient, of the patient not as a human being but as a holder of so many relevant body parts (Morin and Nair, 1997). This is the medical manifestation of the wider phenomenon of the dehumanising effects of bureaucracies (Bauman, 1989).

The analytical lens of the customer-oriented bureaucracy also highlights the contested nature of authority in health care. The idea that the 'consultant is king' clearly speaks to the dominance of the authority of medical knowledge. The western form of medical knowledge prioritises scientific, objective, impersonal rationality (Holden and Littlewood, 1991). It prioritises theoretical knowledge of medicine above the object (the patient) to which this knowledge is applied. Clearly, there is a good degree of congruence between this form of authority and bureaucratic authority. It can be termed 'medical rational authority'. But this medical rational authority is subject to two distinct forms of challenge. As Wicks (1998) points out in her study of Australian hospital work, within the everyday work of nurses, in key areas many nurses challenge this authority through 'patient advocacy' where nurses speak up for (often voiceless) patients.[3] Wicks shows that in a number of areas nurses undertake practices which are informed by their view of the authority of the *patient*, a form of authority which can stand in contradiction to medical rational authority. Most notably this occurs in nurses seeking to effect a 'good death' – a concept which is alien to dominant forms of medical rationality.

Another distinct challenge to medical rational authority lies in the attempts of the new cadre of non-medical managers to erect traditional bureaucratic authority behind a façade of the rhetoric of 'the customer is king'. The choice of the label of 'customer' or 'consumer' here is vital.[4] The rhetoric of 'the patient is king' has not been adopted for two main reasons. First, its own contradictions are too blatant. The etymology of the word 'patient' goes back to the Latin word for suffering. It is not easy to picture someone debilitated with pain as a sovereign. This sovereign will surely need an interpreter and this leads to the second problem. If the patient is king it is left to doctors and nurses to fight it out between them over who is the more able interpreter of the interests and voice of the patient. Non-medical managers can have little role here. However, if the *customer* is king, non-medical managers can position themselves with a legitimate role as experts in understanding the voice of the customer and in translating this voice into organisational structures and practices. After all, this is the claimed expertise of managers in commercial areas of other forms of front-line work. As well as challenging the doctor's authority, non-medical managers may, armed with HRM rhetoric and practices, be colonising the 'sanctuary' (Wicks, 1998, p. 73) or 'black hole' (Robinson, 1992) of nursing. Whereas previously the domain of nursing has largely been regulated within the nursing ranks, managers may seek to extend their role and create authority by entering this domain in the name of good HRM practice. The contested nature of this is brought out well by Bolton (2000, p. 5), who reports that performance appraisals, although described by managers as an opportunity to 'communicate with management', were seen by nurses as putting them at the 'mercy of the manager'. The main political discourse of the battle of authority in health care may be dominated by the opposition between the consultant as king and the customer as king. However, the preceding analysis suggests that the key terrain of the debate *within everyday health care work* lies between medical rational authority, patient (rather than customer) authority and traditional bureaucratic authority. These are the more meaningful debates that citizens in many advanced economies need to take part in.

The concepts of spaces, tensions and fine lines illuminate key aspects of the experience of health care work. The socially embedded relationship with patients provides a space for real pleasure and meaning for health care workers. Indeed, this aspect of work is intensified by the heightened empathy and attachment felt by many health care workers to patients (Hughes *et al.*, 1958, p. 214). A selection of quotations from nurses and nursing aides brings this out:

> I just love the close contact with the patient. I love the chance to sort of be involved in their lives. (Nurse in Wicks, 1998, p. 85)

> A couple of years ago there was one lady in particular who was a ... stroke patient and when she finally walked out the door I knew it was through us busting our guts and her really trying and that was one of the happiest days of my life and I still remember her. (Nurse in Wicks, 1998, p. 84)

> She [favourite patient] asks about my kids. And when I go home I talk about her to my kids. I try my best for her. (Nursing home aide in Foner, 1994, p. 51)

Notably, key changes in the division of labour towards 'primary care' will markedly increase the spaces for these deeply significant aspects of the work.

However, the key structures within which health care workers work are contradictory. The contradictions between the bureaucratic imperative to deliver health care efficiently and the desire of health care workers to give meaningful, personalised care to patients create the central tension of the work. As Wicks states, nurses' 'identification of negatives revolved around situations where their goal of caring for a patient was impinged upon by other factors' (1998, p. 86). Central to these other factors were the increasing requirements for bureaucratic, quantitative efficiency.[5] These tensions have been heightened with the efficiency requirements increasingly being translated into an intensification of nursing labour, manifest most plainly in rising staff–patient ratios (Pratschke, 2000; Ackroyd and Bolton, 1999). The acute tensions experienced by nurses are expressed best by nurses themselves:

> The most frustrating thing for me is the time thing. The tension between the time allocated for duties and the time to offer comfort in doing those duties.
>
> I feel myself constantly torn between those two and compromising, staying for five minutes and perhaps racing through the observations and not asking the next lady how she is. (Nurses in Wicks, 1998, pp. 112–14)

As Benner and Wrubel (1989, p. 191) put it, 'the consequences of delivering inadequate care due to work overload erodes the nurse's self-esteem and causes real anguish.' Nurses tend to hold deeply held values relating to the care given to patients, not least in Germany where the tradition of *Liebesdienst* is still vital. This relates to the importance of Christian ethics and the idea of service for reasons of charity. Tensions are likely to be especially acute where the measures of performance prioritise the easily measured quantitative aspects of work (such as number of patients given a bath per shift, length of stay on patient in hospital beds, length of waiting lists). In the USA, for instance, only the time undertaking medical procedures, rather than the time spent talking to patients, and comforting them, are paid for by health care insurers (Baker *et al.*, 1995, p. 191). Similarly, state regulations of nursing home care in the USA tend to prioritise bureaucratic quantitative measures over patient-oriented processes (Eaton, 2000; Foner, 1994).

Notably, unlike in call centre work, the relationship with the service recipient tends not to give rise to direct tensions (Wicks, 1998). Historically there has been no place for the enchanting myth of sovereignty for patients. Without the myth of sovereignty to be peddled, there is no enchantment and hence no disillusionment that can spark abuse to front-line workers in other settings. However, the mimicking of private sector customer service practices in health care may give rise to a fledgling sovereignty myth among health care patients.

For instance, in the UK considerable management attention is given to alerting patients to the standards that they can expect and to the complaint procedures to use if these standards are not met. Bolton's (2000) study suggests that this is increasingly leading to patients who adopt the role of a sovereign private sector customer. This in turn leads to the signs of systematic tensions between the nurse and the patient (also see Ungerson, 1999).

As yet, these tensions are but fledgling and so nurses need not walk along the same fine line as so many front-line workers who have to act with customers in ways that preserve the myth of sovereignty. However, Dunlop (1986) has noted another important patient-related 'tightrope' along which nurses must walk. Here, the tightrope is one between closeness, stemming from their patient empathy and advocacy, and distance from the patient. This 'distance' stems from both the bureaucratic imperative of efficiency and the nurse's role as technical assistant to scientific medicine. In keeping with the idea of a fragile social order in contemporary front-line work, Dunlop argues that there is an inherent risk of nurses falling one way or the other on this fraught tightrope walk. Certainly, there can be pain for health care workers from the death of patients with whom they have formed attachments (Foner, 1994; Wicks, 1998). For Benner and Wrubel (1989, p. 3) this is part of the dialectic of real nursing: 'involvement and caring may lead one to experience loss and pain, but they also make joy and fulfilment possible'.

Overall, the increasingly frequent moments of the fragile social order of health care breaking down speak to a view of health care as involving a surface calm which is prone to be disrupted in a number of ways by the potentially contradictory logics of customer/patient orientation and rationalisation. Wicks (1998, p. 132) captures this idea very well in stating that 'it is in work environments, such as the hospital ward, that supposedly functional work arrangement can be seen to be conflictual at their very core. In such an environment deeply felt latent and overt tensions are unavoidable.'

Conclusion

> It seemed to me important to allow nurses a voice about what they actually enjoyed about their work and how they experienced pleasure in what they do. To do otherwise is to regard them as powerless or misguided or both, and to see them as caught within structures over which they have no control. (Wicks, 1998, p. 89)

A selective research approach and a selective reading of the research allows an easy development of an overwhelmingly negative picture of front-line work. Certainly, tensions and pains exist, but a picture of front-line work which does not also highlight the pleasures and meaning in the work shows not only poor scholarship but also an implicitly condescending attitude to the people who undertake front-line work – as Wicks implies in the quotation immediately above. Indeed, a crucial test for the use of a theoretical approach is whether it is able to illuminate front-line workers' answers to *both* of the following questions: 'What is the best aspect of your job?' and 'What is the worst aspect of it?' Too often, researchers focus on only one of these questions. This chapter has shown how the concept of the customer-oriented bureaucracy can illuminate answers to both of these questions offered by front-line workers in call centres, health care and hospitality. Indeed, it is only by asking both questions together that one is able to reach proper conclusions regarding answers to each individual question. The dual logics at play in front-line work mean that the experience of work is often dualistic and contradictory, so what is part of the best aspect of the job may also be part of the worst aspect of it.

The examination of three types of work in this chapter has shown a range of important and distinctive features of the worker–customer interaction. The chapter has also highlighted a range of roles for HRM in the creation and maintenance of a fragile social order on the front-line. Table 5.1 summarises the important features of the customer–worker interaction and the roles of

Table 5.1 Distinctive features of customer–worker interaction and the role for HRM in three types of front-line work

Type of front-line work	*Distinctive feature in worker–customer interaction*	*Role for HRM in constructing a fragile social order*
Hospitality work	Tipping instrumentalises relationship, but also potential for deeply embedded relationships.	Tipping as mechanism for (individualised) social order, tends to create managerial vacuum; HRM increasingly fills this vacuum.
Call centre work	Technological distance between worker and customer disembeds relationship.	Central role for HRM, *re* selection, appraisals etc. for finding points of 'balance' for individual workers.
Health care work	Workers hold very strong patient empathy, and often act as voice for powerless patients. Little sovereignty myth.	HRM emerging as part of invasive practices by non-medical managers.

HRM in the three types of work covered. This highlights the fact that if we are interested in the experience of different types of front-line work then the nature of the worker–customer interaction is a critical factor to be considered, particularly the degree to which the interaction can be embedded in meaningful wider social relationships. The previous chapter suggested that HRM is likely to play a critical role in management attempts to construct a (fragile) social order in many front-line workplaces. The table shows that while this is clearly the case for call centre work, it is also increasingly the case for hospitality work. Its role in health care work, however, is more ambiguous. This plurality in the meaning and role of HRM in different front-line workplaces has been illuminated by the analytical approach informed by the concept of the customer-oriented bureaucracy. This concept must be used as a heuristic device, as a way into examining specific contexts of front-line work. It is not meant to suggest that exactly the same dynamics are played out in exactly the same way in all front-line contexts. This chapter has shown how it can illuminate both the experience and management in a number of important types of front-line work.

Notes

1 There is a point of general relevance here. Front-line work will have more customer-oriented pressures, structures and values, while back office work will tend to be more bureaucratically structured (also see Lash and Urry, 1994, p. 203, and Timo, 2000). Hence, there is likely to be a degree of structural lateral conflict between the front-line and back office – both at the staff level and within management.

2 A number of authors (Wood, 1992, pp. 44–7) have also argued that tipping is used to justify low wage levels.

3 Patients themselves have also challenged medical and bureaucratic rationality (Ungerson, 1999; Oliver, 1996).

4 See Neuberger (1999) and Irvine (2000) for a debate on the language of 'patients' and 'customers'.

5 Medical rationality is the other key factor that systematically clashes with nurses' goal of caring for patients. It is important to be aware that reality may be more complex than a simple clash between doctors holding to medical rational authority and nurses holding to patient authority. Hence, many sensitive studies reveal evidence of dual discourses or frames of reference held by many health care workers (James, 1993; Bebbington, 1998; Wicks, 1998).

CHAPTER 6

Sales work

Sales workers already comprise a significant proportion of the labour force in many advanced economies, and estimates show that the growth in the numbers of people employed in sales work is set to continue (Castells and Aoyama, 1994; Rothman, 1998, p. 152). Hirschhorn (1985) suggests that selling will become central to what he calls 'the new services game', and it is clear that sales aims form a significant part of the management agenda in the restructuring of front-line work. The spread of sales has been such that Grimshaw *et al.* (2000) are able to report that even the job of school lunch catering in the UK increasingly involves an active sales element – in this case an active attempt to sell food to schoolchildren.

The key defining aspect of sales work is that the job involves the front-line workers actively stimulating demand, encouraging customers to purchase a good or service. The implicit contrast here is with service work, which involves front-line workers satisfying customer requests, performing transactions, providing information and so on, without the immediate aim of stimulating the customer to make a purchase. This means that just because a job features customers purchasing products it is not necessarily a sales job. In many instances, the role of mass media advertising ensures that a customer has been 'pre-sold' prior to the interaction with the front-line worker (Glazer, 1993), so there is no need for the active stimulation of demand by the worker. 'Sales assistants' may often effectively be service assistants.

Because sales work involves a direct stimulation of a purchase it is more likely than other forms of front-line work to bring out the often hidden *instrumental* relationship between customers and firms that is part of the essence of capitalism. The market relationship between firm and customer in capitalism means that the firm is interested only in the customer to the extent that the customer has money to pay for goods or services. The aim of the producing firm is not to maximise customer well-being but to make what will sell, and to sell, at a profit, what is made. Adam Smith pointed this out over two hundred years ago: 'it is not from the benevolence of the butcher, the brewer or the baker that we expect our dinner, but from their regard for their own interests. We address ourselves, not to their humanity but their self-love' (1776/1910, p. 13). In sales work this instrumentalism is more likely to come to the fore because of sales work's direct concern with the customer's money.[1]

It is this instrumentalism that makes sales work, at its most extreme, the form of front-line work that *has fewest parallels with the model of the customer-oriented bureaucracy*. The most extreme forms of sales work can be seen as being sales-oriented rather than customer-oriented. Chapter 4 argued that the customer should be seen as socially constituted. That is to say that the customer should not be seen as atomistic, pre-existing, or a priori. The customer is not wholly *self*-constituted. Customers are social actors, constituted by themselves in relation to, and in dialogue with, other customers, with firms and with the state. At its most extreme form, sales work tends to prioritise the role of the firm, and its front-line sales workers, in constituting the 'real' interests of the customer, and to marginalise the role of the customer in this process. This is captured clearly in the widespread belief among insurance managers and sales workers that 'life assurance is never bought, it is always sold' (Clarke, 2000; Morgan and Knights, 1992).

With the importance and definition of sales work established, the rest of the chapter is structured as follows. First comes an examination of the extreme form of sales work, that is, where the role of the firm in constituting the customer is prioritised. The chapter then turns to consider jobs involving both sales *and* service.

Extreme forms of sales work

This section begins with a discussion of the key distinctive aspects in the management and experience of extreme forms of sales, before turning to consider models that have been put forward to capture these aspects.

The management of extreme forms of sales work has two key common characteristics. The first is that sales workers are paid on a commission system, so that the more cars, houses or insurance policies are sold, the higher will be the income of the sales worker. Research has shown that payment by a low base salary with a significant commission element is common to a wide range of sales jobs: insurance and financial service sales (Leidner, 1993; Clarke, 2000), estate agency sales (Clarke *et al.*, 1994), car sales (Browne, 1973), home or pyramid sales (Biggart, 1988; Connelly and Rhoton, 1988), retail sales where products are of high value (Woody, 1989; Prus, 1989) and product sales to intermediaries like supermarkets (Lopez, 1996). Often accompanying this, but dependent on the state of the labour market, is the tying of employment security to the achievement of a target number of sales in each week or month (Rothman, 1998, p. 135; Frenkel *et al.*, 1999; Clarke, 2000, p. 131).[2]

Surprisingly, little attention has been given to explaining the predominance of commission payments in extreme forms of sales work. Rather, it tends to be taken as a given, almost 'natural' part of sales work. However, the analytical definition of sales work given above provides the key starting point in explaining the widespread nature of commission payments in sales. Commission payments encourage a sales-oriented rather than a customer-oriented approach from sales workers. It encourages a constitution of the customer that prioritises the role of the firm and the sales worker. The tying of payment (commission) to the outcome of the sales worker–customer interaction also encourages a more instrumental orientation from sales workers. This allows them more easily to turn the customer round to their product. As Oakes (1990) points out, the customer becomes a means to an end (the commission payment), rather than an end in him or her self.

Just as tipping represents a managerial vacuum in hospitality work, so a commission payment system can engender a management vacuum in sales work. The studies cited above which showed the centrality of commission payments for overall remuneration also tend to show that other typical aspects of HRM practice, such as selective recruitment, training, teamworking and the development of an overall service culture, were absent. Clarke (2000, p. 152), for instance, found that UK financial service firms typically only provided thirteen days' training to sales staff before they were 'allowed out in the field alone'. Indeed, many discussions describe forms of sales work as quasi-independent contractors. For instance, Hodson and Sullivan (1995, p. 355) state that 'in effect, [some sales] workers are independent contractors who are offered a desk in the firm but who have few of the other characteristics of steady employment'.

The second common characteristic in the management of extreme forms of sales work is the development of an ideology which legitimises the techniques of manipulation which sales workers may apply to customers. This ideology may take two forms. It may involve the inculcation of a belief in the beneficial qualities of the product being sold. Thus, Biggart in examining pyramid sales structures, or direct sales organisations, stresses the importance of the 'business of belief' and of 'product ideologies'. She argues that 'direct sales organisations are driven by . . . a belief in . . . the transformative powers of products' (1988, p. 99). This is echoed by Leidner's study of the training of insurance sales (1993, p. 114). Here, an important part of the firm's training in the development of a 'positive mental attitude' among its staff was the development of a belief in the usefulness of the product. Similarly, Morgan and Knights (1992, p. 40) acutely observe that, 'there is high pressure at the point of direct contact with the customer. In order to justify this pressure, both to him/herself and to the client, the salesperson draws on the language of morality and insurance.' In this case, the justification lay in the morally beneficial qualities of life insurance, and in a paternalistic imagery of the customer as someone who needs the help of the salesperson to see the true benefits of the product. Developing an appropriate imagery of the customer is the second main way to legitimise manipulation in the sales interaction. One appropriate imagery may be a paternalistic one, but in other cases a negative imagery of customers as potential manipulators themselves comes into play. Although it may not feature as part of a formal training programme, management will often do little to discourage its perpetuation in workplace culture. For instance, Browne's study of car sales showed that a key part of the sales worker's view of the customer was the belief (to quote a sales worker) that 'the customer will absolutely tell you fifty lies to every one of yours' (1973, p. 37). The message is clear – the sales worker is justified in telling a few lies because these pale in comparison to the number of lies told by the customer:

> Some of the aspects of the con are present in [the salesman's] behaviour, and he is more than willing to admit this, although he sees nothing dishonest, peculiar or immoral about it. Part of the reason he feels that he is playing a relatively harmless game and that it's 'no big deal' is that he sees the customer as either playing the same game or wanting to play the same game. (p. 57)

Clarke *et al.* (1994) found a similar imagery of customers prevalent in estate agency sales work. The title of their book, *Slippery Customers*, is meant to reflect not only customers' views of estate agents but also estate agents' views of customers. Rothman, therefore, is correct to highlight that 'sales workers sometimes develop stereotypes about customers that serve to justify and rationalize manipulating customers' (1998, p. 140).

Not only is this extreme form of sales work 'customer'-oriented in a qualitatively different way from other forms of front-line work, but it is also less subject to the pressures of rationalisation. Leidner's (1993) study of an insurance firm shows the significant degree to which management routinised the sales process, but she is surely right to add the caveat that 'Combined Insurance's extensive routinization of the work of insurance agents makes it *unusual* among insurance companies' (p. 87).

Indeed, the absence of features of bureaucracy in forms of sales work have led Biggart (1988) and Frenkel *et al.* (1999) to suggest that alternative theoretical models of work should be developed to take into account the distinctiveness of sales. Biggart explicitly offers her model of the direct sales organisation as an alternative to Weber's model of bureaucracy, arguing that 'the logic of the direct sales organisation is a challenge to the bureaucratic logic' (p. 7). She argues that compared with bureaucracies, direct sales organisations 'have almost no rules, and ... few managers'. She stresses the importance of emotional attachment and of charismatic authority in the pure type model that she derives from her research.

Biggart largely presents her model as an idyllic alternative to bureaucracy. She eulogises the direct sales organisation most strongly when contrasting the bureaucratic 'man's world' (p. 85) with the way in which the 'feminist agenda parallels in important ways the reality of network direct sales organisations' (p. 90). For Biggart, this means that direct sales organisations tend to be flat, participative; they promote nurturing rather than individual competitiveness, and they value intuition. Such a picture, however, is hard to sustain in the light of Biggart's own admission of very high labour turnovers in these organisations (p. 156). If they are so idyllic, why do so many people leave them? An answer to this is suggested by Butterfield (1985), who as an ex-member of a direct sales organisation argues that 'the system probably alienates more people than it converts. The turnover in the business...was staggering' (p. 109). Rather than the nurturing and positive aspects of emotional attachment that Biggart focuses on, Butterfield provides a chilling account of how a direct sales organisation colonises and instrumentalises all aspects of a member's life (p. 53):

> Amway begins to change your life the first time you approach your friends and family members to sell the products or recruit them into the business. Hitherto you related with them as friend, brother, sister, son, daughter. Now you are relating as a salesperson to customer. As soon as you list all your friends in a notebook as potential customers and distributors, they become *prospects*. With a friend there is no ulterior motive for your association...But when you put a friend on a prospect list, then you are guiding the friendship in a preconceived direction; the friendship is no longer primary, it is a means to an end.

Where Biggart's theoretical model is a narrow one, pertaining only to direct sales organisations, Frenkel *et al.*'s (1999) exposition of an entrepreneurial form of work organisation is meant to capture general features of sales work. Further, where Biggart focuses mainly on the positive aspects of a particular form of sales work, Frenkel *et al.* use their model to highlight key ambiguities for sales workers that derive from the way their work is organised. Table 6.1 reproduces Frenkel *et al.*'s summary of an entrepreneurial model of work organisation that is mean to capture key aspects of sales work.

Frenkel *et al.* use this model as a benchmark against which to assess the evidence they glean from their studies of a number of types of sales job. Although the empirical evidence highlights some differences from this ideal type, overall, they suggest that 'sales work...resembles the entrepreneurial ideal type' (p. 268). Frenkel *et al.* are effectively proposing an 'independent-contractor' model of sales work. Each dimension of their model is based on this premise. There is an arm's-length relationship between the sales worker and the firm's management. The sales workers are given considerable discretion on how they complete their tasks, but if they are not able to produce the sales results then their pay falls and employment security comes under

Table 6.1 Frenkel *et al.*'s (1999) entrepreneurial model of work organisation

Dimension	Entrepreneurial ideal type of work organisation
Work relations	
Basis of work rules	Defined by market requirements
Competencies	Broader than in bureaucracy; seize market opportunities, self-discipline, contextual knowledge, social skills
Employment relations	
Reward system	High variable element, pay related to performance
Career structuring	Reliance on external labour market
Control relations	
Employee discretion	High regarding work process
Form of control	Mainly output related
Co-worker relations	
With immediate colleagues	Individualised work; little interdependence
With workers in other sections	Dependence on others for completing transactions; tension
Customer relations	
Role of worker	Affective/instrumental; sales and service provider
Triangular (customer–worker–management) relations	Complex; worker has instrumental relations with customer and with manager

pressure. HRM here plays a peripheral role, for this form of work organisation effectively represents a managerial vacuum.

Among the merits of this model is that it does accord well with the many instances of a commission-based, managerial vacuum found in studies of sales work that were mentioned earlier. Further, it does help provide an understanding of positive *and* negative aspects in the experience of sales work. It is clear that one of the most satisfying aspects of sales work stems from the considerable autonomy in the process of work. This is apparent in the way sales workers often value the consideration that their job does not 'pin you to a desk' (Browne, 1973, p. 54). Browne (p. 19) also argues that the smiling façade of the sales worker interacting with customers may be driven not just by instrumentalism but also by the challenge that their autonomy over the work process gives them.

Butterfield, reflecting on the key areas of satisfaction when he worked in a direct sales organisation, notes the pleasure of feeling in control of the work process: 'the [sales] techniques give me control over the situation: I ask the questions, I maintain the format of an interview, I have the power to build up or squelch the prospect...I alone know where the conversation is going'

(1985, p. 66). Howton and Rosenberg (1965, p. 298) capture this idea well when arguing that sales workers glorify the entrepreneurial, self-dependent ethic, and the way that this constitutes an escape from bureaucracy. This is echoed in Hodgson's (1999, p. 1) study of a financial services sales force in which he finds strong evidence of 'a specifically masculine and fiercely *autonomous form of subjectivity* among the salesforce' (italics added). Collinson *et al.* (1990, p. 137) similarly note the linking of ideologies of masculinity and fierce independence: 'the task of selling is described ideologically in terms of a heroic drama in which "intrepid" and autonomous males stride out into the financial world and against all odds return with business'. And so the pleasures of the autonomy of the sales work process becomes entwined with the pleasures (and accompanying pains) of experiencing a specific form of masculinity. This is likely to be a significant factor, particularly in the more extreme forms of sales work. As Hodson and Sullivan note, there is a strong gender segregation in the USA in sales work. While women predominate in sales of low-value items, in jobs which have less autonomy, 'men still dominate jobs selling higher-priced items, such as motor vehicles, furniture, electronic equipment, and appliances...Two-thirds or more of insurance sales workers and securities sales workers are men' (1995, p. 358).

This analysis of extreme forms of sales work also suggests potential areas of pleasure in the work from interactions with customers. Although there is a stronger instrumentalism at play than in many other types of front-line work, where there is also a paternalistic imagery of the customer, as discussed above, there can also be real pleasures to be taken from interacting with customers. For instance, Clarke *et al.* note that many estate agents experience a real feeling of 'satisfaction from service to clients' (1994, p. 108). They note that 'the small gestures of appreciation, a card, flowers, a bottle of wine, from satisfied customers were repeatedly referred to as part of what makes the job worthwhile – and compensates for the contrariness of some members of the public' (p. 136). This 'contrariness' of customers derives from customers' perception of the instrumentalism present in some forms of sales work, and this can be a source of not inconsiderable dissatisfaction for sales workers. As one estate agent in Clarke *et al.*'s study notes (p. 109),

> People will come in, they won't acknowledge your smile or your greeting. Whether they are naturally rude or whether they are slightly nervous and they have got it into their heads that we are going to trap them into signing something...I think it's just a lack of manners basically.

As Clarke *et al.* argue, this form of 'rudeness' is not a reflection of a customer's 'natural' character, but rather derives from the structure of the social situation he or she is in. It reflects the fact that the instrumentalism between firm and customer that is always present to some degree in capitalism is closer to the surface in sales work.

Many studies of extreme forms of sales work highlight the high levels of turnover in this work (as well as that in direct sales organisations) (Knights and Morgan, 1990; Browne, 1973). Clarke (2000), for instance, shows turnover rates of around 40 per cent within a year in financial services sales jobs in the UK. Although there has been little research examining the causes of turnover, the Frenkel *et al.* (1999) model does suggest two key sources of tension and dissatisfaction that might inform turnover. First, there are the considerable insecurity and pressures that come from the independent-contractor model of work organisation. Second, there is the tension in the relationship with customers relating to instrumentalism. Clearly, where instrumentalism is combined with a negative imagery of customers, to justify manipulation, the sales worker is located in a highly dehumanised set of relationships. This may be an important factor informing decisions to leave sales jobs – especially after the initial dream of a quick, easy, high income fades (Clarke *et al.* 1994). Further, even where there are more paternalistic images of customers, instrumentalism may also be a factor driving turnover. Oakes (1990), in a brilliant analysis of the experience of insurance sales work, argues that ultimately those who survive in this extreme form of sales work are those who have a 'will to ignorance' (p. 87) regarding the tensions between instrumental manipulation of customers and paternalistic images of customers. He argues that the experience of conflicts between these factors remains below the cognitive horizon of the sales workers who survive in the industry (p. 87):

> In order to develop their competence as sales personnel, agents need to know how to ignore the kind of knowledge that compromises their own effectiveness and endangers the viability of the practice of personal sales . . . The illusion most indispensable to agents is their belief in the coherence of the sales process itself and the consistency between the two idioms that define their occupational identity and make their work possible.

The clear implication of this is that those who are unable to master this 'will to ignorance' are those who leave the job. In many cases, the immediate cause may *appear* to be their inability to make enough sales, but Oakes's analysis suggests that underlying this failure of practice will often be a 'failure' of a 'will to ignorance'.

In keeping with the focus of this chapter, this analysis of sales work has focused on the analysis of the management and experience of sales work. However, in this case, it is also worth examining a key systematic implication *for customers* of extreme forms of sales work, namely mis-selling. In the UK, this word has entered everyday language following the revelation of a series of 'scandals' in which *several million* customers have been systematically sold financial products, particularly pensions and mortgages, which are highly inappropriate to their circumstances (Clarke, 2000). For instance, in the late 1980s millions of customers were persuaded by pension sales workers to leave relatively lucrative and secure pensions schemes run by their employer to take up personal pensions. This change left millions of people facing retirement financially much worse off. Evidence of mis-selling has been so widespread and so significant in the industry that the regulatory body overseeing the industry has ordered a range of firms to ensure that millions of customers are recompensed for their losses. From the earlier analysis, it comes as little surprise that this massive and systematic mis-selling was driven by the commission payment system. For instance, Clarke (2000, p. 87) notes, regarding endowment insurance, that,

> At the height of the boom in the late 1980s and early 1990s mis-selling was undoubtedly rife, with customers being induced to surrender or abandon existing policies, being sold unsuitable policies, and policies with elements they did not need, *because these generated commission*. (Italics added)

Similarly, a study by the *Guardian* newspaper (9 October 1998) into pension selling by a leading financial services firm with some nine million customers found that their reporters, who posed as would-be customers, were:

> recommended poor value pensions;
> quoted future growth figures banned by the Financial Services Act;
> Shown...deliberately misleading competitor statistics.

The sales worker 'attempted to sell policies that *maximised earnings* for both the salespeople and the company' (italics added). Clarke (2000) argues that attempts to prevent further mis-selling have sidestepped the key issue of the commission payment system driving mis-selling. It is the commission payment system that heightens the instrumentalism in the sales worker–customer interaction and leads to a form of customer orientation in which the voice of the customer is marginalised, and the voice of the sales worker is given centre-stage.

Mixing sales and service

In turning to examine less extreme forms of sales work it is necessary to consider the implications of the application of the key pressures of other forms of front-line work – namely customer orientation and bureaucratisation. The Frenkel *et al.* model only provides insights into sales work when the firm is relatively unconcerned with customer perceptions of the quality of the service–sales interaction. In many cases, however, the firm will be concerned with customer perception of service quality *and* the generation of sales.[3] The move in emphasis away from a sole focus on direct revenue generation (in sales) will also bring with it increasing pressures to rationalise to increase efficiency. Indeed, the restructuring of many front-line jobs has involved a meeting of these pressures. Rather than this being a case of a managerial vacuum, management must once again enter to construct an ever more precarious fragile social order.

The problems facing management are best separated into two scenarios. There is the problem of constructing a fragile social order, first where there is a restructuring of extreme sales jobs to encompass service elements, and second where there is a movement in the opposite direction, where restructuring brings sales aims into service jobs. Evidence suggests that both forms of restructuring have been important currents in contemporary front-line work. Examples of the restructuring of extreme sales to encompass service elements can be found in estate agents, in financial services and in claims concerning the development of 'relationship sales' and 'relationship marketing'. In the case of estate agents in the UK there has been a market-led dynamic away from extreme sales work (Clarke *et al.*, 1994). The growing rhetoric of 'relationship sales' and 'relationship marketing' also suggests a market-led movement away from extreme forms of sales in other areas (although see Fitchett and McDonagh, 2001). The idea of relationship sales is that the focus should not just be on the immediate revenue generated by a sale, but rather on the maximisation of longer-term revenue generation which can be enhanced by forming an ongoing relationship with a customer. This is likely to be accompanied by a greater focus on (longer-term) customer perceptions of service quality. In UK financial services, by contrast, the dynamic away from extreme sales has been led predominantly by the state and regulating bodies. Following the widespread mis-selling that was widely discussed in the mass media the government has strengthened the bodies regulating the industry.

There is also evidence of the other form of restructuring, away from 'pure' service work to encompass an active sales element. Notably, a major international study of the financial services industry is entitled *From Tellers to Sellers* (Regini *et al.*, 2000) – highlighting the way the work of bank tellers has moved from being predominantly service-based, reacting to customer requests, towards a focus on the active generation of sales. Prosaically, the movement to add sales elements to service jobs is manifest in the fast-food worker routinely asking 'Would you like a coke with that?' (Leidner, 1996). Chapter 1 noted that cross-selling was an important aim in the mergers and restructuring of service firms, and this has been confirmed among financial services and estate agency firms (Clarke *et al.*, 1994; Clarke, 2000). Cross-selling involves selling products which are related to the main product or service being delivered. Hence it is likely to lead to more jobs involving both service and sales.

Table 6.2 summarises the different problems facing management, and the key role for HRM in the two routes taken towards sales/service jobs. The discussion of the role of HRM in both routes will follow after the examination

Table 6.2 Problems for management and HRM role in restructuring towards service and sales jobs

	Restructuring sales *jobs into sales/service jobs*	*Restructuring* service *jobs into sales/service jobs*
Key management aims	Introduction of customer orientation rather than pure sales orientation. Increase rationalising focus on efficiency	Introduction of sales orientation.
Consequent key new policies	Management intrusion into autonomy of work process – standardising procedures, and increasing measurement of work process.	Rise in workforce discretion regarding work process.
	Move away from payment being mainly commission-based. Introduction of metrics obtained from customers concerning service quality.	Move towards greater element of performance (sales) related pay. Introduction of sales targets, rather than targets related to work process.
Key obstacles arising from existing workforce	Workforce seeks to preserve process autonomy – possibly deep-seated resistance related to specific form of masculine identity tied to sales work. This may be carried over into resistance to change in payment system. New tensions within worker–customer relationship.	Workforce may resist greater instrumentalism in relationship with customers, but may enjoy greater autonomy and be seduced by possibilities for increasing pay.
Overall role for HRM	HRM practices as driving change and seeking a cultural transformation.	HRM practices as driving change and seeking a cultural transformation

of the main problems facing management in both routes. In the switch away from sales to sales/service, management aims not only for increased customer, rather than sales, orientation, but also for greater efficiency as the emphasis moves away from short-term revenue generation to also encompass cost minimisation. There are a number of concrete policy implications of these general aims. Both aims inform a greater management intrusion into the work process. The workforce's autonomy in deciding the details of how to carry out their jobs is systematically eroded as management introduces standardised customer-oriented procedures to be followed. With a greater focus on the process of the service encounter, not merely the outcome of it, these proced-ures allow management to start measuring aspects of the process of the service encounter. To cement the move in emphasis away from a sole focus on sales outcomes, management may often change the payment system, shifting the balance of payment away from commission based on sales and possibly towards a greater salary element and/or an element of payment based on performance against service quality, rather than sales performance. Clarke *et al.* (1994) for UK estate agents, and Hodgson (1999, 2001) for UK financial services, give evidence of these managerial policies being imple-mented. Hodgson (2001), for instance, acutely points out that the increased measurement of the work process of the 'sales' workers is used not only to comply with the customer-oriented standards demanded by the industry regu-lating bodies but also to pressurise staff to increase the efficiency of their work. Clarke *et al.* (1994, p. 134) highlight that the move from pure sales generated by entry of large corporate estate agency firms meant a greater emphasis on *both* bureaucratisation and customer orientation. They argue that the increasing 'report systems are linked to another critical feature of corporate estate agency: proceduralisation and the maintenance of quality of service'.

These studies also highlight substantial resistance to the policies. Hodgson, for instance, argues that the sales workers he studied had built a particularly masculine form of identity based around their autonomy and mastery of the sales process in which they were autonomous figures free from management intervention. The increasing management intervention in the sales process, however, meant that 'many staff seriously resented the threat to their auton-omy they perceived in the intensification of the system of surveillance' (1999, p. 14). This was because in part the construction of their masculine self-identity was being threatened. As one branch manager in Hodgson's study puts it, 'I mean the guys don't like being monitored, I mean they're in sales to be salesmen, they don't want to be in some clerical job ... They want to be in charge of their own destiny, their future!' (1999, p. 16). Although research into the introduction of service into sales jobs is not substantial, it seems likely that Clarke *et al.*'s conclusion will not be an untypical one. The study shows resistance to the introduction of service elements into sales jobs, arguing that there was a 'culture clash' (1994, p. 136) between the prevailing workforce norms and the aims of new corporate estate agency firms.

There have been rather more studies of the introduction of sales orientation into what had previously been service jobs. In some senses the obstacles to this form of restructuring seem rather less substantial. The move to sales often involves a rise in the discretion given to front-line workers. There are fewer standardised procedures to be followed when a key aim of the job becomes the active stimulation of sales – a process which must be tailored to the specific nature of the interaction with the customer. Such an increase in autonomy is likely to be strongly welcomed by the workforce. A move to sales is often accompanied by the introduction of a performance-related payment system, where performance is to an important degree related to sales achieved. For instance, this is true of the changes made at the UK financial services firm Alliance & Leicester, when management systematically restructured front-line jobs to actively stimulate sales (*Guardian*, 24 July 1999). Such a change in the payment system may be welcomed by a section of the workforce who see the short-term possibility of a rise in income as attractive.

Such positive features in the restructuring of the sales jobs are likely to be emphasised by management. But accompanying these changes are some potentially negative aspects that could inform serious resistance from front-line workers. As has been noted earlier, for many front-line workers in service jobs one of the key areas of satisfaction and meaning in the job involves relating to customers as people whom they can help. Management demands for the achievement of sales, with a portion of salary dependent on meeting these demands, lead to a more instrumental approach to customers. There is less emphasis on the customer *per se*, and more emphasis on getting at the customer's money. There is increasing evidence that many front-line workers resist this approach. For instance, Bradley reports bank workers opposed to the new approach they are expected to take towards customers. One bank worker stated that, 'I don't like the hard sell attitude that we're told to do. It's got worse here' (1999, p. 120). Korczynski *et al.* (2000) explore this issue more systematically with respect to call centre workers whose jobs were increasingly involving an active sales element. This shows that a significant proportion of the workforce in the call centres often refused to carry out managerial demands to actively stimulate sales (also Lankshear *et al.* 2000). This refusal was related to their preference for a relationship of empathy and identification, rather than instrumentalism, with customers. A selection of quotations from call centre workers brings this out:

> I was never against cross-selling when it was meeting customer needs but it's a really different focus now, trying to push things on people.

> I'm bad with sales. I hate doing that to people.

> I went at it [sales attempts] and got five negatives in a row and I'm like hiding under the desk and crying. Rejection, it hurts, because *I can hear myself* at the other end [of the phone line].

Taylor and Bain (1999b, p. 9) confirm the importance of this by showing that from their widespread study of UK call centre workers, many call centre workers commented that one of the major problems with aggressive sales targets was that their introduction had led to a deterioration in the level of supportive customer care, which had been integral to the service in the early years of the call centre.

A further negative aspect of the move to sales that can lead to resistance is the tying of job security to the achievement of sales targets (Bradley, 1999, p. 120). Above, it was suggested that in 'pure' sales work it is often standard practice to link job security to sales performance, and there is evidence that management in some firms are 'borrowing' this element of organisation of sales work and using it to effect the restructuring of service jobs into sales/service jobs. Indeed, the worst excesses of the management of labour in call centres involve the linking of job security to the achievement of sales. Taylor and Bain (1999a) show that failure to reach sales targets in some call centres has led to workers facing disciplinary action, with a real threat of dismissal if their sales do not improve.[4]

Role of HRM

It is likely that HRM will be central to the restructuring of front-line jobs to encompass sales *and* service. Indeed, the discussion so far has highlighted changes in a number of HRM practices as playing key roles in such restructuring, whether from previously service or previously sales jobs. Changes in the nature of the payment system and in the degree of 'empowerment' or autonomy in the work process are HRM elements central to the restructuring. In addition, changes are likely to be made in recruitment, in the management of performance, and in training to help effect the changes. The recruitment profile for candidates for sales/service jobs is likely to be significantly different from the recruitment profile for either 'pure' sales or 'pure' service jobs. As Collinson *et al.* (1990) and Frenkel *et al.* (1999) have pointed out, recruitment criteria for sales jobs tend to emphasise the candidates' 'hunger' for the job, and their ability to be 'self-starting'. By contrast, as has been noted earlier in the book, recruitment criteria for service jobs tend to emphasise attitudes of customer empathy. However, neither criterion on its own is likely to be appropriate for the sort of hybrid demands arising within sales/service jobs. Further research is required into how management is defining the sort of qualities of candidates suitable for the requirement to be both sales- and customer-oriented.

Important changes in performance management are also likely when a shift occurs towards sales/service jobs. This is particularly the case when it is a movement away from pure sales work where an arms-length quasi-contractor model of sales work has existed and where performance management is based almost exclusively on the achievement of sales targets to give potentially attractive commission payments and employment security. Frenkel *et al.*'s (1999) study of sales workers showed that although formal policies for systematic and frequent performance appraisals existed for the sales workers they studied, in practice these paper policies were a fiction. Performance appraisal meetings merely involved a brief checking of sales achieved against targets. In sales/service jobs, by contrast, performance appraisals are likely to be important arenas where the manager attempts to find a point of 'balance' for each front-line worker between the competing demands of sales orientation, efficiency and customer orientation. However, such attempts to locate such individual points of 'balance', or points where overt manifestations of contradictions are minimised, will be systematically hindered by the hierarchical nature of performance appraisals which limit the ability of individual workers to express their voice.

Training is another important area for the input of HRM in restructuring towards sales/service jobs. Management may see the issue of moving towards a service/sales approach as requiring a fundamental change in the culture of the organisation. Indeed, Clarke *et al.*'s (1994) description of a 'culture clash' between the culture of sales workers and the culture of the estate agent corporations seeking a move towards a sales/service approach gives support to such a managerial view. As Hopfl (1993) has illustrated with regard to British Airways, managers in service firms seeking to embark on a cultural transformation of the organisation tend to focus their attention on training sessions which are symbolically important, being accorded considerable status by senior managers in the organisation, and which are meant to impart the new culture to the workforce.

Two levels of problem exist with this approach, however. First, there is a considerable debate concerning how far 'culture' can be managed, especially through the top-down delivery mechanism of training sessions. As Legge (1995, p. 186) argues, 'in the use of the term "corporate" culture many writers seem to be imputing a culture created by senior management for the lower orders to swallow'. This approach implicitly sees 'culture' as something an organisation has; it is an independent variable open to manipulation. It is something which the leaders of an organisation have a key role in creating. By contrast, many commentators argue that culture is best conceptualised as something emerging from social interaction – it is something an organisation 'is' (Meek, 1988; Morgan, 1997). It should be seen as a system of shared knowledge and beliefs, and as a system of shared symbols and meanings. As Legge puts it, 'if culture is seen in these terms, it is questionable to what extent – or even whether – senior management can successfully manipulate or unilaterally change it' (1995, p. 186). In Kunda's (1992) terms, 'engineering culture' is a process fraught with contradictions.

This first level of problem is one common to the 'management' of culture in all organisations. The second level concerns problems arising from the *specific* change to a sales/service culture. Although more research is required into the area, it is likely that a key symbolic way in which management will seek to create a sales/service culture is through adoption of the rhetoric that 'service is sales', and 'sales is service' (Korczynski *et al.*, 2000). This rhetoric posits that a customer orientation is equivalent to a sales orientation. While in some customer–worker interactions the two orientations may be highly compatible, it is nevertheless the case that in the two orientations there are very different imageries of, and roles for, the customer. In one the customers are a means to a sale, cannot independently voice their interests and must be actively coaxed into a sale. In the other, the customer is more of an end than a means, and is a figure to empathetically serve. Cultural management becomes doubly difficult when it is based on a rhetoric that denies differences that are clear to front-line workers (Korczynski *et al.*, 2000).

Conclusion

This chapter has examined sales work. It has argued that sales work can be identified by the degree to which the worker is expected to actively stimulate demand from customers. Sales work warrants its own separate consideration because of the distinctive aspects of the customer–worker relationship and of the way in which sales work is managed. 'Pure', extreme or 'hard' sales work tends to promote a greater instrumentalism in the relationship between worker and customer. Hand in hand with this is the extensive use of a commission system by which front-line workers are rewarded according to the number of sales made. Also accompanying this is the development of an ideology which legitimises the techniques of manipulation sales workers may apply to customers. The commission system and an ideology legitimising manipulation are the key elements underlying some major instances of mis-selling that have been identified. These features of sales work also mean that it is not usefully analysed in terms of the model of the customer-oriented bureaucracy. Extreme sales work tends to be sales-oriented rather than customer-oriented. Further, because the focus is on revenue generation there are fewer pressures of cost-minimising rationalisation. The systematic differences between sales work and other forms of front-line work have led Biggart and Frenkel *et al.* to put forward alternative models of the organisation of sales work. Frenkel *et al.*'s is the more wide-ranging. Their entrepreneurial model was analysed as effectively an elaboration of a form of contracting-out model of sales work.

The rest of the chapter suggested that there are strong pressures for the restructuring of many sales jobs and many service jobs into sales/service jobs and sought to analyse these developments. The discussion highlighted the tensions, workforce reactions and management policies consequent to the meeting of the entrepreneurial logic with the pressures of customer orientation and rationalisation. The role of HRM in trying to effect these changes and in trying to establish a fragile social order amid the competing demands was highlighted.

Notes

1 Regarding non-sales work, we can go back to Parasuraman *et al.*'s SERVQUAL model of service quality, and recall the finding that customers value empathy from the service worker, defined as the *caring* individualised attention provided to each customer. This in effect turns Adam Smith's famous quotation on its head. It appears, in fact, that customers do expect benevolence from the butcher, brewer and baker (or at least their front-line workforce), and that they do address themselves to the humanity rather than the self-love of the butcher, brewer and baker's front-line workforce.

2 Also see Arthur Miller's classic play (1949, p. 34) *Death of a Salesman,* in which the ageing and fading sales worker, Willy Loman, is fired by his manager because he has not been able to meet his target sales. Loman famously retorts: 'I put thirty-four years into this firm, Howard, and now I can't pay my insurance! You can't eat the orange and throw the peel away – a man is not a piece of fruit!' (p. 64).

3 Collinson *et al.* (1990, p. 138) argue that there two different ways in which work is organised in insurance sales. The mode of direct sales involves a form of work organisation very similar to the entrepreneurial ideal type outlined by Frenkel *et al.* Where sales involve the use of intermediaries, such as lawyers, to locate customers, a different form of work organisation pertains with secure employment status and a paternalistic management strategy. This form of insurance sales using intermediaries effectively involves a mix of service and sales. Management here is concerned not only with immediate sales to end-customers but also with the degree of service given to a network of intermediaries.

4 Call centre modes of extreme sales work are also likely to be the most oppressive form of call centre work because the control system there can marry the unambiguous output measurement of sales achieved, with the tight, IT-based monitoring of work processes.

CHAPTER 7

Empowerment on the front line?

One of the great symbols of the empowerment of the front-line workforce is the traditional organisational chart turned upside down on the office walls of senior management (Canning, 1999). Through this inversion, the front-line workforce are portrayed as the leaders, to whom the rest of the organisation must respond. While even service management writers admit that this is symbolic rather than actual leadership which is bestowed on the front line, there are still widespread arguments that front-line workers must be, and increasingly are, empowered. This chapter examines how far the empowerment of front-line workers matches the reality of these claims. It is structured in the following way. First, a brief overview is given of the debate on empowerment of front-line workers between the new service management school and those writing from critical perspectives. Arguing that analyses of empowerment and control should be conducted in tandem, the chapter then turns to examine the distinctive problems of control in front-line work for management, before examining specific issues in the empowerment of front-line workers.

Debates on empowerment

As with the general debate on empowerment in the workplace, the debate on empowerment in the front-line workplace is a polarised one, with either 'bouquets or brickbats' given out by analysts (Wilkinson *et al.*, 1997, p. 799). Too often there is an absence of appreciation of the nuances and complexities that exist. In this section it is argued that the concept of the customer-oriented

121

bureaucracy provides a way into analysing empowerment in a manner which is more than one-dimensional.

From Chapter 2 it will be recalled that one of the key arguments that the new service management school uses in constructing a win : win : win scenario for the service workplace is that competition is pushing firms towards the empowering of front-line workers. Only with an empowerment approach can service firms hope to deliver service quality. Within the service management school, however, there are some differences over what exactly 'empowerment' means in the context of front-line work. For some writers, it pertains to the degree of latitude or discretion in decision-making given to the front-line worker (Heskett *et al.*, 1997; Zemke and Schaaf, 1989). For others, it relates to the 'freedom' from the requirement to follow policies and procedures, and the 'freedom to take responsibility for ideas, decisions and actions' (Carlzon, 1987). Others still believe that 'empowerment is a "state of mind"' (Bowen and Lawler, 1995, p. 276) – a definition which focuses on psychological features of individual workers.

Writers from critical perspectives have been quick to criticise this management literature which heralds the arrival of the empowered front-line worker. For instance, Willmott (1995) acidly takes issue with the promise of empowerment that has accompanied business process re-engineering (BPR) – a management technique often used on the front line. Willmott argues that in BPR, 'empowered' work is assumed simply to be the opposite of fragmented and degraded work. However, this may simply take the form of working on integrated tasks which are made possible by the introduction of expert information technology systems and relational databases. Thus the new service work in fact may not involve any expansion of discretion or even task variety. Willmott also stresses that in this version of empowerment the determination by the workforce of the framework in which job decisions are made is placed off-limits.

As Rosenthal *et al.* (1997, p. 481) note, critical writers tend to see management rhetoric of empowerment as involving 'sham empowerment', often accompanied by 'work intensification and increased surveillance'. For instance, while Bowen and Lawler discuss the provision of customer feedback as an integral part of the empowerment of front-line workers, Fuller and Smith (1991) point to the use of customer feedback and mystery shoppers as new and pervasive forms of monitoring in the front-line workplace.

At this level, however, the debate is often a frustrating one. The new service management school is clearly at fault in failing to address issues of control, but too often critical writers are too ready to dismiss potentially meaningful changes in levels of discretion by arguing that the really important changes at work concern control. Two things are needed to advance the debate. First, there is a need for a conceptual approach that *links* the analysis of empowerment and control. The concept of the customer-oriented bureaucracy can inform such an approach. Within this concept there is no priority given to *either* empowerment or control. Rather, both can be seen as dimensions of an overall form of work organisation structured by two dominant logics. The second thing needed to advance the debate on control and empowerment is the disaggregation of the concepts to allow a more careful evaluation of them. The subsequent two sections in this chapter, on control and empowerment respectively, follow this requirement.

Control

Control can be thought of as 'the ability of ... managers to obtain desired work behaviour from workers' (Edwards, 1979: 17). The first stage in analysing control, therefore, is establishing what form of behaviour management desires from workers. It is clear that the pressures to deliver service quality mean that management is increasingly looking for more than compliance from the front-line workforce. Rather, it seeks an active commitment to allow customers to consume the enchanting myth of sovereignty. But the bureaucratic logic has not been completely supplanted – for instance, management does not just require emotional labour in the form of customer empathy, but wants a rationalised, efficient display of emotional labour. It wants quality and quantity.

The difficulties management has in obtaining these desired behaviours are propounded by three distinctive problems of control in front-line work that stem from the presence of the customer in the work process. These are the problem of *variability*, the problem of *observability* and the problem of *output measurement*. They are critical problems because, as is outlined below, their presence can severely undermine the operation of key forms of control.

The problem of variability derives from the potential variability of individual customers – a characteristic of front-line service work introduced in the first chapter. As Fuller and Smith (1991, p. 2) note, 'to perform quality service labour an employee must tailor delivery to the idiosyncratic and changeable needs of individual customers'. Management can organise matters to guide and teach customers in their behaviour, but the need to perpetuate the myth of sovereignty means that the control management has over customers in front-line interactions is incomplete. The myth of sovereignty systematically creates the possibility that the customer will step outside the routines that management attempts to impose upon him or her. For instance, Benson's (1986) excellent account of work within a department store argues convincingly that 'managers had little, if any, success ... in controlling the substance of customer–salesperson interactions; the attempt to maximise and satisfy each customer's needs enduringly resisted routinization' (p. 286). Herzenberg *et al.* (1998) argue that the variability of individual customers means that the engineering approach to job design, where tasks are pre-programmed, is highly problematic in front-line work. Relying solely on bureaucratic control (Edwards, 1979) becomes problematic because it is difficult to pre-design standard tasks and rules against which to assess workers' performance.

The problem of the observability of front-line work arises in part because the customer–worker interaction is likely to be affected by the physical presence of a supervisor monitoring the interaction. The presence of a supervisor runs the risk of harming the customer's satisfaction of a service interaction – it is likely to disrupt the enchanting myth of sovereignty. In addition, given that front-line work supervisors require not only visual information but also audio information, it is difficult for one supervisor to observe the labour process of several workers at the same time. This means that simple direct control, in the form of direct monitoring by management, becomes problematic.

Another traditional form of control – that based on measuring outputs (as distinct from measuring or observing the work process) – also becomes problematic in the contemporary service workplace. The output of front-line work, in part, relates to how customers have perceived the interaction with the worker and is intangible. As such, management may be faced with a problem of clearly and unambiguously measuring outputs.[1] Even when management does receive feedback information from customers it is often very difficult to link this information directly to the performance of individual workers, and therefore it is often not possible to use this information for control purposes (although see Snape *et al.*, 1996). An important caveat here is that for pure forms of sales work, output measurement is not a problem for management. The number of sales achieved is a clear, unambiguous measure of output, and as discussed in the preceding chapter the control system for sales work tends to rest on tying output measurement to payment through a commission system.

The new developments in control in front-line service work are attempts to address the problems of control while trying to engender the required efficient customer-oriented behaviour. Theoretically, the model of the customer-oriented bureaucracy suggests that service management will address these problems in *both* bureaucratic and customer-oriented ways. The classic bureaucratic response to the above problems is for management to seek to increase their knowledge and measurement of the labour process. If managers themselves are unable to easily observe the labour process they can turn to alternative sources of information – cue the entry of mystery shoppers and the use of IT in monitoring front-line work. Mystery shoppers are employed by service firms to pose as customers in order to assess the standards of service, including the attitudes and behaviour of the front-line staff. Research suggests that mystery shoppers are coming to be employed extensively in service settings (Fuller and Smith, 1991; Van Maanen, 1991; Leidner, 1993; Rothman, 1998). In the UK, one agency claims to have a potential of 2500 mystery shoppers ready for clients to call upon in monitoring the service delivered by their front-line staff (*Guardian*, 9 October 1996).

Technology is also being used to monitor the work of service workers without the direct physical presence of a supervisor. Information technology is unlike previous forms of technology in that it not only automates work processes but it also 'informates', that is, it reflexively provides information on its own activities (Zuboff, 1988). In front-line workplaces, this informating capacity is frequently used for monitoring purposes. If the front-line worker's job involves extensive use of IT then management is able to access this information to provide a good picture of what its front-line staff are doing (for example, Ball and Wilson, 2000). A report in the UK by the Institute of Employment Rights (Ford, 1999) suggests that the use of IT in monitoring front-line work is most extensive in call centres.

Monitoring by mystery shoppers and IT has been compared by some authors to the operation of a panopticon (Fuller and Smith, 1991; Fernie and Metcalfe, 1997). The concept of the panopticon dates back to the nineteenth-century political economist Jeremy Bentham, but has received recent consideration because of the work of Foucault (1979). Bentham sought to design a prison on the principle of a panopticon by which all the inmates could be observed at all times without being able to observe the observer. The detail of this design (a circular building of cell blocks with a central observation tower) is not centrally relevant. What is important is that Foucault saw in the panopticon a rich metaphor for the workings of much of contemporary society. The idea was applicable and in operation in more spheres than just prisons, for 'prisons resemble factories, schools, barracks, hospitals, which all resemble prisons' (1979, p. 83). A further key element in the operation of the panopticon is that the perception of being observed comes to be internalised by the people observed such that it is no longer necessary for an observer to be actually present. The observation tower in the prison may be empty, but the inmates cannot know this and still feel themselves under the gaze of the guard. And so it can be argued that mystery shoppers and IT function as a modern panopticon in the service workplace. The front-line workers can be observed without knowing whether they are being observed. But they know that there is the potential that they are observed so they may come to internalise the perception that they are permanently observed.

This comparison of mystery shopping and IT-monitoring to the panopticon is useful if it is seen as a way of highlighting the response of management to garner more information on the work processes – to see it as a bureaucratic response to its inability to directly monitor front-line work. It is less useful, however, if the metaphor is seen to imply that the control system becomes complete, and that there is no space for front-line workers to contest and reframe the control of their work lives (for example, see Taylor and Bain, 1999b). Indeed, as Chapter 5's discussion of call centres observed, technology only gives information in quantitative terms, but not in terms centrally relevant to important elements of service quality. It is notable that studies which make reference to the operation of the panopticon in the service workplace fail to provide data on how the modes of surveillance (either by IT or by customers) alter the consciousness of workers – this is despite the fact that central to Foucault's use of the concept is an argument about internalisation, or changes in consciousness. Finally, it should be noted that while it is the case that IT-monitoring has increased considerably, there is a danger that debates concentrate too much on call centre work. Indeed, it appears to be the case that many front-line workers in other areas remain relatively unaffected by IT monitoring – think of health care work, for example. Grant and Higgins's (1989) survey of 1500 front-line workers in 50 Canadian firms showed that as few as 5 per cent of respondents reported that IT 'checked the way work is done'. 35 per cent of respondents stated that IT monitored the number of transactions undertaken, with this being the element of work that the highest per cent of respondents reported as being monitored by IT.

There are clear indications, then, that management has responded to the problems of control in front-line work in a bureaucratic way by increasing its information of the labour process from other sources. What of responses to these problems driven by the logic of customer orientation? The appeal of the adoption of the mystery shopper is that it serves a dual bureaucratic and customer-oriented purpose. It not only supplies information to management on work behaviours, but it supplies it in a way that is related to customer perceptions of the service process. But there is another significant response driven by the logic of customer orientation – namely the use and development of *customer-related norms and values*.

If management wants customer-oriented behaviour, it can monitor the work process only imperfectly, by proxy, and must seek to cope with the increased variability of customers; a response has been to use customer-related values that will guide the front-line workers to deliver the behaviour that management would desire but which it increasingly cannot observe or set standard procedures for. Most obviously this approach can be seen in the substantial and widespread shift in recruitment criteria for front-line jobs towards the primary importance of the candidate having the appropriate customer-related personality and values (Stanback, 1990). It is here that it becomes possible to see concrete implications of what the alleged existence of 'consumer capitalism' and the 'service society' actually means for the organisation of front-line work. Only in consumer capitalism, first, would management seek to recruit on the basis of customer-related values, and, second, would these recruitment criteria be apparently readily met by job candidates. Abstract arguments from Bauman (1988, p. 220) that 'features of the consumer culture ... spill over all other aspects of contemporary life', and Ritzer (1999a, p. 189) that 'consumption pervades our consciousness' come to have real meaning when it is clear that many hiring decisions for (service) production roles relate to the existence of such a consciousness informed by consumption. Front-line workers are often hired on the basis of their identity as and identification with customers.

Service management does not just use such values as customer empathy and customer identification, but it also seeks to *develop* these values through socialisation, training and performance appraisals. Lashley (1997, pp. 48–9) describes a typical training session aimed at developing customer service values, at Marriott Hotels:

> The programme intended to develop a sense of empathy in the staff to customer experiences. Each employee was encouraged to look at things from the guest's point of view. The contents of the programme helped employees to consider who is the customer, what it is they are buying from the company, and the importance of employees in both creating impressions and in delivering customer satisfaction. The programme ran through guest experiences using role plays.

The extensive use of role plays in these settings is no accident, for not only is the message that the workers should think of situations from the customer's point of view, but the medium of role plays reinforces this, because workers are asked alternately to play the role of the customer. Korczynski *et al.* (2000) also note that service training sessions tend to be run on particpative lines with trainers seeking to elicit an active role from workers in the development of customer-related values. Recalling the discussion of culture management in the preceding chapter, the active participation of front-line workers in the creation of an overall service culture is likely to be crucial if management aims are to be met. Less research has been conducted into the process of perform-ance appraisals in front-line work, but it is likely that customer values will be further developed in this forum, with an emphasis on drawing out the active role of the front-line worker in the construction of these values.

The use and development of customer-related norms can be termed a process of *consuming commitment*. The contrast here is with Burawoy's (1979) famous concept of *manufacturing consent*. Burawoy sought to understand why class conflict, between labour and capital, was apparently declining, despite the enduring nature of exploitation and alienation in capitalist production. On the basis of a detailed observational study of a manufacturing plant in the USA, he argued that consent from the workforce came about not because of any consciousness imported from outside the manufacturing plant, but rather from the practices within the plant. Specifically, workers played (and were allowed to play) elaborate games involving informal rules and practices aimed at creating spaces, controlling earnings and making work more inter-esting. These games not only created spaces for workers but also generated consent to the overall system in which they were located. Burawoy argued that 'one cannot play a game and question the rules at the same time; consent to rules becomes consent to capitalist production' (1981, p. 92). The work of Burawoy is a good example of a manufacturing-based study generating concepts which have only limited relevance to contemporary front-line work-places. His argument about the lack of relevance of 'imported' consciousness is most likely to be resonant in workplaces where there is a buffer between production and consumption. Where production and consumption occur simultaneously, as they do in front-line work, there is a much greater potential for a significant role to be played by an 'imported' consciousness related to consumer identity and authority. Further, Burawoy's stress on the importance of *consent* does not accord with the demands for *commitment* made by service management. The use of an imported consumer consciousness is useful to management precisely because it can lead to active commitment, rather than just minimal consent.

In many existing approaches to control there is a tendency to see the development of normative forms of control as alternatives to bureaucratic forms of control centred on measurement and standardisation (Ouchi, 1979; Etzioni, 1961). But the concept of the customer-oriented bureaucracy points to the likelihood of a widespread *dual* existence of these forms of control in front-line workplaces. This analysis suggests two key levels of contradiction in the operation of this form of control (Korczynski *et al.*, 2000). First, there is the contradiction between the continued measurement/monitoring and the generation of customer-related values. While the former tends to rest more easily with low-trust, command dynamics leading to compliance on the part of workers, the latter tends to be associated with high-trust dynamics supporting active worker commitment (Fox, 1974). Fuller and Smith (1991) give a good illustration of this point. They report a 'smile strike' (that is, a withdrawal of commitment) by hotel desk clerks, who were 'angry' when they found out that they were being monitored by mystery customers. Korczynski *et al.* (2000) report a telling response from a call centre worker regarding the practice of the monitoring of phone conversations with customers: 'It's like in the factory with a leading-hand. We're all adults and should be trusted to do our work.' Trust necessary for commitment to values is undermined by monitoring.

This tendency is likely to be exacerbated when the fragile social order of the front-line workplace periodically breaks down. In periods of surface calm the combination of being monitored and being asked to be committed to customer-related values may not be experienced as a galling contradiction. However, this may change when the same combination is placed in the context of labour-stretching as customer demand rises unpredictably, and in the context of customer abuse. Contradictions in control that were latent may become manifest. Management can act, however, to try to turn a situation of contradiction into one of mutuality and symbiosis. Management will justify monitoring and measurement by arguing that these processes are needed to ensure customer satisfaction (Korczynski *et al.*, 2000). The logic of this is that given that the front-line workers are committed to giving good customer service then they should have no quarrels with the procedures that are in place to ensure that this occurs. The rhetoric of management and HRM become as important as the actual practices that are put in place.

The second level of contradiction lies *within* the use of customer-related norms. Analysis must be sensitive to the active role of workers in the creation of customer-related norms. Norms cannot simply be imposed in a top-down exercise (Kunda, 1992). Crucially, systematic and significant differences may arise between management's view of the customer and that of front-line workers. Specifically, the fact that management's actions are underpinned by the dual logics of customer orientation and efficiency means that it will prefer workers to identify with a collective, disembodied concept of the customer. Such a disembodied image of the customer will encourage workers to deal with individual customers efficiently, because they will be conscious of the concerns of other customers waiting in a queue. Front-line workers, however, may be more likely to identify with embodied individual customers, because interactions with specific customers are an important arena for meaning and satisfaction within the work, as detailed in previous chapters. This analysis suggests that the many front-line workers who identify with customers are likely to often welcome the development of customer-related values and associated initiatives (Rosenthal *et al.*, 1997), but that the translation of these values into the sort of behaviours that management desires will be rather more ambiguous (Peccei and Rosenthal, 2000). Importantly, for resistance, the dual logic informing front-line work means that their are dual legitimate languages or discourses in service work. This provides front-line workers and their representative bodies with the potential to call on one of these legitimate discourses in order to contest and reframe management decisions. As Rosenthal *et al.*'s (1997, p. 481) study shows, front-line workers can use the language of customer service and customer orientation 'as resources in their struggles with managers in order to bring managers into line with workforce expectations'. There is a process of consuming commitment, but *it is not a process of all-consuming commitment.*

Empowerment

Elements in the above analysis of control have already given indications of important developments in the empowerment of front-line staff. For instance, the increased need to cope with the variability of customers, and the managerial recognition that norms not just procedures are increasingly needed, both have implications for empowerment. To analyse the issue of empowerment further, however, it is useful to break down the concepts into distinct areas. Here I focus on downward and upward communication, task-based participation, teamworking and self-management, and empowerment in relation to customers.

Downward and upward communication

Paradoxically, perhaps, the pressures of the customer-oriented bureaucracy suggest an increase in both downward *and* upward communication. In the bureaucratic setting, standardised procedures and products tend to stay in place for lengthy periods, with little new information generated that needs to be transmitted downwards to front-line workers. With competitive pressures driving service firms to be more customer-oriented, however, this situation has changed, and such firms constantly develop an array of new products, services and offers to attract customers. Further, the aim towards the development of a customer relationship means that the front-line division of labour has been reconfigured so that there are fewer hand-off points between staff to be experienced by customers. This means that the front-line staff must have a greater array of information at their disposal to communicate as necessary to the customer. Both these factors point to the need for systematic and frequent mechanisms for service firms to cascade information downwards to staff. Hence the rise of the 'team' or group briefing in the front-line workplace (Frenkel *et al.*, 1999), and the redefinition of the supervisor role towards a greater emphasis on communication and teaching or 'coaching' (Korczynski *et al.*, 1996; Larkin and Larkin, 1996).

If front-line workers are receiving greater amounts of downward communication, they are also more likely to communicate upwards than they were two decades ago. Readers of the new service management literature will not have to wait long for the injunction that management must learn to 'listen to the front-line'. This sudden attention to the voice of the front-line workforce, however, is based not on an interest in the voice of the workforce *per se*, but rather on a view of the voice of the front-line as a *proxy* for the voice of the customer. It is this vision of the front-line that underpins the symbolism of the inversion of the organisation's traditional pyramid. Bowen and Lawler (1995, p. 283) are correct to point out that forms of upward communication are easily compatible with a production line approach to service management, and their choice of example underscores this point:

> Suggestion involvement can produce some of the gains possible with empowerment, without altering the basic production line approach. McDonald's, for example, really listens to the front-line. The Big Mac, Egg MacMuffin, and McDLT were all invented by individual employees within the system.

The words 'McDonald's . . . really listens to the front-line' can be delivered without irony only if the implicit assumption is that the front-line voice is only that of the customer by proxy. This is a very limited and unitarist view.

Another important limit to the role of front-line workers as disseminators rather than receivers of communication has also been suggested by Frenkel *et al.* (1999, p. 175). Their research into call centres showed that management imposed severe restrictions on email communications *between* front-line workers, even when they were related to business and customer service matters. Here management imposed conditions that the front-line could receive and send messages only from and to supervisors. The supervisors were to be the arbiters of what information to distribute to other front-line staff. Management justified this in terms of the need for customers to receive consistent and reliable information from staff. If workers could communicate freely with each other, they argued, there would be the possibility of half-truths regarding policies and services that would be reproduced to customers. This concern speaks directly to the 'reliability' element of Parasuraman's model of customer perception of service quality (reviewed in Chapter 4). This need for reliability is likely to serve to limit the communication role of front-line staff to *'information receivers rather than knowledge-creators'* (Korczynski *et al.*, 1996, p. 83).

Task participation

This element of empowerment, by contrast, does challenge key parts of the production line approach to service work. Task participation relates to the design of the front-line job itself, and whether there is more scope for the workforce to take decisions in their everyday worklife.

The ever more competitive requirement of customer orientation means that firms must deal increasingly with the variability of customers. As noted above, this means that front-line work will be structured less by standard policies and procedures which customers must be expected to adhere to. The corollary of this combined with the inability of supervisors to directly monitor the work is that there is a strong logic driving an increase in the discretion available to front-line workers in dealing with more and more variable customer situations. Similarly, the customer orientation logic pushing towards a division of labour based more on a customer relationship means that the scope of tasks that a front-line worker will undertake is likely to increase. Finally, from the discussion in the preceding chapter, it is clear that the rise in discretion in some front-line jobs may be due to a reconfiguration of roles to encompass sales aims. Little surprise then, that there is now widespread evidence that front-line workers do have significantly more discretion in their jobs than in the recent past. This evidence comes from a range of settings – hospitality (Lashley, 1997; Jones *et al.*, 1997), call centres (Frenkel *et al.*, 1999), retail (du Gay, 1996; Rosenthal *et al.*, 1997), airlines (Wouters, 1989) and public welfare workers (Foster and Hoggett, 1999).[2] Lashley's discussion of task empowerment in the hospitality context brings out aspects common to many of these instances of increased discretion:

Empowerment is largely related to attempts to generate improved service quality by improving responsiveness of front-line employees in the immediate service situation. Empowerment consists chiefly of authority to operate within prescribed boundaries. This could be a cash value to be given to the guest as a refund for a complaint, a reduction on the bill, a free meal, a complementary drink or bottle of wine...In the main this form of empowerment consists of empowering employees to provide extra service...The employee takes ownership of the service encounter and provides a level of service not normally given without reference to a supervisor or manager.

To a degree this form of empowerment suggests a reuniting of conception and execution in service work. The traditional Taylorist production line approach separates conception from execution, with management taking over the conception element of work and creating procedures to be followed – with workers merely following procedures, or executing tasks. Offe (1985) makes the case that the simple application of rationality to service work is problematic, for some autonomy must be given to the front-line worker to cope with customer variability. Herzenberg *et al.* (1998) take this point further by arguing that contemporary service work is increasingly ill-suited to a form of Taylorist, or engineering approach to job design. They argue that an 'interpretive' model of work is more applicable to contemporary service work: 'the interpretive model takes as problematic what the engineering model takes as given: the prior definition of the product and the independence of the production process from the design of the product' (p. 87). Herzenberg *et al.* would see important strands of this interpretive form of job design in the studies cited above.

Even studies heavily critical of the gap between managerial rhetoric of empowerment and the reality of workplace practices are often forced to concede that there has been *some* rise in front-line workers' discretion. For instance, Hales's (1999) critical discussion of the limits of empowerment in a fun park notes that there was some increase in task participation: 'any employee choice in how they performed their jobs arose mainly from operational necessity and pressure of work and was restricted to trying to "take ownership" of customer complaints' (p. 13). Similarly, his study of high-quality hotels in Holland found a great disparity between managerial rhetoric and reality, but nevertheless it was the case that even the worst instance involved greater though 'highly circumscribed discretion in responding to guest requests/complaints' (p. 10).

Critical studies are useful when they point to important caveats. Two specific caveats need to be raised. First, although there is widespread evidence that discretion has increased, it must be borne in mind that, in many cases, increases came from a very low starting position, suggesting that the levels of discretion remain circumscribed to an important degree. Rosenthal *et al.*'s (1997) careful study of a large UK supermarket chain is a case in point.

The authors note on the one hand that, 'discretion and responsibility have increased noticeably at Shopco' (p. 491). On the other hand they state that previously there had been a 'virtual absence of discretion under the old regime' (p. 492). They conclude therefore, that 'we would assess this empowerment as being fairly limited' (p. 492). Indeed, the model of the customer-oriented bureaucracy would suggest this finding. Management is not introducing empowerment because they have a sole focus on customer orientation and service quality. Rather, these aims have joined the rationalising aims focusing on efficiency. It is likely that empowerment *must exist*, but it *must also be limited* if efficiency in dealing with customers and in running the organisation is not to be lost. As Bowen and Lawler put it, 'the helpful hotel receptionist who allows a disgruntled guest to check-in early doesn't always think through the implications for that day's housekeeping plan' (1995, p. 285).

The second caveat is that many of the cases of task empowerment concentrate on the 'service recovery' (Bowen and Lawler, 1995) aspect of the job. The rise in discretion and latitude tends to be concentrated in resolving a guest's complaint, or in taking 'ownership' of a particular customer's problem. A key question, not properly addressed in many studies so far, is how far discretion has risen in the original service offer, rather than in the service recovery aspect of the job. Bowen and Lawler make two important points here. First, they argue that empowerment approaches are best suited to the service recovery aspect of the job, but that there is considerable scope for the application of the production line or bureaucratic logic to the original service offer:

> the real challenge is to fine-tune the service delivery systems so that employees don't need to scramble to recover because they get it right first time ... The strength of the production line approach to services is its delivery of reliability and consistency. (pp. 285–6)

Second, they suggest that management should be proactive in applying the hard tools of total quality management to ensure that service is delivered correctly first time, so that instances of service recovery remain limited. But it is service recovery where task empowerment is more prevalent. Hence, task empowerment will remain systematically limited.

Teamworking and self-management

Following Marchington and Wilkinson (2000), teamworking and self-management are defined as incorporating: responsibility for a complete task; working without direct supervision; discretion over work methods and time; encouragement for team members to organise and multi-skill; and influence over recruitment to the team. Clearly, this form of participation or empowerment is more far-reaching than those considered already. The literature examining the rise in teamwork is centred on studies of either manufacturing work or knowledge-intensive work (Proctor and Mueller, 1999). A limited number of studies of teamwork in front-line settings can be found, however (Mathews, 1994; Griffiths, 1997; Lashley, 1997; Foster and Hoggett, 1999; Leverment *et al.*, 1998; Ostroff, 1999, ch. 7). Lashley, for instance, describes the creation of 'autonomous work teams' in the UK restaurant chain Harvester. Management here introduced teams as part of an overall restructuring of the firm in line with an empowerment philosophy, and Lashely's description suggests a greater direct participation by staff in a wider range of decisions than is experienced by staff empowered only at the task level. He notes that the teams in the restaurant

> will be responsible for guest service, guest complaints, sales targets, ordering cutlery and glassware, cashing up after service and team member training. In the more advanced cases, teams take part in the selection and recruitment of new team members. (pp. 44–5)

Mathews (1994) describes the teamwork set up at an Australian insurance company. He draws analogies between the 'one-stop shop' idea that underlay teamwork at this firm and the cellular approach to manufacturing which is conducive to teamwork in that setting. The team, made up of a number of specialists, provided service to a set of customers to whom they would seek to render an integrated insurance service. Just as car workers in teams, in cellular systems, work in a coordinated and interdependent way around cars, so insurance workers worked around a group of customers, clustered in a defined segment of the market. Mathews makes some sweeping claims for this approach, arguing that 'it represents a prototype that will sweep through the service sector, eliminating the previous Fordist, fragmented work organisation' (see also Bellamy's (1996) discussion).

Nevertheless, most of the few studies of 'teamwork' in front-line settings that do exist turn out, on inspection, to be studies of rather more dilute forms of teamwork than in the definition given above (for example, Belt *et al.*, 1999; Lloyd and Newell, 1999). Indeed, Frenkel *et al.* (1999) seek to cut through the pervasive management rhetoric of teams by showing that what managers called 'teams' in the service and sales workplaces they studied were in effect administrative work groups of individual workers under the jurisdiction of one supervisor. They shared none of the characteristics in the definition above.

An appropriate conclusion would appear to be that teamwork and self-management have not followed Mathews's prediction, and swept through the service sector, but rather remain isolated in incidence (Cully *et al.*, 1999, p. 44; Hunter, 2000). This is not to say that teamwork based around the one-stop-shop concept is not likely to feature increasingly as part of the reorganisation of service work. On the contrary, a *form* of teamwork around this concept fits well with the dual requirements of customer orientation and efficiency. It is a basis of a division of labour that allows for the creation and maintenance of a customer relationship, while also potentially doing little harm to quantitative customer-throughput measures, for instance (for example, see the Xerox case in Heskett *et al.*, 1997, p. 110). What is at issue is the degree of empowerment and self-management that will be built into such forms of teamwork. At present, it seems that service management, like management in other settings, is reluctant to cede the degree of influence to the front-line that would allow many cases to be seen as fully fledged examples of teamwork and self-management.

Empowerment in relation to the customer

The discussion so far has focused on the degree of empowerment of front-line workers within the organisation. This is where most analyses of empowerment stop. However, for front-line work it is also necessary to consider front-line workers' empowerment with regard to customers. For some critical writers, the rising customer orientation of firms increases the degree of subservience and servility of front-line workers to customers. This theme was partly examined in relation to feminist perspectives on service work discussed in Chapter 3. But the argument of subservience is put forward by others as well. Rothman (1998, pp. 134–5), for instance, argues that

> in most cases, the sales or service workers occupy a social role of implied subordin-
> ation or even explicit subservience... 'Customer' carries the connotation of being
> served and the right to define and direct the relationship. 'Service' shares linguistic
> roots with 'servant', 'servitude', and 'slave'.

The idea of the disempowerment or subservience of front-line workers in relation to customers is also implicitly present in the arguments of du Gay and Salaman (1992, p. 622), who state that 'the language of the sovereign customer is increasingly embedded in a wide-ranging series of organisational structures, practices and technologies'. If service management is using the language and imagery of sovereign customers then it is forcing front-line workers into subservient positions with regard to customers.

The key word in that last sentence is 'if'. Despite one or two counter-examples (Sosteric, 1996; Eaton, 1996), it is clear that management rarely uses the norms and imagery of customer sovereignty to directly inform the way front-line workers should deal with customers.[3] The key norms that are promulgated are ones of customer empathy and identification rather than customer sovereignty. The usual approach is not for a manager to say to the front-line worker that the customer is always right, but rather for the manager to ask workers to put themselves in the customer's shoes, to ask them to think about what the customer must be feeling. In a subtle way, however, customer empathy and identification also brings with it an element of the concept of customer sovereignty – namely that the customer should be allowed to consume the *myth* of customer sovereignty. The story of contemporary service work is not one of the simple subservience of the front-line worker to the customer. Rather, the concept of the customer-oriented bureaucracy can highlight ways in which elements of *both* empowerment and disempowerment in relation to customers are present in the relationship.

Empowerment exists in two senses. First, as noted above, front-line workers have a greater ability and power to act for a customer – in resolving problems, in providing extra services, in going outside simple policies and procedures. They are also more likely to interact with them in a relationship or at least a pseudo-relationship, and so see through policies enacted, rather than having to hand off the customer to another department or unit. The second form of empowerment results from the continuing bureaucratic imperative in front-line work. Service firms still need customers to be dealt with efficiently. In order to ensure that this occurs, front-line workers are trained in how to *take control* of interactions with customers (Rieder *et al.*, 2000; Korczynski, 2001) – to ensure that the appropriate service can be delivered rather quicker than if the customer is allowed to dictate the flow and direction of the interaction.

The key fine line of much of front-line work rests on taking control of the interaction in a subtle way that does not overtly disturb the myth of customer sovereignty. It is when this myth is disturbed and when customers become abusive as enchantment turns to disillusionment that the major form of disempowerment with regard to customers occurs. In contemporary service work, front-line workers are systematically more likely to face, and have to put up with, customer abuse. As service firms must compete with each other for customers in increasingly fierce ways, so management increasingly instructs front-line workers to put up with irate customers, to see them as 'opportunities' to turn around (Korczynski, 2000b). Here, disempowerment is real, and Rothman's arguments in this area are valid: 'the whims of an ill-tempered or rude person, which would be inappropriate in communication among equals, must often be endured by service persons, lest customers take their business elsewhere or complain to management' (1998, p. 134). As the following chapter shows, these manifestations of disempowerment can occasion real pain for front-line workers. In part the pain arises from the experience of a degree of empowerment turning into an experience of subservience as this fragile order crumbles.

This examination of empowerment in front-line work has excluded sales work from consideration. As the preceding chapter suggested, sales work tends to have very different patterns and dynamics. The analysis in that chapter already highlighted some important aspects of, and limitation to, empowerment in sales work. The high discretion over the process of sales work identified speaks to high levels of task-level empowerment. The greater propensity to manipulate customers into sales speaks to a greater empowerment of sales workers with regard to customers. But what of the other aspects of empowerment in sales work? The arms-length relationship between the sales worker and the organisation will tend to work against any substantial amount of downward or upward communication. Typically, sales workers may attend short briefings, perhaps monthly, focusing on product characteristics, and may attend an annual conference, drawing together the sales worker of a firm nationally or by region (Frenkel *et al.*, 1999). Upward communication will be limited particularly by the lack of incentive for sales workers to deliver this. Commission payment systems drive instrumentalism. It is sales achieved that reap commission and there is little incentive for sales workers to volunteer information upwards on customers if this will not directly affect their sales numbers (see Lloyd and Newell, 1999, for an example of sales workers withholding information). Potentially, teamworking and self-management could be compatible with the arms-length relationship with the firm that is part of the entrepreneurial model of sales work. However, teamwork appears to be noticeable by its absence in sales work. This can be explained by the emphasis on *individual* competitiveness that management places as central to its control mechanisms in sales work (Lloyd and Newell, 1999).

Conclusion

This chapter began by highlighting the terms of an increasingly sterile debate between a literature celebrating the arrival of the empowered front-line worker and a critical literature which tends to argue that the rhetoric of empowerment hides an intensification of control and effort. The chapter has provided equal space for an analysis of both control and empowerment and has drawn out connections between the two areas. Particularly, the dual presence of the logics of customer orientation and rationalisation leads to ambiguities and contradictions in both areas.

In the sphere of control, three key problems for management increasingly present themselves in the front-line workplace – the problems of variability, observability and output measurement. These problems prevent an easy application of traditional bureaucratic forms of control, such as standardisation of procedures, measurement of work processes, and direct monitoring. Nevertheless, management has continued to pursue bureaucratic approaches by seeking to use alternative sources for information on the behaviours of front-line workers – namely IT systems, customers and sometimes pseudo-customers. But management does not just desire bureaucratic, compliant, efficient behaviour; it increasingly needs front-line workers to act in committed customer-oriented ways. Hence, the restructuring of control on the front-line has also involved a significant role for the use and development of customer-related norms and values. Important ambiguities and contradictions in this dual, customer-oriented and bureaucratic form of control were highlighted. A process of consuming commitment may be generated, but is unlikely to be a process of all-consuming commitment.

A clear connection between control and empowerment is that management relies on the customer-related norms to direct the behaviour of front-line workers within the greater scope for discretion that exists for many front-line workers. Front-line workers' empowerment at the task-level has increased, but there are limits to this – and the model of the customer-oriented bureaucracy suggests these limits are systematic and likely to be enduring. Front-line workers find themselves both receiving more downward communication and offering more upward communication than in the past. Within this, however, there is a tendency for many of these workers to remain more information-receivers than knowledge-creators. The potential for more teamwork and self-management was highlighted, but it was argued that this opportunity has yet to give rise to widespread enactment. The implicit sense of the dynamic within the concept of the fragile social order allows a view of the simultaneous empowerment and subservience of front-line workers in relation to customers. A sense of empowerment gives way to an experience of subservience as the irate customer disrupts the fragile social order of the front-line workplace.

Notes

1   Indeed, at the macro level there is a considerable debate regarding the ability of official statistics to adequately capture the outputs of service industries (Dean and Kunze 1995; Herzenberg *et al.* 1998).

2   Further note that Chapter 5 presented detailed workplace-based research which indicated that even where highly standardised procedures existed on paper the necessary variability of front-line work meant that these procedures were not followed in practice. This is true for rigid paper procedures in restaurants (Paules, 1991), tight scripting of interaction in call centres (Frenkel *et al.*, 1999) and rigid medical protocols in health care work (Bolton, 2000). See also Adler's (1986) more detailed discussion of this relating to bank work.

3   This is not to say, therefore, that the norm of customer sovereignty will not be used by management to legitimise wider organisational facets. It is merely to stress that it is not a norm used to directly inform the customer–worker relationship.

CHAPTER 8

Managing emotions

Car workers are not expected to smile at cars, computer programmers are not expected to behave empathetically towards software, but for many front-line workers expectations related to emotions are central to their job roles. Staff at Sheraton hotels, for instance, are issued with the instruction that 'every time you see a guest, smile and offer an appropriate hospitality comment. Speak to every guest in a friendly, enthusiastic and courteous tone and manner' (Boella, 1996, p. 280). More succinctly, 'Smile', and 'Be Friendly' are the directives of signs hanging in the staff-only space of a US supermarket (Tolich, 1993). In the terms of a growing academic literature, these front-line workers are expected to deliver *emotional labour*. There are some small differences in emphasis in definitions of the concept of emotional labour in the front-line context (Hochschild, 1983; James, 1989; Noon and Blyton, 1997). However, common to most approaches to the topic is the idea that emotional labour involves the front-line worker managing feelings, and behavioural displays associated with feelings in interactions with customers. Hochschild (1983, p. 11) estimates that 'roughly one-third of American workers today have jobs that subject them to substantial demands for emotional labor', and that 'of all women working, roughly one-half have jobs that call for emotional labor'.

As competition has intensified, firms have sought to differentiate themselves through the quality of the service interactions with customers, and key parts of this service quality have implications for emotional labour. Indeed, emotional labour can be seen as relevant for four of the five dimensions in the SERVQUAL model of Parasuraman *et al.* (1991) (discussed in Chapter 4). This model suggests that front-line workers' *appearance and demeanour* should be positive for customers, that they should demonstrate *willingness to help* customers, that they should be *courteous* to customers and appear *trustworthy* and that they should show *individual empathy* to customers. The logic is clear: if management is concerned with ensuring that customers receive high service quality, it must also be concerned with emotional labour.

This rise in the importance of emotional labour over recent decades should not mean that a simple contrast can be drawn between the present and the unemotional bureaucratic past, however (Merton, 1962; Lipsky, 1976; Prottas, 1979). Such a sharp contrast may be informed in part by real changes in the nature of front-line work. However, the contrast is also partly informed by pervasive conceptual blinkers which had prevented both academic researchers and management from seeing emotional labour in action in the past. For academic researchers, the most important conceptual blinkers were a legacy of Max Weber. With a few exceptions, most academic studies of work until the 1980s and 1990s were written with an unstated acceptance of Weber's image of the ideal type of bureaucracy, unsullied by 'love, hatred and all purely personal, irrational and emotional elements' (Gerth and Mills, 1958, p. 216). Management's unwillingness to recognise emotional labour was informed by a mixture of gender inequality and direct economic benefits. Feminist analyses have pointed out that 'because emotional labour [was] seen as "natural" unskilled women's work... the significance of its contribution and value... [was] ignored' (James, 1989, p. 22). Male employers and managers could get a double benefit from marginalising emotional labour – they could gain as men in perpetuating a system of female subordination, and they could benefit as an economic class by being able to keep down the wages of the female emotional labourers.

Although largely ignored by academics and managers, emotional labour has been performed in many front-line jobs for many years. As the very title suggests, workers in 'caring' occupations have always understood that emotional labour has been central to their work (James 1986). With the growth of welfare systems in advanced economies, the labour of caring has shifted significantly from the unpaid domain of the private household to the paid domain of the public (sector) workplace (although see Glazer, 1993). As such, emotional labour has been a central aspect of paid work for a key sector of advanced economies for many years.

For academic observers of the workplace, the blinkers to emotional labour were effectively ripped off by Hochschild's (1983) groundbreaking study of emotional labour among flight attendants and debt collectors. Hochschild wrote about the work of flight attendants not just in terms of the physical labour involved, e.g. serving meals, but centrally in terms of the emotions that management expected them to display. Hochschild developed C. Wright Mills's (1957) earlier pessimistic visions into a sustained critique of the way in which capitalism was increasingly commercialising and commodifying emotions. Here was a study which demanded attention, and put emotional labour on the centre-stage of academic interest in the 1980s and 1990s. As noted already, emotional labour was also appearing centre-stage for service management in the same period. As Fineman (1996, p. 557) observes, 'in the last decade or so we have witnessed an acceleration in the institutionalization of managerial control over emotional display.'

It is, therefore, important to examine the management of emotional labour in the front-line workplace. 'Who does the managing, how, and with what consequences?' are the key questions that drive the rest of this chapter. The following section lays out Hochschild's pioneering and critical work on the experience of emotional labour, and reviews criticisms and elaborations of her arguments. Flowing from this is an analysis of key HRM practices related to the delivery of emotional labour.

Experiencing emotional labour – Hochschild and beyond

Some writers from the new service management school suggest that the emotional acting that is required of front-line workers is little different from the sort of emotional acting that people undertake in their everyday lives. This implies that there is little that can be particularly harmful about emotional labour. Hochschild's book, *The Managed Heart: Commercialization of Human Feeling* (1983), takes direct issue with this approach. This section begins with a detailed summary of Hochschild's important argument that has set the terrain for much subsequent analysis. Key assumptions in her approach are brought to the surface and are then subjected to critical analysis. This critical analysis calls on a range of other research into emotional labour.

The first half of Hochschild's work lays out general rules and contexts of the 'emotion work' that is done in the private sphere of people's lives. The second half focuses on the 'transmutation' (p. 19) of emotions and their management from the private sphere to the commercial sphere. For Hochschild there are a number of key differences between the two spheres. In the commercial sphere of front-line work, a feeling becomes a 'commodity', something to be bought and sold, and to be used instrumentally. Adopting a Marxist perspective, she argues that just as other forms of labour become commodified in capitalism, so too does emotional labour. This leads to the alienation of the feeling from the self of the front-line worker: 'when the product – the thing to be engineered, mass-produced, and subjected to speed-up and slowdown – is a smile, a mood, a feeling, or a relationship, it comes to belong more to the organisation, and less to the self' (p. 198). There are two other key factors that make emotional labour in the commercial sphere fundamentally different from emotion work in the private sphere. First, the emotional labour of the front-line worker takes place in the context of an unequal relationship with the customer, while there tends to be greater equality in relationships in the private sphere. As Hochschild puts it,

in private life, we are free to question the going rate of exchange and free to negotiate a new one ... But in the public world of work, it is often part of an individual's job to accept uneven exchanges...Where the customer is king, unequal exchanges are normal. (pp. 85–6)

Second, there is the fact that it is management who impose systematic feeling rules for service workers, while in the private sphere these rules on the display and experience of feelings stem from 'deep private bonds' (p. 56) and social roles. These management-imposed feeling rules are seen as being increasingly standardised, serving to deskill front-line jobs.

These distinctive aspects of emotional labour performed in the commercial sphere – commodification, the structured inequality in relation to customers and the managerial imposition of feeling rules – mean that emotional labour has deeply harmful consequences for front-line workers. Hochschild argues, mainly on the basis of her study of flight attendants in the USA, that the consequences are particularly harmful because the management-imposed feeling rules demand that workers do not just put on a façade, or 'surface act', to customers. Rather, management are concerned that front-line workers 'deep act' their emotions with customers. It is not just a front that management want; they want workers to internalise the feelings they are meant to display. They want to manage the hearts, rather than just the faces, of workers – hence the title of Hochschild's book, *The Managed Heart*. These demands cause harm to the front-line workers – regardless of the individual coping strategies these workers take. She outlines three such coping strategies and concludes that there is 'harm in all three'. For instance, if the worker clearly distinguishes herself from the job she is less likely to suffer burnout; but she may blame herself for making this very distinction and denigrate herself as 'just an actor, not sincere' (p. 187).[1]

Many analyses of emotional labour in different front-line occupations continue to use Hochschild's framework with little modification (for example, Ogbonna and Wilkinson, 1988, 1990; Taylor, 1998; Stenross and Kleinman, 1989; Smith, 1992). Other commentaries on emotional labour tend to accept the main tenets of Hochschild's work while also 'bolting-on' certain points raised in criticism of her arguments. A case in point is Ashforth and Humphreys' (1993) argument that Hochschild's range of options for front-line workers' response to emotional labour is incomplete. They argue that front-line workers need neither 'deep act' nor 'surface act' emotional labour, for the possibility exists that the expected emotional display may be fully consistent with the worker's own inner feelings. There is no need to act, because the required emotions flow naturally from the worker's own identity and personality. This is an important but limited point if it is made simply as an addition to Hochshild's overall approach. Central to Hochschild's approach is the idea that emotional labour delivered in the commercial sphere is necessarily estranged and alienated because it has become commodified, a product that exists apart from the worker. This is true even if there is an apparent match between emotional requirements and personality, and the implication of this is not considered by Ashforth and Humphreys's 'add-on' point.

A critical evaluation of Hochschild, therefore, needs to go beyond *ad hoc* criticisms and should examine more fundamental conceptual issues in her arguments. As Tolich (1993) points out, Hochschild's arguments provide no basis for a systematic understanding of customers as a key source of *both pain and pleasure* for front-line workers. Her analysis and emphasis on the pain and the harmful effects of emotional labour is inadequate, for it is an absolutist approach that sees harm in all forms of emotional labour, and does not locate the tensions of emotional labour in relation to the managerial demands for *rationalised* emotional labour.

An important problem in Hochschild's work is that although her analysis exists at two levels she shows no awareness of the distinction between these levels and leaps from one to the other inappropriately. One level relates to the 'objective' alienation of emotional labour that she sees as occurring in capitalism. This is an argument, exactly like Marx's arguments on alienation, that is conducted at the level of a political understanding of the nature of capitalism. It does not pertain to the *subjective* experience of emotional labour by front-line workers. An instructive analogy can be drawn with how Blauner (1964), a US sociologist, sought to use Marx's political-philosophical concept of alienation to construct various hypotheses of the alienation that would be *experienced* by production workers in different settings. However, as Grint (1998, p. 270) notes,

> Blauner's subjective version of alienation is qualitatively different from Marx's objective notion of alienation (that is, for Marx, it is an inherent and undifferentiated element of all capitalist societies and therefore immune to the articulated attitudes of . . . individuals).

So Hochschild should see her arguments about the *subjective* experience of alienated emotional labour as being at a qualitatively different level from her arguments about the *objective* status of emotional labour as alienated within capitalism. But this is exactly what she does not see. Rather, she imports her absolutist, universalist conclusion of the objective alienated nature of emotional labour and uses this to imply that the subjective experience of emotional labour will be necessarily harmful. This is a fundamental flaw in her argument (see also Smith, 1999, p. 126).

Another key weakness in Hochschild's work is that she fails to use the idea of the social embeddedness of economic interactions (Granovetter, 1985). As Chapter 4 argued, the idea of social embeddedness allows a view of the pleasures that workers can gain from the social interactions that are *part of* the economic interactions. Indeed, Hochschild's own data point to this. She writes that 'many flight attendants spoke of enjoying "work with people"' (p. 107). It is noteworthy that it is the socially embedded 'people' that flight attendants liked working with, rather than the 'customers' of the simple economic exchange. This sentence of Hochschild parallels many other findings of front-line work, and it should be central to analysis. Instead, it is a quick sentence dusted off before turning to the real topic for Hochschild, which is the *tensions* of emotional labour. As Wouters (1989, p. 112) puts it, 'Hochschild's concentration on the costs of emotional labour...distorted her empirical results'. Where in Hochschild's work is the space for seeing the pleasures of working emotionally with customers that are so meaningful to front-line workers?

This leaves unevaluated in her analysis the focus on the unequal, deferential, relationship with the sovereign customer, and the focus on the managerial imposition of feeling rules. Chapter 7's analysis of empowerment vis-à-vis the customer shows Hochschild's point regarding the customer to be only partly true. It is the case that the front-line workers are in a subservient position when they have to put up with customer abuse and anger. To this degree, Hochschild's argument has merit – there will be pain to be suffered by front-line workers from customer abuse, particularly because front-line staff are expected to be, and often are, empathetic towards customers (Korczynski, 2000b). Indeed, Hochschild's own data support the idea that incidences of facing 'irates' represent critical incidents in the experience of emotional labour. She gives three examples of flight attendants recalling 'personal breaking points' in the job (p. 128). Each of these examples involves either customer abuse or customer behaviour with which it was impossible to empathise. So there is merit in part of Hochschild's argument. However, her assumption that the axial principle of the customer–worker interaction is that of subservience to the sovereign customer is misplaced – as the previous chapter argued.

The final point to consider in Hochschild's approach is her argument regarding how the hierarchical imposition of feeling rules informs the harmful effects of emotional labour. This is an important and sound point that has received considerable support in subsequent research. How far the experience of emotional labour is harmful and painful relates to the degree of autonomy that front-line workers have – particularly in determining the feeling rules of emotional display. When it is management that tightly circumscribes the rules of emotional labour then the front-line worker is more likely to suffer from the tensions within the potentially contradictory situation of the customer-oriented bureaucracy. Conversely, when front-line workers have greater freedom in deciding when to smile, how to smile, or even if to smile, then, systematically, emotional labour will have less harmful consequences for staff. As Hochschild puts it, the harm of emotional labour 'could be reduced ...if workers could feel a greater sense of control over the conditions of their work lives' (p. 187).

A number of studies have lent support to the general thrust of this argument (Morris and Feldman, 1996; Ashforth and Tomiuk, 2000; Troyer *et al.*,

2000). In Wharton's (1993) quantitative study of over 600 banking and health service workers in the USA a key finding was that the front-line workers performing emotional labour were less likely to experience emotional exhaustion if they had greater autonomy over how they carried out their work. Similarly, a significant finding of a large-scale international quantitative study of call centre workers was that the more influence was reported over how they undertook their tasks the less likely it was that the workers reported experiencing stress (Frenkel *et al.*, 1998). From her qualitative study of the emotional labour in nursing in the UK, Smith (1992, ch. 7) argued that a critical factor influencing how far student nurses experienced emotional labour in a negative way was the degree of hierarchy within the nurse management structure. When work was organised in a more collegial way, and where the 'individuality' and individual feeling rules of student nurses were recognised rather than repressed, then emotional labour could be experienced in a predominantly positive way. Aiken and Sloane's (1997) careful study of nurses in the USA lends strong support to the idea that the degree of autonomy in the job is perhaps the key factor influencing the effects of emotional labour. They examined the factors that influenced the experience of emotional burnout among nurses providing care to patients with AIDS. Their findings were striking in a number of ways. First, the findings ran counter to the intuitive proposition that nurses in wards dedicated to caring for patients dying with AIDS would experience higher emotional burnout than nurses who provide care for general patients. Second, this counter-intuitive finding could not be explained because there was in any sense a better 'job fit' between the individual nurses and the dedicated AIDS units where they worked.[2] Rather, the key explanation was in the way the dedicated AIDS units were organised. The basic pattern was that nurses who worked in less hierarchical settings where they had greater say on how to do the work suffered less burnout – even when compared with nurses not constantly caring for dying patients.

Tolich's (1993) acute ethnographic study of emotional labour among supermarket workers in the USA carefully delineated between the emotional labour where front-line workers have to follow managerially imposed feeling rules and emotional labour where the staff autonomously determine the feeling rules. He argues that it is the former which cause the greater tension and estrangement for workers, and the latter which occasion the greater pleasure and satisfaction. This is an important study, for it opens up the debate to allow a consideration of the pleasures as well as the harmful effects of emotional labour. A particularly debilitating effect of the terms of analysis being set by Hochschild is that studies tend to follow her in focusing almost exclusively on the harmful effects of emotional labour (Wouters, 1989).[3] Some of the real pleasures related to emotional labour were highlighted in the discussion of health care work, call centre work, hospitality work and even sales work in Chapters 5 and 6. Combining the importance of autonomy with the importance of socially embedded relationships with customers, a strong proposition is that front-line jobs involving emotional labour will bring greatest pleasure and meaning when workers have autonomy in feeling rules and have socially embedded relationships with customers (also see Himmelweit, 1999).

An analysis of emotional labour guided by the concept of the customer-oriented bureaucracy suggests that frustrations and tensions for front-line workers may come as much from an inability to deliver the degree of individual care and attention that they desire as from an over-delivery of such emotional labour under management's feeling rules. Again, Hochschild's own data (but not her theoretical approach) suggest this. She paints a historical picture of the evolution of emotional labour experienced by flight attendants in the USA. She argues that in the 1950s and 1960s emotional labour was actually quite easy to deliver, and the flight attendants suffered relatively few harmful effects. But in the 1970s and 1980s deregulation of the industry brought in heightened competition, which meant management policies informed by the rationalising logic, seeking efficiencies. She terms these policies, which led to a considerable intensification of work, an industry 'speed-up'. She writes (p. 126) that 'before the speed-up, most workers sustained the cheerful good will that food service requires. They did so for the most part proudly'. It was only after the speed-up, 'when asked to make personal human cost at an inhuman speed' (p. 126), that is, when emotional labour became increasingly rationalised, that the tensions of emotional labour became significant. Hochschild's own data rest well with the analysis of emotional labour suggested by the concept of the customer-oriented bureaucracy. Unfortunately, her theorising from this data, with its sole focus on the harm of emotional labour, is too often found wanting.

The discussion so far has suggested the need to be critical of writers who accept Hochschild's terms. An exception to this is Nickson and colleagues, who present their work on *aesthetic labour* as an extension of Hochschild's analysis of emotional labour (Nickson *et al.*, 2000; Nickson *et al.*, 2001). While Hochschild concentrates on emotions and their *internal* management, the concept of aesthetic labour highlights the importance of the *outward* – visual and aural – display of service workers. They (Nickson *et al.*, 2000, p. 2) formally define aesthetic labour as:

> a supply of 'embodied capacities and attributes' possessed by workers at the point of entry into employment. Employers then mobilise, develop and commodify these capacities and attributes through processes of recruitment, selection and training, transforming them into 'competencies' and 'skills' which are then aesthetically geared towards producing a 'style' of service encounter deliberately intended to appeal to the senses of customers, most obviously in a visual or aural way.

The rising importance of aesthetic labour is set in the context of service firms increasingly seeking to 'tangibilize' the intangible element of the service process. It is worth recalling that 'tangibles' is one of the five dimensions of Parasuraman *et al.*'s (1991) model of service quality, and that the definition of 'tangibles' refers to the appearance not only of physical facilities but also of personnel. Service managers increasingly consider that front-line workers 'physically embody the product and are *walking billboards* from a promotional standpoint' (emphasis added) (Zeithaml and Bitner, 1996, p. 304). Nickson *et al.* show how aesthetic labour pervades increasingly large parts of the hospitality, retail and even financial services industries in Glasgow, particularly in the 'style labour market' in these industries. The personnel manager at one firm stated that they sought 'a "tasty" and "stylish" appearance: "They had to be pretty attractive looking people...with a nice smile, nice teeth, neat hair and in decent proportion"' (2000, p. 10). For some firms, the code of aesthetics demanded of their front-line workers was becoming stricter. One service worker stated that, 'if I was to have my hair done or anything...if you're going to cut your hair in any way, well drastically or highlights, you've got to discuss it with the manager first' (p. 12). In one supermarket, 'one person was sent home to shave her legs' (p. 12). The aural as well as the visual aesthetics were important. For call centre workers this was especially true, with managers seeking to recruit staff who could project an 'aural smile' (p. 11).

A tentative finding from this research has been the 'acceptance by the employees of their company's aesthetic demands' (Nickson *et al.*, 2000, p. 14). The authors explain this by suggesting that management made use of the workers' identity with, and identification as, customers. In the previous chapter, it was argued that this approach has become central as part of control mechanisms in front-line workplaces. Nickson *et al.* reason that workers came to accept management's aesthetic standards because they were encouraged to think of the service interaction from the customer's point of view. Indeed, in cases, management encouraged front-line workers to become more cultivated as *consumers* in the belief that this would impact the approach to appearance and style as service *workers*. This acceptance of aesthetic standards could also be related to the fact that if workers adopt a particular style of self-presentation then they are afforded entry in a form of community with customers who have a similar style. This suggests a degree of social embeddedness of relationships with customers and hence scope for meaningful spaces in their work. By contrast, when aesthetic standards are more closely tied to a context of deference to the customer, then front-line workers are more likely to reject and contest such standards. For instance, Nielsen (1982) and Hochschild (1983) have described how flight attendants' unions in the USA have resisted company aesthetic standards which were seen as sexist and demeaning.

Managing for emotional and aesthetic labour

So far the discussion has focused on the nature of emotional labour, the importance of who manages the emotions, and the importance of the worker's relationship with the customer. This section turns to examine HRM's role in managing emotions. Following the analysis of HRM presented in Chapter 4, there is a focus on HRM engendering emotional labour and on HRM as seeking to cope with the subsequent inevitable tensions.

HRM engendering emotional labour

It may be tempting to believe that soft HRM policies are required to engender suitable emotional labour, and that hence soft HRM policies will come to pervade front-line workplaces. 'Suitable' emotional labour for management increasingly means both internalisation and outward expression. In Hochschild's terms, management wants 'deep acting'. The argument of the general prescriptive HRM advocates is that if management needs commitment rather than just compliance they must increasingly turn to soft HRM polices to engender this (Walton, 1985). The requirement for deep acting can be seen as the front-line equivalent of the need for commitment in other spheres of work. Hence the logic suggesting an inevitable move towards soft HRM policies in service work.

Certainly, the need for emotional labour increasingly requires the *systematic* application of human resources policies, from recruitment to training, through to appraisal. If committed emotional labour is required then recruitment can no longer be seen as a separate, marginal task, as Storey (1992) suggests was the case under the less systematic approach in the era of personnel management and industrial relations. Canning suggests that 'hiring friendly, caring people is your number one priority' (1999, p. 80). Similarly, Schlesinger and Heskett's (1991a) cycle of capability stresses the need for a strong emphasis on recruitment. As alluded to in Chapters 4 and 5, the need for emotional labour translates into a systematic approach to recruitment which focuses on customer-related values and attitudes – which are taken by management as the best indicators of the potential for a candidate to deliver deep, committed emotional labour. There have been a number of studies examining the increasingly systematic ways in which recruitment is undertaken (Simmons *et al.*, 1996; Schneider and Schechter, 1991). Such recruitment methods extend beyond the structured interview to include work simulations and role plays. For instance, Schneider and Schechter (1991) describe work simulation exercises for telephone service and sales jobs. Job candidates had to handle three types of simulated calls involving persuading a customer to buy more products, and dealing with irate and complaining customers. Central to the assessment of how a candidate dealt with these calls was the rating of the candidate's delivery of emotional labour during the calls. Despite the rise in more systematic recruitment practices focusing on emotional labour, a number of studies have suggested that recruitment for jobs involving emotional labour can involve discriminatory stereotyping. This is explored in more detail in the following chapter.

The need for emotional labour suggests a need not only for systematic recruitment, but also for systematic training and appraisal by management. The previous chapter examined the training and appraisal practices related to the development of customer-related values. The development of such values is the central way to generate committed emotional labour. As discussed in the previous chapter, the soft HRM characteristics of 'nurturing' and 'facilitating' (Storey, 1992; Frenkel *et al.*, 1999) appear to be in evidence in the way these practices are conducted in many front-line workplaces. A hierarchical, directive form of performance appraisal is unlikely to generate the sort of emotional labour that management requires. Being ordered to smile will rarely result in the display of a meaningful smile. When appraisal is structured more as a dialogue, however, subtle managerial skills can encourage appropriate emotional display, particularly by making reference to customer-related attitudes. Further, managers and supervisors increasingly present themselves as 'coaches' to the front-line staff (Korczynski *et al.*, 1996). In this way, within performance appraisals, managerial attempts to correct behaviour, particularly relating to emotional labour, can be presented in the language of training and development for the individual worker. Front-line workers will tend not to be directly reprimanded for emotional display which falls below the required standards, but rather will be offered the opportunity to 'develop' themselves by attending training courses or by being mentored by a more senior colleague (Frenkel *et al.*, 1999). It may be tempting to consider the development of systems of performance appraisal in terms of a move 'from control to development' (Bratton and Gold, 1999, p. 219). However, a more useful approach is to consider them as forums for the generation of control and discipline *through* (limited, task-based) development. Certainly, it appears that when emotional labour is required then the *language* of HRM becomes softer. Individuals, for instance, are 'counselled' rather put through a disciplinary procedure if they fail to meet their targets.

This discussion of policies to engender emotional labour has suggested that 'soft' and systematic HRM policies are often in place, but that entwined with these 'soft' elements are 'hard' elements. Already, the paint is beginning to chip away from the picture of win:win:win accompanying the arrival of emotional labour. Further analysis shows the picture to be a systematic fake. The discussion earlier in this chapter pointed out that emotional labour will be more likely to be harmful when front-line workers lack autonomy, particularly regarding feeling rules, and when they are placed in a position of subservience to customers. Importantly, analysis and evidence presented in the previous chapter suggested that the task-level empowerment of front-line workers, although increasing, was likely to stay circumscribed to an important degree. It was also argued that subservience to customers, while not a dominant motif in front-line work, nevertheless was felt most keenly when customers became irate and abusive. The forces of competition increasingly press management to force front-line workers to put up with irate customers. This is brought out well by Taylor and Tyler (2000, p. 84), who quote a trainer addressing call centre workers: 'if a man's having a go at you...don't get ruffled... *He can really talk to you how he wants. Your job is to deal with it'* (emphasis added). Though rarely so plainly expressed, this is one of the principles underlying the organisation of front-line work. It is a principle that will systematically lead to pain in the experience of emotional labour on the front-line.

HRM coping with emotional labour

If management wants committed emotional labour and if the organisation of front-line work means that pain will arise in the experience of this emotional labour, management must also use HRM policies to *cope with* the pressures and pains of emotional labour in an attempt to keep together a fragile social order. If management does not instigate coping processes then turnover and absences are likely to increase. Mann (1999) suggests the following approaches for coping with emotional labour: creating 'downtime' for front-line staff, developing calming strategies, and encouraging 'cognitive restructuring' among front-line staff. This section examines each of these in turn. In addition, the role of workplace rituals highlighting the pleasures of customer service work is examined. Finally, there is an analysis of how coping with emotional labour is often a collective process for front-line workers. This suggests important limits to the extent of individualising managerial policies in front-line work.

It is reasonable to assume that stress, tension and pain from emotional labour will be easier to bear if staff are given time away from the emotional demands of front-line work (Morris and Feldman, 1996). As James (1989) puts it, 'as with physical labour, after a sustained period of emotional labour, an alternative or rest is necessary'. Mann (1999) outlines how management can create 'downtime' for workers, not away from work *per se*, but away from the emotional demands in front-line work. The most progressive policy is a shift rotation system tied to a degree of multi-skilling. Halford *et al.* (1997) suggest that a system of job rotation on and off the front-line is common in UK banking. Hunter (2000) shows that as many as 46 per cent of service firms covered in a large survey in the USA practised job rotations, but it is not clear how far this applied to front-line staff. One significant factor working against the development of such policies at the front-line is the way that the distinctive focus on personality and attitudes in recruiting for front-line jobs may in effect create a segmentation of these workers from the rest of the firm, minimising the ability to swap workers between jobs. Employing front-line workers on part-time contracts is an alternative way of limiting the amount of emotional labour asked of front-line staff in a working week. As the following chapter shows, part-time work is common for women in many front-line occupations. The two factors may be causally connected – as Scott's (1994b) data on management decisions in structuring retail employment suggest (see p. 250).

A different approach allowing downtime is the managerial sanctioning of 'off-stage' areas. As Fineman and Sturdy note,

> Rest rooms, galleys, corridors and other 'off-stage' areas provide an opportunity for employees to drop their corporate mask, free from the scrutiny of supervisors and customers. 'Undesirable' emotions, such as fear, anger, hurt and frustration can be vented or expressed. In such settings the otherwise consented-to social order can be attacked, deprecated, or ridiculed in the presence of a 'willing' audience of colleagues. (Boje, 1991; Gabriel, 1991; Martin, 1992)

Managers may formally or informally sanction such areas. A clear example of a formal sanctioning would be the 'venting' sessions for call centre workers advocated by Barlow and Maul (1999) (discussed in Chapter 4). Mann also advocates formal sanctioning in the creation of 'real feelings schedules' (p. 135), for instance in the form of diaries provided by management in which front-line workers can anonymously record incidents that have caused them difficulties. Such forms of downtime, of course, are a palliative, and do nothing to alter the social situation that gives rise to the tensions and stresses experienced by emotional labourers.

As Mann notes, downtime may not always be available 'for those with unsympathetic employers who may not take kindly to requests for downtime' (p. 136). This leads on to her advocacy of calming strategies and cognitive restructuring. Her suggested calming strategies include taking a few deep breaths 'when faced with the prospect of having to hide boredom or anger from a customer' (p. 136), and deep relaxation techniques to unwind at the end of a stressful day. She also says the emotional labourer can use 'displacement' techniques, where anger is expressed but deflected away from the person or situation that provoked the negative reaction. For example, Sutton's (1991) study of debt collectors noted that after calls with abusive debtors, collectors frequently punched their desks and aired curses. Alternatively, Mann recommends visualisation techniques involving going through a painful or stressful event in your mind, but in the visualisation scenario 'you say exactly what you feel ... Be as forceful, rude and abusive as you like' (p. 143). This leads into Mann's suggestions for cognitive restructuring. Cognitive restructuring may involve front-line workers restructuring their view of their own emotional work. They are recommended to reflexively consider their own work as an act, and to take pleasure in skilful acting. An alternative form of cognitive restructuring is to restructure the view of an incident. Here Mann eagerly calls on an example from Hochschild's book on the training of flight attendants. Flight attendants were encouraged to view a passenger constantly demanding attention not as an irritant but as someone with problems that may cause them to act in that way. Training at Delta airlines recommended that the flight attendants should 'pretend something traumatic has happened in their [the customers'] lives', allowing the workers to replace their anger with empathy.

There is some evidence that the sort of techniques prescribed by Mann frequently feature in ongoing training sessions for front-line workers (see Eaton, 1996; Zemke and Woods, 1999). Hochschild, for instance, notes that in the 'Recurrent Training' programme that flight attendants went on yearly, the focus was on 'avoiding anger' (p. 113). Hochschild (p. 113) makes an acute analysis of training involving these calming and cognitive restructuring techniques:

> From the beginning of training, managing feeling was taken as the problem. *The causes of anger were not acknowledged as part of the problem.* Nor were the overall conditions of work – the crew size...the company's rigid antiunion position. These were treated as unalterable facts of life. The only question to be seriously discussed was 'How do you rid yourself of anger?' (Emphasis added)

Training in such calming and cognitive restructuring techniques is a part of what Newton *et al.* (1995) refer to as a discourse on 'stress management' that involves conceptions of stress as individualised, ahistorical and apolitical. Training programmes and counselling services in service and other types of firms emphasise making the individual worker more 'stress fit', better able to cope with the causes of stress and hence more productive. Newton *et al.* argue strongly that this way of individualising stress means that there is less likelihood of seeing the *organisational* and social causes of a *collective* sense of stress. Further, by supporting implicit constraints on the voicing of negative emotions, these techniques mean that it is less likely that front-line workers will see their commonality of feeling, and hence it will be less likely that front-line workers will challenge the root causes of the common feeling.

A final managerial approach to encourage front-line workers to cope with the emotional labour is to establish workplace rituals which emphasise the pleasures of emotional labour with customers. The message that management wishes to convey is that it is worth putting up with some pain and some stress in order to glean the rewards from emotional labour. In my own research into five call centres internationally, it was common practice for managers to run such celebratory rituals. These rituals involved a manager reading out letters of praise from customers, regarding service received, in front of an audience of customer service representatives (CSRs). After reading out a letter the manager would instigate applause directed at the staff member praised in the letter. Workers were keen to join in applause in recognition of the work of a colleague. In addition, it appeared that the praised CSR felt pride in receiving this praise. The CSR typically smiled and occasionally blushed, partly from pride. This ritual placed managers, literally, as the mouthpiece of the customer and so potentially strengthened their legitimacy in the eyes of the CSRs. In addition, the pleasure that the praised CSRs felt and exhibited demonstrated to the other CSRs the benefits that could accrue from their work when carried out with commitment. Overall, the ritual created a sense of shared aims and the benefits of pursuing these aims.

This examination of practices for coping with the strains of emotional labour so far has focused on approaches directed by *management*. But there are also coping mechanisms directed by *front-line workers themselves*. Data from research into a variety of front-line jobs show that workers tend to cope communally and socially. Fineman (1993, p. 21) observes that 'field social workers...would regularly seek solace from one another in informal gatherings at work'. Meyerson (1989) noted a similar phenomenon at one of the work settings of medical social workers that she studied. Benner and Wrubel (1989) and Norbeck (1985) show the importance of nurses' collectively coping with the emotional strains of their work. Indeed, the work of Menzies (1959), Satyamurti (1981) and Handy (1990) all indicate that collective forums may help in dealing with stressful situations. Benson (1978) has pointed out the importance of the 'clerking sisterhood' in providing friendship and support among retail workers to help them cope with their jobs. Mennerick (1974) has suggested that the collective informal creation of client typologies among front-line staff functions as a method of coping in the job (also Blau, 1974, pp. 181–2). Korczynski (2000) has noted the spontaneous sharing of painful experiences among call centre workers. This echoes Sutton's (1991) observation of debt collectors at work. The displacement technique, noted above, of desk-thumping and cursing was used as a signal for the *sharing* of experiences. Smith (1999, p. 126) vividly describes the need for *communities of coping* at the Samaritans' crisis helpline:

> This is gut wrenching, fearful, demanding, heart-destroying, rewarding, exhausting, invigorating, absorbing, and skilful, deep-acted emotional labour. The management have arranged the telephone cubicles off a central area for communal rest and recuperation and mutual care. They have thought with great care about sustainability. The counsellors care for each other in bucket-loads. When a voice at the other end of the phone threatens the helper by shaking a bottle of pills at them down the phone...it brings out...our concern with decency, fraternity, sorority, social solidarity and for the people who care.

This description of a form of off-stage arena also alerts us to the fact these off-stage areas are important in part because they are *social* areas. In the quotation from Fineman and Sturdy on this topic given earlier, the 'audience of colleagues' is a key factor which makes these galleys and rest rooms meaningful spaces. Even writers from within the new service management school acknowledge the role of communities of coping. Berry and Parasuraman (1991, p. 162) argue that 'an interactive community of co-workers who help each other, commiserate and achieve together is a powerful antidote to service burnout'. Similarly, Zemke and Schaaf (1989, p. 65) note that, 'in hospitals and airlines, frontline employees sometimes form support groups to help each other deal with the stresses and frustrations experienced on the job'. Hochschild suggests that the communal nature of coping with the strains of emotional labour is so important that it constitutes a form of 'collective emotional labour' (1983, p. 114).

Communities of coping, often spontaneous, informal and crucial to survival in the job, set potentially important limits to the extent of individualising HRM policies in front-line work. Communities of coping are most likely to arise when there are cooperative relations between front-line workers. By contrast, if managerial policies promote individual competitiveness among front-line workers, then communities of coping are less likely to arise, and harmful aspects of emotional labour are more likely to become manifest in other ways, perhaps through rising turnover levels. While the extent of individualising HRM policies (Storey and Bacon, 1993) has been examined in other work settings, little research has systematically explored this in the specific context of front-line work. The communal, collective aspects of coping, however, may explain apparent limits in the application of performance-related pay where this is determined at the individual level. The existing research on this factor has been conducted mostly in call centres. Marshall and Richardson (1996, p. 1855) report that team-based performance evaluation developed in call centres after 'initial attempts to link *individual* pay to performance . . . caused internal dissension'. Research by Korczynski (2000b) into call centres also demonstrates resistance by call centre workers to policies designed to increase individual competitiveness. Further, Fernie and Metcalf (1999) find that performance-related pay in the UK call centres only enhanced productivity where it was constructed on a team basis rather than on an exclusively individualised one. This suggests benefits to management of performance-related pay *only where it does not undermine supportive relations among front-line workers*. Indeed, the authors also find that where performance-related pay was based on an individual basis (alongside a whole centre basis) this actually weakened financial performance. Wider research into performance-related pay suggests that it frequently operates in a contradictory fashion. Kessler (2000, p. 283), for instance, describes it as a 'double-edged sword'. The horns of the specific dilemma for the manager in the front-line workplace is that while performance-related pay may potentially increase effort in the display of emotional labour, it may also systematically undermine the communities of coping crucial for survival in the job. Foster and Hoggett's (1999) analysis of performance-related pay in public welfare work suggests exactly this.

Conclusion

The rising importance of the quality of the service encounter in the terrain of competition between service firms has meant that service management is increasingly concerned with the delivery of rationalised emotional labour by front-line workers. Who does the managing of emotional labour, how, and with what consequences? have been the key questions driving this chapter. The point of departure to explore these questions was an analysis of Hochschild's work, which continues to dominate the way in which emotional labour is considered. Wouters (1989, p. 119) puts it well: 'Hochschild has written a very stimulating book, but also a strongly irritating one'. Hochschild decisively put emotional labour central to the agenda of understanding service work through her eloquent polemic focusing on the *harm* incurred through emotional labour. But there are a number of important flaws in her argument. For Hochschild, the harm of emotional labour in paid employment in contrast to the emotion work of people's private lives stems from three factors – the process of commodification, the structured inequality of the front-line worker in relation to the sovereign customer, and the managerial imposition of feeling rules. Each factor was examined in turn. It was argued that it is conceptually inappropriate to draw conclusions about the subjective experience of work from arguments about the objective nature of labour in capitalism. Next it was argued that while Hochschild's point about the relative power relationship between the front-line worker and the customer was an important one, her assumption of structured servility to the sovereign customer was inappropriate. Finally, strong support, backed up by wider research, was given to her argument concerning the importance of how far management imposes feeling rules on front-line workers. In addition, Hochschild's sole focus on the harm of emotional labour was criticised, and it was suggested that a fuller understanding of the social embeddedness of the economic exchange between service worker and customer allows a richer appreciation of the potential pleasures and meanings in emotional labour. The concept of the customer-oriented bureaucracy also allows an understanding that one of the key frustrations of some front-line workers is that the job is structured such that workers are unable to deliver the form of emotional labour they would like to. Before examining the HRM polices driven by the need for emotional labour, reference was made to the important work of Nickson *et al.* (2000), who highlight the growth of aesthetic labour.

There are two functions of HRM polices with regard to emotional labour. One set of policies seeks to engender committed emotional labour. Just as with HRM in other types of work, the need for commitment from the workforce brings with it a logic of the development of soft HRM policies. But soft HRM policies around recruitment, training and appraisal are intertwined with hard elements (Marchington and Grugulis, 2000). Further, the structuring of front-line work in which workers increasingly face abusive customers, and in which there are important limits to how far workers' own feeling rules are used, means that as well as there being pleasure there will often also be pain in emotional labour. A range of HRM policies to aid front-line workers in coping with the harmful aspects of emotional labour were examined. These included creating 'downtime' for workers by allowing them time away from customer contact, perhaps through a shift rotation system or by creating off-stage areas. In addition, ongoing training in service workplaces frequently focuses on calming strategies and strategies for cognitive restructuring. These policies were interpreted as part of a growing managerial and popular discourse on stress management which places the responsibility on the *individual* to cope with stress. This means that the organisational situations which give rise to stress escape criticism. Finally, the importance of the social, communal ways that front-line workers cope was highlighted, and it was argued that this may place limits on HRM policies which seek to develop an ethos of individual competitiveness in the front-line workplace.

Examining emotional labour can be potentially confusing. On the one hand, readers are presented with images, from the past, of the unemotional, impersonal hell of life as a street-level bureaucrat filling in forms, processing people and following procedures. And yet, on the other hand, readers are also presented with images, from the present, of the hell of working in jobs which are too full of emotional labour. This chapter has suggested that the way through this confusion is to focus on issues of the power and autonomy of the front-line worker vis-à-vis management and the customer. Whose feeling rules? And in what sort of relationship with the customer? These are the key questions to address in considering the experience of emotional labour. The analysis in this chapter suggests rather ambiguous answers to these questions for many front-line workers. Despite all the rhetoric of soft HRM, it is clear that allowing management to make all the key decisions within the context of the forces of competition will increasingly leave front-line workers in positions of vulnerability. The ways in which service workers themselves can organise to protect themselves, and the ways in which the state may impose regulations on service management decision-making, are the focus of the following two chapters.

Notes

1 Hochschild also makes the important point regarding the role of emotional labour in representing and reproducing gender inequality. This will be discussed in the following chapter.

2 This is an important finding, for it runs counter to the sort of argument proffered by Ashforth and Humphreys (1993), who see the effects of emotional labour on front-line workers as being influenced centrally by the identity and personality of the worker. Aiken and Sloane call this the 'job fit' hypothesis. They also conclude that wider research shows that 'burnout has more to do with characteristics of the workplace than with characteristics of the worker' (p. 455).

3 Smith's study of emotional labour among student nurses includes a number of passages highlighting the way in which adopting Hochschild's focus on the harm of emotional labour prevents a consideration of the pleasures and rewards of emotional labour. Even Fineman and Sturdy's (2001) recent overview of emotional labour, which is otherwise nuanced and sensitive, continues the focus on the harm of emotional labour, without adequately considering potential positive aspects for front-line staff.

CHAPTER 9

Gendered segregation and disadvantage

This chapter and the following one focus on the regulation of service work. In this context, regulation means any action by the state or an independent body, such as a trade union, to constrain the behaviour of service management. For the new service management writers it is axiomatic that service management should be left free to make the key decisions regarding the nature of service work. Their win:win:win arguments relate to the forces of competition pushing service firms to be more accommodating to customers and workers alike. When the triangular relationship falls out of equilibrium, the market creates a self-correcting system. Key weaknesses in these arguments, however, have been highlighted throughout this book. For meaningful gains to be distributed to front-line workers it is not enough to leave decisions to service management. Take the issue of gendered segregation and disadvantage in front-line work – the subject of this chapter. Despite the fact that the topic of gendered segregation and disadvantage is well documented and highly significant in a range of front-line occupations, and the fact that service management has a key role in its enactment, it is not a subject broached by new service management writers. This chapter first of all shows the extent of gendered segregation and disadvantage in front-line work and outlines how it is systematically enacted. The second half of the chapter examines how regulation can challenge these processes and outcomes.

Segregation and disadvantage in front-line jobs

A prevailing management rhetoric in service firms concerns the need to become customer-oriented. This is a rhetoric that brooks no opposition;

there is an assumption that only benefits can flow from being customer-oriented. But what if the customers to whom the firm is being oriented hold systematic prejudices? Does this not inevitably mean that the firm's internal structures and practices will come to reflect the prejudices of its customer base? Even when the rhetoric of customer orientation is not taken at face value – when, by contrast, a view of the service firm approximating the customer-oriented bureaucracy is taken – there is still the potential for the systematic *organisational internalisation of customer prejudices*.[1]

For all its failings, and for all the criticisms levelled at it concerning a hidden gendered subtext, a potentially positive characteristic of the bureaucratic organisation was that it erected a barrier between customers/clients and the principles of the producer organisation. Here workers were shielded from the direct effects of the potential prejudices held by the customers. However, in the contemporary service firm this shield is being increasingly taken down. Although general discussions stress the role of the parties in the management-worker dyad, particularly management, in creating gendered segregation and disadvantage, the potential for systematic 'consumer-led discrimination' (Philpott, 2000) to be enacted in service organisations is also real. In front-line work, both management *and* customers have key roles to play in the gendered segregation and disadvantage that exists. This section first outlines the extent of gendered segregation and reviews explanations of this, and then outlines the extent and enactment of disadvantage experienced by workers in the front-line occupations that are women-dominated enclaves.

In terms of the whole economy, women tend to work in female-dominated occupations (rather than workplaces – the difference is important). This is true for the major European economies (Rubery *et al.*, 1999) and for the USA (Stromberg and Harkess, 1988). In the UK, Rubery *et al.* (1999) estimate that 67 per cent of women work in female-dominated occupations, while Scott (1994a) estimates the figure to be 76 per cent. Along with secretarial and clerical occupations, a range of *front-line occupations* are the ones that have the highest levels of female density. Understanding gendered segregation on the front line is, therefore, central to understanding it more generally. Hochschild's (1983) analysis of the USA labour market data shows that for the vast majority of non-professional front-line occupations women considerably outnumbered men. For instance, women made up 86 per cent of bank tellers, 67 per cent of counter clerks, 66 per cent of personal service workers, 88 per cent of health service workers and 89 per cent of waiting staff (also see Geschwender, 1999, and Berheide, 1988). In the UK, research has shown that women comprise 77 per cent of counter clerks and cashiers in the finance sector (Rubery *et al.*, 1992), nearly 100 per cent of cashier clerks in building societies (Crompton and Sanderson, 1990), around 70 per cent of call centre workers (NTO Tele.com, 1999), 78 per cent of bar staff and waiting staff (Rubery *et al.*, 1992) and around two-thirds of all retail staff (including sales jobs) (NIESR, 1986). The main exception to this pattern of female-dominated front-line occupations is sales work involving objects of relatively high value, where men overwhelmingly predominate (Berheide, 1988; and Chapter 6) and where jobs are remunerated more highly. Nor is this segregation a thing of the past that will naturally fade away over time. Lorence (1992), for instance, shows that in the USA from 1950 to 1990, 74 per cent of all new low-skill service sector jobs were filled by women, and Rubery *et al.* (1998, p. 289) state that 'there is strong evidence of continued and in some sense intensified segregation' of occupations.

There are two broad explanations of the segregation of women into specific occupations with relatively poor conditions (Scott, 1994b). One explanation is that management seeks to take advantage of women's weak labour market position, and therefore creates (often deskilled) jobs that can be filled by women who will accept low wages. The other broad explanation points to the social construction of gendered jobs. The idea is that jobs are not empty positions to be filled by a man or a woman depending on individual aptitude, but have gender assumptions built into them which often systematically bias the recruitment process (Bradley, 1989). It is the gender of individuals, rather than their individual aptitudes, which influence the recruitment process for many jobs. Further, jobs are gendered in such a way as to reflect and reproduce gender inequality prevalent in the wider society. Regarding these two explanations, Scott (1994b, p. 239) argues that 'nowadays, few sociologists would support an extreme version of either approach, and most would argue for some combination of the two'. She, however, notes that 'the theoretical basis for their combination is unclear' because while the first explanation emphasises the rational economic decision-making of management, the second emphasises social processes and pressures that may stand in contradiction to rational economic goals.

For segregation in front-line work, the model of the customer-oriented bureaucracy suggests that these two processes will often work systematically together. The concept of the customer-oriented bureaucracy highlights that service management must increasingly act in response to dual pressures – pressures to be economically efficient, to rationalise production, and pressures to be customer-oriented, particularly by allowing the consumption of the myth of customer sovereignty. For the majority of front-line occupations both of these factors point to the likely predominance of women.[2] It is often cheaper, more economically efficient to employ women because they can be paid less, partly because of their weaker labour market position. But this is not the only criterion guiding recruitment decisions. For instance, Scott (1994b) shows clearly how retail employers do not simply focus their recruitment on the section of the labour market that would accept the lowest wages. Rather, it makes sense for service managers to employ women socialised in a certain way because these staff allow an easier consumption of the myth of sovereignty.

Consumption of the myth of sovereignty can be affected by three factors directly connected with the behaviour and identity of the front-line worker.

First, the myth is more likely to be consumed if the wider – socially embedded – status of the front-line worker is a low one. This allows an easier envisioning by the customer of implicit superiority within the service encounter. Second, the myth is more likely to be consumed if the appearance is maintained that the customer is in control of the service encounter, that he or she is in charge of its terms and its pace. These first two factors are clearly interrelated in that the appearance of customer control will be easier to maintain if the customer's socially embedded status is higher, or at least not lower, than the front-line worker's. Finally, consumption of the myth will be affected by the degree of empathy to the customer shown by the front-line worker. By acting in ways that demonstrate an attempt to see the service encounter through the customer's viewpoint, the front-line worker in effect communicates to the customer that it is the customer's viewpoint that is the legitimate one.

Crucially, all three of these factors are likely to lead to an over-representation of women in front-line jobs. Women generally have lower status than men in contemporary economies. Further, women are more likely to be socialised into roles in which they readily give the appearance to another party within an encounter that it is the other party that is in control of the encounter (Holtgrewe, 2000). It is also the case that women are more likely than men to be socialised into roles involving empathy-giving (Wicks, 1998).[3] Because women more readily fit the three criteria derived from the consumption of the myth of sovereignty they are recruited into front-line jobs in disproportionate numbers. As Trentham and Larwood (1998) put it, service managers show a discriminatory 'rational bias' regarding women by making hiring and other decisions based on the real or perceived customer preferences about the 'proper' gender of the front-line worker.

Belt (2000) provides an interesting analysis of the gendered recruitment criteria for call centre agents. This is an important study, for it highlights the continuing strong gendered segregation in a new and expanding front-line occupation. Belt reports that, for the call centres that she studied in the financial services industry in Ireland, the Netherlands and the UK, women made up between 70 and 91 per cent of the call centre agents. When asked why women made up so many of the call centre agents, managers replied that it was because more women applied for these jobs. As Belt notes, however, this begs the question of why call centre jobs attract more women than men. The answer to this lies in the way the call centre jobs are constructed though a gendered subtext. Crucially, the recruitment criteria related to characteristics of roles into which women were more to have been socialised. Management wanted to recruit candidates who had patience, empathy, listening skills and outgoing, bubbly and lively personalities. Belt also shows that the marketing by these financial service firms to customers promoted (and also reflected and reproduced, I would argue) a gendered aspect to the myth of customer sovereignty. These companies used images of smart, smiling female call centre agents in their advertising. Taylor and Tyler (2000) suggest that the gendering of jobs leads easily to the use of sex-typing discrimination in recruitment, with women applicants chosen for call centre jobs primarily because they are women.

These findings echo those of other studies regarding the use of sex-typing assumptions in recruitment for front-line jobs (Curran, 1986; Collinson *et al.*, 1990). This process is likely be intensified through the increasingly customer-oriented approaches of service organisations. Wider studies of the process of discrimination in recruitment (Jenkins, 1986) have suggested that discrimination is most likely to enter the process of recruitment when selectors adjudge the character and personality of a candidate – rather than, for instance, their technical aptitude or qualifications. Scott (1994b, p. 247) makes a similar argument regarding retail work: 'in the absence of objective measures of skills, hiring decisions clearly rested on employers' subjective perceptions of the applicant's suitability, leaving plenty of scope for sex and age stereotyping' (also Adkins, 1995). Because personality is a key recruitment criterion, recruitment for front-line jobs may be becoming more discriminatory. As MacDonald and Sirianni put it (1996, pp. 14–15):

> Even though discrimination in hiring ... exists in all labor markets ... in no other area of wage labor are the personal characteristics of the workers so strongly associated with the nature of work ... Traits such as gender, race, age, and sexuality serve a signalling function, indicating to the customer/employer important cues about the tone of the interaction.

Similarly, the rise of aesthetic labour also has clear discriminatory implications.

So far, this analysis has highlighted the key factors, leading to an over-representation of women in many front-line occupations. On its own, however, this does not necessarily mean that women are disadvantaged in service work. That next step requires an examination of the conditions of employment of these front-line jobs in which women predominate. Here, I will briefly review, in turn, evidence relating to pay levels, full- or part-time status of employment and its implications, working hours and sexualised labour.

Women continue to be paid considerably less than men in employment in general. In the UK, Grint (1998, p. 189) notes that women's hourly earnings are 79 per cent of men's. An important element of this comes from job segregation (Geschwender, 1999) – women are predominantly found in occupations which are low-paid. Foremost among the low-paid, predominantly female occupations are a range of front-line occupations. Take the case of the UK national minimum wage, introduced in 1999 at the level of £3.60. The Low Pay Commission's report (1999) on its introduction shows that of the one and a half million workers whose pay was raised, two-thirds were women. The occupations which made up the majority of those benefiting from the minimum wage were care assistants, cleaners, sales assistants, bar staff, kitchen porters, counterhands, childcare workers, security guards and hairdressers. Front-line occupations in which women predominate are the majority here. The retail and hospitality sectors had the largest numbers of workers affected by the minimum wage, and not surprisingly, a strong majority of beneficiaries in these sectors were women. That the minimum wage had its main effect for women in front-line occupations matches a wider pattern of evidence suggesting that front-line occupations in which women predominate tend to be low-paid. Evidence suggests that it remains the case that typically the front-line worker in the USA continues to be the lowest-paid and least-trained member of the organisation (Barbee and Bott, 1991). Even the new service management writers Zemke and Schaaf accede that 'people who deal with the public are usually the lowest-paid employees in the company' (1989, p. 10). Nelson (1994, p. 240) notes that in the USA, 'service workers are more likely than manufacturing workers to have lower incomes'. Although Nelson does not disaggregate his data to compare front-line jobs with other jobs within service organisations (indeed official statistics make this difficult), his comparison with income levels in manufacturing is likely to be indicative of the relative position of many front-line service workers. Bluestone and Harrison (1988, p. 126) suggest that the move towards services in the USA will bring with it 'a proliferation of low-wage jobs'.

The relatively poor pay in many front-line jobs is linked to the over-representation of women in these jobs. Important here is a tendency for skills deployed in jobs predominantly occupied by women to be undervalued (Acker, 1989). Language has an important role here (Fearfull, 1996). As Poynton and Lazenby (1992, p. 7) note, the ways in which managers, researchers and even the front-line workers themselves 'refer to the skills used by women workers often reinforces their images as natural attributes or "gifts", as personal qualities... rather than industrial or workplace skills'. When important skills used by front-line workers are not recognised in language, it is little surprise that these skills often are not recognised in pay levels. This undervaluation or non-recognition may be entrenched in organisational practices through job evaluations which either ignore the presence, or undervalue the worth, of women's 'natural' skills and 'common sense'. This process is likely to be particularly important for front-line jobs. The Equal Opportunities Commission (1999, p. 22) reports that frequently overlooked job characteristics in job evaluation exercises include 'providing caring and emotional support to individuals', 'dealing with upset, injured, irate or irrational people', 'representing the organisation through communications with clients and the public' and working in conditions of 'stress from dealing with complaints'. These are all central aspects of front-line jobs.

Not only are front-line occupations dominated by women relatively low-paying ones, they are also ones with a high incidence of part-time employment status. For instance, hotel catering is 'characterised by high levels of female and part-time employment... and low wages' (Crompton and

Sanderson, 1990, p. 139). This is a triumvirate of factors found in many front-line occupations. The overlap between feminine domination and part-time status in front-line occupations is to be expected from the macro statistics which show that 44 per cent of UK women worked part-time in 1994 (Rubery *et al.*, 1999, p. 255). Further, Rubery *et al.* (1994, p. 206) note that 'part-time work appears to be highly segregated, confined mainly to feminised occupations in the service sector'. The high incidence of part-time work in female-dominated front-line occupations is significant because there is strong evidence suggesting that part-time jobs involve lower skills than full-time ones, are connected to lower training provision and involve limited access to a wider range of employment benefits (Rubery *et al.*, 1994).

Another key relative disadvantage of part-time work (which is primarily significant only in front-line occupations) is that it involves far greater demands on workers for 'unsocial and flexible working hours, involving weekend working, variable days, and evening and some nightwork' (Rubery *et al.*, 1994, p. 229). The issue of the time at which the work is undertaken is a very significant one for front-line workers, more generally. As the concept of the customer-oriented bureaucracy highlights, service organisations increasingly have to configure themselves to meet the variability of overall customer demand. Further, deregulation and intense competition mean that service firms in the UK are moving towards the twenty-four-hour, seven-day model of opening, a pattern set by the USA (Kreitzman, 1999). So front-line workers are increasingly being called on both to alter their working patterns at relatively short notice and to work outside standard hours. Dupuy (1999, p. 82) argues that whereas bureaucracies could externalise costs on to customers (through inconveniently restricted opening hours, for instance), intensified competition and deregulation have 'extinguished the opportunities for externalisation and forced members to find other solutions, which are by definition more difficult in so far as they will now have to split the costs among themselves.'

In deregulated economies with relatively weak labour standards, such as the UK and the USA, almost inevitably this means that the (predominantly female) front-line staff are the ones who end up bearing the costs. The Daycare Trust (2000) reports that nearly one in four of the UK's workforce now works at some point between 6 am and 6 pm. Fifteen per cent now work all night. Although the study is unable to break down the percentage exactly, it is clear that front-line workers make up a significant part of this. The study points out not only that workers' out-of-work social lives are severely disrupted, but also that the system leads to children being 'passed like batons' between parents caught in the demands of consumer capitalism. The study also shows that 'there has been an erosion of premium payments for working outside the old nine-to-five hours so people often receive no extra money for this either'. Data from the comprehensive UK Workplace Employee Relations Survey show the systematic coincidence of female labour, part-time status, low pay and flexibility (Cully *et al.*, 1999, p. 45). The authors state that one important route to flexibility in private sector workplaces is

> based on . . . extensive use of part-time, female, relatively low-skilled employees. This is most likely to be found among workplaces in wholesale and retail, hotels and restaurants and financial services. Typically, these workplaces were part of very large organisations.

Finally, some women in the predominantly female front-line occupations are expected to take part in a labour process that can be sexualised to a significant degree (Adkins, 1995). This was raised in Chapter 3's discussion of feminist analyses of service work. As Hochschild (1983) has argued, the job of a female front-line worker is different from that of a male worker, not least because women are often expected to use sexuality as part of their job. This is likely to be strongest in hotel, catering and other 'leisure'-related services (Preece *et al.*, 1999, p. 179). For instance, Adkins's (1995) study of a hotel and a fun park carefully shows how management's rules regarding aesthetic labour were much tighter for women than for men (also Woolf, 1990). She argues that these rules contributed to a sexualisation of the women's work. Although the women in the study were adept at 'laughing it off', real costs can be borne by female front-line workers. A number of studies suggest that both management and male customers expect women front-line staff to routinely put up with sexual harassment from male customers (Guerrier and Adib, 2000; Adkins, 1995; Hughes and Tadic, 1998). The enchanting myth of customer sovereignty is one that can be played out in sexualised terms and when fine lines are transgressed sexual harassment may be the outcome.

This, still, however, is not a complete picture of the disadvantage experienced by women in service work. For instance, if service organisations have career ladders which allow a progression for front-line staff, then, even if women are over-represented in front-line jobs with poor conditions, disadvantage may be mitigated. However, as Herzenberg *et al.* (1998) note for the USA, internal career ladders (which were often inadequate for women in the first place; Berheide, 1988) have begun to fall apart, particularly in service organisations. There have been a number of reasons for this that apply across many sectors of advanced economies. However, specific reasons can be identified why this process might be intensified for many front-line jobs.

In short, *it is more likely for strong internal career ladders to function within a bureaucracy than within a customer-oriented bureaucracy*. Indeed, the idea of clear and linear career progression was part of Weber's original statement of what constituted a bureaucracy. Front-line workers are recruited for their customer-oriented personalities and values, their bubbliness and liveliness, but find that these attributes are not those that are relevant for career progression within the service organisation away from the front line. They become trapped in 'occupational ghettos' (Goffee and Scase, 1995, p. 127). A number of examples can bring this idea out. Crompton and Sanderson (1990) and Cressey and Scott (1992) suggest that UK bank branch staff are increasingly becoming isolated from the traditional strong career ladders that have existed in banks. While somewhat sceptical of this argument, Halford *et al.* (1997, p. 118) nevertheless concede that their data from the UK banking sector suggest that female front-line cashiers may 'get stuck' in that role. Their data from two UK local government authorities also suggest many (mainly female) front-line workers are located in '"dead zones" as far as career opportunities are concerned' (p. 147). Further, even where there remains a clear career path from the front line, there are systematic factors at work that tend to allow a quicker and easier career path for the (relatively few) men who occupy front-line roles. The case of US and UK nursing is a good example of this. Male nurses make up only a small part of the total nursing workforce, but occupy a considerably disproportionate slice of the jobs in the higher nursing grades (Williams, 1995; Halford *et al.*, 1997). As noted in earlier chapters, within the service organisation informed by the dual logics of customer orientation and rationalisation there is a tendency for a process of alignment of customer orientation with femininity, and of rationality and efficiency with masculinity. In the context of nursing, femininity has come to be increasingly aligned with bedside care, and masculinity with efficient management.

This segregation of (particularly female) front-line workers in career terms from the rest of the organisation is likely to be most significant for (predominantly female) part-time staff. There is strong evidence that part-time jobs are 'associated with long-term career downgrading' for women (mainly front-line) workers (Rubery *et al.*, 1994, p. 230). Although, for some, part-time employment can act as a bridge back into full-time employment (Scott, 1994b), for the majority of female workers it represents more of a trap than a bridge (Tam, 1997).

Challenging segregation and disadvantage

This analysis so far has identified the systematic pressures towards an over-representation of women in front-line service jobs, which tend to have relatively poor conditions of service and which are less and less likely to offer opportunity for internal career advancement, especially for women. Further, there seems little to hope for from any HRM policies inspired by the new service management school. In the HRM policies prioritised, the creation of clear career paths within the service organisation is noticeable by its absence. If the results of unconstrained management decision-making in service organisations are likely to mean systematic disadvantage for women, how can regulation by law or institutions mitigate these problems? The most important point to note here is that the gendered segregation and disadvantage outlined in the previous section have taken place within the context of existing equal employment opportunity and equal pay laws. This is not to say that these laws have not had some significant effects in ameliorating the extent of the disadvantage experienced by women in the service economy, however. For instance, in the UK, the Equal Pay Act 1970, the Sex Discrimination Act 1975 and the Equal Pay Regulations 1983 have been seen by many commentators as playing an important role in the narrowing of income inequality between men and women (Grint, 1998) that has occurred over the last twenty-five years. The legislation has also blocked 'direct' discrimination in which employers offer different conditions and opportunities purely on the basis of the sex of the candidate or employee. The legislation is also designed to prevent 'indirect' discrimination. Indirect discrimination is said to occur when both a selection criterion or employment condition applies to a greater proportion of one sex than another, and where the condition causing this disproportionate effect cannot be justified by the employers as being genuinely necessary for the performance of the job. While front-line jobs may still be gendered in terms of the assumption built into them, the current legal framework is primarily directed at preventing the use of sex-typing discrimination in recruitment. Sex-typing assumptions involve managers assuming that candidates of one sex will be more likely to perform well in a job than candidates of another sex, purely because of their sex.

Table 9.1 outlines the key stages of segregation and disadvantage for female front-line workers and outlines the potential to challenge and ameliorate the conditions for women. As this table suggests, challenging the sort of sex-typing assumptions highlighted by Taylor and Tyler is possible but difficult. As Dickens notes, 'although organisations may be vulnerable to legal challenge, in practice the risk appears small . . . Individual applications to employment tribunals remain relatively scarce and meet with limited success' (2000, p. 155). Even where individuals successfully go through the difficult process of proving sex discrimination in hiring decisions, compensation ordered by tribunals remains low. The formalisation of recruitment procedures promoted by the legislation may have limited the use of sex-typing assumptions in recruitment decisions. However, as Collinson *et al.* (1990) point out, the formalisation of recruitment is a necessary but hardly sufficient condition for equality of opportunity in employment. Indeed, at its worst, formalised recruitment procedures with equality opportunity principles apparently enshrined in them may be subverted in practice and yet provide management with an 'alibi' that conceals and legitimises practices which are unlawful.

As Table 9.1 also shows, there is the potential within the existing legal framework to use the principle of equal value (UK) or equal worth (US) to challenge the relatively poor pay of front-line jobs mainly occupied by women. The principle here is that equal pay should be given to jobs of equal value, irrespective of the sexual composition of the occupants of jobs.

Table 9.1 Stages of gendered segregation and disadvantage in front-line jobs and the potential for segregation and disadvantage to be challenged

Stage within employment relationship	How is segregation/ disadvantage enacted?	Potential for segregation/ disadvantage to be challenged or ameliorated
Identification of job requirements	Gendered job requirements for front-line work related to importance of maintaining myth of customer sovereignty.	Direct discrimination illegal.
Matching of candidate to job requirements	Gendered segregation flows from above; in addition selectors make assumptions based on sex of candidate.	Sex-typing assumptions illegal, but difficult to challenge; formalisation of recruitment may help but may also conceal unlawful practices.
Job conditions	Low pay for front-line jobs with over-representation of women – job evaluation exercises ignore key front-line tasks performed predominantly by women; low pay reflects weak labour market position of women.	Challenge possible (often union-supported), based on principle of equal pay for work of equal value/ worth; equality and upgrading bargaining by unions and imposition of minimum wage.
Internal career opportunities	Segregation of front-line jobs from career ladders into rest of organisation; where limited career ladders exist, women left behind.	Possible but difficult to challenge individual promotion decisions; possible but difficult to challenge career structures through EO Commission investigation; in addition, unions can seek more inclusive career structures, facilitated by regulated systems of training.

This allows women segregated in low-paying front-line jobs within service organisations to make the case that their jobs are of equal value to higher-paying jobs mainly occupied by men, and that hence they should receive pay at that higher rate. For instance, in 1987 a front-line worker, a checkout operative employed by the Sainsbury supermarket chain, compared her job to that of a warehouseman and claimed equal pay for work of equal value. The firm agreed to an out-of-court settlement, and restructured its system of pay grading – a process which meant a 4 per cent increase in the wage bill. Female front-line workers were key beneficiaries here. In addition, 'grading and pay structure revisions followed in other major food retailers' (Dickens, 2000, p. 149). Claiming that jobs are of equal value to other jobs is an inevitably political process. In this process, the increasingly customer-oriented rhetoric of service organisations may in fact be used by unions and front-line staff to make the case for the illegitimacy of existing inequality. It becomes increasingly difficult for service managers to say that 'nobody is more important than our front line', and yet to still pay (predominantly female) front-line staff relatively poor wages compared with staff in the rest of the organisation. This is another way in which the customer-oriented bureaucracy creates spaces, this time in terms of language, which potentially allow front-line workers and their representative bodies to contest and reframe organisational life.

Again, the process of making a claim is a daunting and difficult one for an individual to pursue, and many cases are supported by trade unions as a lever to force employers to restructure their pay-grading systems in a more equitable manner. In other words, the existence of trade unions representing female front-line workers is a key factor in extending the impact of the current legislation. That there is considerable scope for an extension of the implementation of the principle of equal pay for equal value is suggested by data from the extensive UK Workplace Employee Relations Survey, which found that only around 16 per cent of medium and large employers systematically reviewed the relative pay rates for different groups (Cully *et al.*, 1999). Further, unions can increase absolute levels of pay through collective bargaining, and may help the relative pay levels internal to the service organisation though equality bargaining in which they negotiate for higher pay rises at the lower end of the pay structure. Unions in the UK health care sector, for instance, have adopted this approach. One limitation here is that female front-line workers in certain jobs may have little collective bargaining power, and hence unions may make demands but may be unable to force the employer's hand. Realisation of this has gradually spread in the UK union movement over recent decades, leading a movement, backed by many unions, for the introduction of a national minimum wage. As noted above, a large proportion of those covered by the minimum wage in 1997 were female front-line service workers.

The other major way to challenge low pay in female-dominated front-line occupations is to upgrade the skill levels in the jobs (Berheide, 1988), so that there is more productivity or 'value added' (Reich, 1991) at the front line. Front-line workers could then reap some of the ensuing benefits (Herzenberg *et al.*, 1998). This is addressed below regarding training and career advancement, and is also discussed in the following chapter's examination of union strategies. Such a strategy to counter low pay works directly to counter an enduring myth of service work – that of necessarily low productivity in such labour-intensive jobs. This myth can be traced back to Adam Smith's dismissive treatment of service work (see Chapter 1) and more recently to the arguments of Baumol (1967). Baumol's argument rests on taking the playing of music as an exemplar of service work. He argues that the overall 'productivity' of a horn quintet is no higher than that of a horn quartet, despite the fact that it requires more staff. From this analogy, he argues that as service employment keeps growing (as the quintet becomes a sextet) productivity growth in the overall economy will necessarily be low. His argument, however, falls down for two main reasons (also see Stanback, 1979). First, his idea of productivity appears rooted in a Fordist notion of quantity rather than quality. Second, his analogy does not feature service work in which there is a direct interaction between an individual front-line worker and an individual customer. As Chapter 1 outlined, the degree to which the service interaction is part of the product can vary a great deal between types of front-line work (psychotherapy say, as compared with fast-food work). With this acknowledged, the point becomes that of trying to upgrade front-line occupations towards the higher end of the continuum.

Tackling the implications of part-time working again involves a combination of the law and union action. If there are poorer conditions for part-time workers and if part-time workers are disproportionately female, then the law allows a challenge to be made to seek parity with the full-time workers. However, it will often need a union to make an adequate case and to take it forward through the judicial system. Turning to non-standard working hours, here, regulation is likely to rest primarily on trade union action.[4] With the major battles regarding the deregulation of restrictions on opening hours largely lost in most consumer-capitalist economies (Kreitzman, 1999), the issue becomes that of who *controls* the allocation of non-standard working hours and the remuneration of those hours. A poll for the Trades Union Congress (TUC, the UK union confederation) (1998) found that while 43 per cent of workers wanted control over the allocation of their working hours, only 20 per cent had such control. Some unions are focusing on ensuring that decision-making on the allocation of non-standard hours is not left just to service management, but is subject to joint regulation with trade unions. Regarding potential challenges to sexualised labour, again the existing law in the UK provides a basis for action, which to be realised effectively requires union action, or support to individuals from the Equal Opportunities Commission. The principle through which the law can help can be found in a notable victory that was won for waiting staff who were subject to racist abuse from customers at a venue at which a comedian notorious for his racist jokes was on stage. In this case, it was the employer who was found liable – for customer actions towards their staff. Unions can use this principle to tackle sexualised labour by bringing cases against employers who routinely expect women front-line staff to put up with sexual harassment from male customers.

Challenges to career structures which tend to exclude female front-line workers are possible but difficult to enact. The main route for such a challenge within the existing legislative framework is for individuals to claim that they have been discriminated against in specific promotion decisions. Again, Collinson *et al.* (1990) argue that while formalisation of promotion procedures is a necessary step for equal opportunities, it is far from being a sufficient one. From their wide-ranging study of recruitment and promotion decisions, they also note that 'a consistent pattern emerging from the case-studies was that female employees were highly reluctant to challenge decisions...that quite clearly appeared to discriminate against them on the grounds of sex' (p. 189). Many women already employed in the organisations knew that they were being discriminated against but tended to do little about it – partly, the authors argue, because they did not want to disrupt the 'security' of normal relations at work, and because challenging decisions would disrupt their own definition of their, in some sense subordinate, gender identity. In addition, women's reluctance to challenge decisions can be seen as rational given the process that they have to go through, the relatively small likelihood of the challenge being successful, and the fact that even if the claim is successful recompense is likely to be small (Dickens, 2000). Further, individual challenges to promotion decisions will relate mainly to the competition between individual female and male front-line workers for limited points of entry into internal career ladders. Individual challenges will have less effect on a tendency to segregate *all* front-line workers from internal career ladders, however. And it is this which is the more profound issue. Investigation of potentially discriminatory career structures, rather than just individual promotion decisions, can be undertaken by the Equal Opportunities Commission in the UK, but such investigations 'are infrequent, especially since judicial interpretation of their statutory powers restricted their scope for action' (Dickens, 2000, p. 155).

As Table 9.1 notes, trade unions can attempt to open up the segregation of front-line workers by seeking to negotiate more open, inclusive career ladders. Korczynski (1999) describes a case of a union in a large telecommunications firm in Australia adopting such an approach. Korczynski was able to compare the union impact in this call centre against four other call centres in the study. The union influence meant the call centre stood out from the other centres in some significant ways. It was only at this centre that industry-level accreditation of training was on the agenda. Further, at this centre the union ensured that there were significant structures in place to promote training and career development. For instance, the design of jobs at different hierarchical levels in the organisation were being aligned to allow a clearer and easier transition between levels. Thus the segregation of front-line workers from career ladders is not a necessary attribute of service organisations but is one that can be contested and remodelled, particularly through trade union action. A key way to create career ladders for front-line workers is through ensuring that these workers are trained (Collinson *et al.*, 1990, p. 209). Therefore, for the impact of trade unions to be significant in this area, wider issues of the regulation of training also need to be addressed.

Crucially, to facilitate career advancement, training must pertain not just to the customer service skills that are necessary for customer-facing jobs but are less relevant for jobs higher in the organisation. To facilitate career advancement training should also encompass problem-solving and technical skills. Two examples can bring out this point. Herzenberg *et al.* (1998, p. 100) contrast the training approach of most firms in the USA employing home health aides against the approach of the worker-owned cooperative Home Care Associates. In the former, training relates to rules of conduct with patients, and to a set of rules to be followed for common tasks. By contrast, at the worker-owned cooperative the longer training period is

> intended to help new employees think critically and to learn to solve job-related problems on their own...Aides are taught that there is no one right way to solve a problem, that each problem should be viewed from multiple perspectives, and that choices should be openly discussed with clients.

The second example relates to differences in training for retail workers in France and the UK (Jarvis and Prais, 1989). While British retail workers may have gone through some customer service skills training, frequently they receive little training related to associated technical skills that could facilitate career development. The conclusion of this meticulous study is worth quoting at some length (p. 69):

> The typical qualified French salesperson is trained in specialised product-knowledge, has been examined in practical selling, and progressed further in general educational subjects (native language, mathematics, a foreign language) as part of the vocational course. Expectations in Britain are lower: little is required for the main corresponding retail qualifications by way of product-knowledge, and general educational subjects are rarely pursued. To put it in practical terms: the reason British shop assistants so often know hardly anything about what they are selling is that no one has ever taught them.

In addition to there being little doubt as to which approach to training results in the better service, there is also little doubt as to which approach facilitates an easier career development for front-line retail workers.

The relatively poor level of training in the UK is not restricted to front-line service work (Keep and Rainbird, 2000). However, studies which examined training in hotels and retail and in manufacturing industries show that the UK training deficiencies were larger in the service industries (Jarvis and Prais, 1989; Prais *et al.*, 1989). There are a number of factors underlying the UK's poor training record. First, the design of the system of vocational education and training tends to exclude trade unions which would push for a wider skill base to facilitate better pay and greater possibilities for career advancement. Rather, the systems are dominated by employers who tend to have a short-term approach to training, focusing on immediate and narrow skills for task proficiency, which in the case of service work often translates to customer service skills (Payne, 2000) and a marginalisation of knowledge-based skills (Bradley *et al.*, 2000). Second, the training provided by firms, rather than by the general education system, is unregulated. It is left to managers in individual service organisations to make their own decisions on levels and forms of training. The problem with this market approach to training provision is that the 'market' of training is beset by the free-rider problem. In economists' terms, training is a special type of good: it is a public good, like street lighting, in the sense that once it has been provided by a firm that firm cannot restrict 'consumption' of the good to itself. The problem is that a free-rider firm, which has not paid for the training provision, may come along and poach the trained worker. Over time, it becomes rational for the firm which initially provides training to cut down on its training because it sees its investments continually poached by other firms. Hence, the market approach to training leads to a systematic, economy-wide underprovision of training. Further, this problem will be particularly exacerbated in occupations which have high levels of turnover. Because, as noted in earlier chapters, many front-line occupations have high levels of turnover this problem is likely to be exacerbated for these types of jobs.

Conclusion

Overall, in this chapter, the segregation and disadvantage of women in front-line jobs has been outlined and forms of regulation to challenge or ameliorate these problems have been considered. The fact that it is women who make up the vast majority of front-line occupations is no accident. The model of the customer-oriented bureaucracy points to the systematic factors underlying this. It is logical for management acting out of rationalising pressures to take on cheap labour from a weak segment of the labour market. In addition, a key part of the front-line worker's job is the maintenance of the myth of customer sovereignty. Job requirements are drawn up with this aim in mind. These job requirements are likely to be systematically gendered because, in a number of ways, women are generally more likely than men to be able to perpetuate the myth of sovereignty to customers. The tendency towards recruiting women because of the implicitly gendered job requirements may be reinforced through managers basing their recruitment decisions on sex-typing assumptions. In front-line jobs with an over-representation of women, pay levels tend to be low, part-time employment status is common and demands for a degree of sexualised labour and for working unsocial hours may exist. Again this is no accident. For instance, job evaluation exercises may often ignore key front-line tasks performed predominantly by women. The segregation and disadvantage experienced by women in front-line jobs becomes an even more pressing issue when potential tendencies to segregate front-line jobs away from career ladders into the rest of the organisation are considered. The way out of low-paying front-line jobs is doubly hard for women, because even where limited career ladders exist women tend to get left behind compared with men. In considering the ways in which to challenge segregation and disadvantage, it emerged that trade unions are important bodies that can use existing laws to constrain the decisions of service managers in ways that can improve the lot of women service workers. However, in many economies trade union membership has fallen significantly in the last two decades or more. The following chapter considers whether and how trade unions can become (or remain) significant bodies to minimise some of the negative aspects of front-line work.

Notes

1   See Fischer *et al.* (1997) and Mohr and Henson (1996) for an examination of ways, in which customer prejudice can enter organisational practices and structures, but which are not covered in this chapter.

2   Sales work relating to products of high value tends to be dominated by men. This is often an extreme form of sales work, compared with the female-dominated sales work relating to items of lower value which often relies on pre-selling by advertising. So the difference is more between extreme sales and *service* work than between types of sales work (cf. Berheide, 1988). This is important because there is a different social relationship between front-line worker and customer in extreme sales compared with that in service work. The former prioritises the firm and the worker in defining the customer's interests, while the latter revolves around the successful perpetuation of the myth of customer sovereignty. The customer's (gender-based) assumptions are key in service work, while in extreme sales work customer assumptions are more likely to be secondary concerns. Management will be concerned to recruit staff whom they see as able to push the firm's definition of the customer's interests. In recruiting for such jobs they are likely to be guided by sex-typing assumptions (Collinson *et al.*, 1990).

3   For instance, Scott (1994b, p. 256) provides the following quotation regarding young males' approach to checkout working and the lack of male socialisation into the requirements of front-line roles: 'Some of the younger men hate it because they think it's poofy and don't want their mates to see them.'

4   The European Union Working Time Directive is concerned primarily with the regulation of the overall number of hours worked rather than with their distribution outside of standard hours.

CHAPTER 10

Trade unions and service work

This second chapter on the regulation of service work focuses on trade unions. It may be tempting to see trade unions as a dying historical legacy of the era of manufacturing and industrial economies, and to link the decline they have suffered in many countries to the rise of the service economy. Trade union membership in the UK, for instance, has slipped from a high point of 56 per cent of the labour force in 1979 to around 30 per cent at the end of the twentieth century. In the USA, union membership levels stand at around 14 per cent. Whole regional economies, such as the Glasgow conurbation, and the North-East of England which used to be synonymous with heavily unionised, heavy industries such as shipbuilding, steel-making, and coal extraction now seem to be dominated by call centres, and large retail malls. 'Once we made ships, now we take calls' reads a newspaper headline (*Guardian*, 9 November 1998). The accompanying article describes call centre workers as 'docile', with an implicit contrast drawn with militant male workers in heavy industries.

Such a view *necessarily* linking the rise of service work with the decline of trade unions is a misleading one, however. The decline of trade unions has occurred for a number of reasons, only some of which pertain directly to the rise of service employment. Important factors in the UK which have fuelled decline have been high unemployment, low inflation, employer polices of union marginalisation[1] and anti-trade union legislation. These are not caus-ally linked to the rise of the service economy. Other factors fuelling decline, which do have specific relevance to service work, are the declining average size of the workplace, the changing composition of the workforce, and sec-toral shifts in the economy. In addition, turnover levels must be considered as affecting relative unionisation levels in service occupations. Each of these is briefly examined in turn.

Research has consistently shown that union membership tends to be higher the larger the size of the workplace (Bain and Price, 1983). Manufacturing production can be centralised in larger workplaces because there is a buffer between production and consumption. In front-line service work production and consumption are simultaneous. Thus service production tends to be decentralised and located around multiple nodes of consumption, and front-line service workplaces tend to be smaller. Wial (1993) calculates that in the USA the average service workplace has 13 workers, while the average manufacturing workplace has 51 workers. Millward *et al.*'s (2000, p. 27) analysis of the four comprehensive UK workplace surveys concludes that 'workplaces in private sector service industries tend to be the smallest, although their typical size has increased gradually [since 1980].' The changing composition of the workforce has been seen as affecting union membership levels because traditionally male, full-time workers have been more likely to be union members than female part-time workers. The rise in service employment has brought with it a shift in workforce composition that makes union membership less likely. As noted earlier in this chapter, many front-line occupations are made up predominantly of women. Further, the pressures for flexibility to match unpredictable customer demand, as noted in Chapter 4, have meant that many front-line workers are employed part-time, especially in the UK (Walsh, 1990), and also in the USA where Tilly (1992) has noted 86 per cent of part-time workers are located in service industries, with a rising trend. The sectoral shifts in the economy have been alluded to in the introduction to this section. Research has suggested that this may be a significant factor in union decline (Waddington, 1992). Research suggests that more service industries than manufacturing industries have what researchers term a 'residual industry effect' which disposes them towards low union membership. This residual industry effect is meant to refer to something affecting union membership in an industry even when other important factors such as workplace size and workforce composition have been taken into account. In effect the label is an admission of failure by researchers to understand social processes that appear to be specific to certain industries.[2] Finally, the high turnover levels that occur in certain front-line occupations are also likely to contribute to low levels of unionisation. Unions find it harder to recruit and keep up membership when workers have a propensity to leave employment within a short period. Indeed, as Bain and Price (1983, p. 25) note, 'a high degree of labour turnover may indicate that workers are leaving unsatisfactory work as an *alternative* strategy to improving it through unionisation' (emphasis added).

Overall, then, there are important barriers to sustained union organisation in service work, especially front-line work. However, they do not necessarily determine union failure. Consider the case of flight attendants, for instance. This is a front-line service workforce mainly composed of, often young, women. These staff work in small clusters, with often little continuity in work group composition between one day and the next (Wouters, 1989). This gives little opportunity for the sorts of deep, non-unitarist 'associational solidarity' (Heckscher, 1988) that can inform union organisation. Such factors are likely to be the sort of things that might underlie unidentified industry residual effects noted above. Further, within a stereotypical image, flight attendants may appear 'docile'. Such an imagery may be informed by the presence of the customer in the labour process. Images of militancy seem to sit better in the simple management–workforce dyad of manufacturing work. The unspoken assumption is that conflict may exist for flight attendants, but that such conflict is more likely to pertain to relations with customers. Even then, conflict will only rarely become open: attendants tend to take a deep breath and smile back at the irate customer. Such images of docility, however, stand badly beside the high levels of unionisation of flight attendants in many countries (Nielsen, 1982; Hochschild, 1983; Williams, 1989). Behind the public image and aesthetic labour of flight attendants lies a history of union–management confrontations. As Hochschild notes, these unions 'have challenged company regulations affecting whole territories of the body and its adornment, regulations on facial make-up, hairstyles, undergarments, jewellery and shoe styles' (1983, p. 126). One of the largest and most highly publicised disputes in the late 1990s in the UK concerned unions challenging management policies for changing working conditions at British Airways. As Linstead (1995) notes, the 'perfumed picket line' is part of the landscape of the service economy.

Indeed, against the factors that make unionisation harder in front-line work the analysis of this book points to factors which can work systematically in unions' favour. First, unionising front-line service work may be easier because employers are unable to use the threat of the geographical relocation of production as a tactic against unions. These employer tactics are widespread in other work settings, especially in the USA (Bronfenbrenner, 2000) and have been theorised by Burawoy (1985) as a central part of a 'hegemonic despotic' phase of capitalism in which unions are quietened. The colocation of production with consumption that marks a key aspect of front-line work (except where technologically mediated) takes this important tactic away from employers. Second, unions are likely to confront management whose position on a range of work organisation elements is unlikely to be definitively fixed. This book has stressed that management faces a series of dilemmas in trying to establish a (fragile) social order that can generate profit. While management may espouse a rhetoric that is substantively systematic, practices and policies are likely to be informed consistently by ambiguous compromises between the dual logics. Within this setting unions are likely to systematically discover that management finds room to accommodate a range of their demands. Third, unions can look on the informal, but often dense and crucial, communities of coping that appear widespread in service workplaces (see Chapter 8) as an important form of collective solidarity deriving from the nature of the labour process from which unionism can grow, and has grown historically (for example, see Price, 1980).

Trade unions can have a role in the front-line workplace. In Canada, for instance, there has been a growth of service sector unions (Murray, 1998).

Further, while research into the *history* of union growth and decline suggests some important obstacles in certain service industries, trade unions can re-define themselves and change *in the present and in the future*, adapting to the new environment (Cobble, 1996). But what sort of approach should trade unions take to extend their membership in front-line service work? Given the considerable size of front-line employment, and given the predictions of its continued growth, this is a pivotal question for the future of the unions. The question drives this chapter. First, there is an overview of union strategies in relation to recruiting and organising front-line workers. Then the chapter turns to examine strategies concerning the questions of who unions should organise, and what interests they should prioritise. This is followed by an examination of strategies in relation to the questions of how unions should organise, and what forms of sustaining ideology they can put forward.

Analysing union strategies

Mirroring debates in other countries, the debate on union strategies within the UK centres on examining the merits and demerits of the (social) *partnership* approach and the *organising* (or social movement) approach respectively (Heery, 2001).[3] Differences in these approaches can be best examined by extending Hyman (1997b) in breaking down the concept of union strategy into four key questions: Who should unions organise? What interests of their members should they prioritise in their actions? How should they organise and represent their members? and What is the ideology underlying their actions? Table 10.1 summarises the answer to these questions offered by the advocates of the partnership and organising approaches.[4] The final column lays out an approach informed by the concept of the customer-oriented bureaucracy (COB).

As Heery points out, how far one is persuaded by the case for either the partnership or the organising model is centrally determined by one's view of the nature of contemporary work. If contemporary service work is seen as offering a greater potential for interests shared between management and workforce then a partnership approach makes sense. It makes sense to build on existing cooperative relations with *employers* by extending recruitment where good relations exist with employers and by concentrating activity on areas offering clear potential for mutual gains. Here, unions must still be democratic, but in a representative rather than participative sense, and the sustaining ideology of trade unionism is one of placing trade unions as a legitimate actor within a stakeholder organisation and society. However, if service work is seen as increasingly steeped in conflict between management and the workforce, then an organising model is the more appropriate one.

Table 10.1 Three union approaches to organising front-line service workers

	Partnership approach	*Organising approach*	*Approach informed by COB analysis*
Who to organise?	Focus recruitment efforts on core workers in organisations in which union presence is already established.	Bring in members from occupations and workplaces with little union presence, covering both core and contingent workers.	Recognise limited union presence in many service workplaces; hence main focus on non-union workplaces and occupations.
What interests to prioritise?	Interests should be prioritised where areas of common interest are forged with management, e.g. 'pay to hire and keep the best people', training and development.	Engender membership growth by focusing on issues of conflict with management, e.g. countering low pay, and resisting intensification of work.	A range of pay and conditions, directly relevant to front-line workers – see text; enforce cooperation through conflict; and use management rhetoric of customer service.
How to organise and represent interests?	Representative democracy; relatively passive membership, with union officials engaged in centralised and 'back-stage' discussions with management.	Participative democracy; active role for membership at workplace level in mobilising to force concessions from management.	Recognise barriers and limits to participative democracy; potentially build union organisation around centralised nodes of consumption; organise with gender composition of workforce in mind; periodic mobilisation for customer support.
The ideology of unionism	Union as legitimate actor in stakeholder organisation, and stakeholder society.	Union linked with ideology of class conflict.	Unionism as civilising production and consumption simultaneously.

Here unions seek to break into the non-unionised areas where the workforce is likely to be subject to greater exploitation, and to focus their action on issues of conflict with management. By forcing concessions from management a union can appear attractive to new members, whom it will seek to actively involve in the union. Participative democracy is important because the mobilisation of the membership may be necessary to keep forcing the employer's hand, and the sustaining ideology is that of class conflict. Heery suggests the utility of breaking out of conceptualising union approaches in terms of an apparent strict dichotomy between the two approaches. An implication is that if a central characteristic of contemporary work is its *contradictory* nature, then union strategies must reflect this, implying an interplay and dynamic between elements of the two approaches. The analysis of service work centred around the concept of the customer-oriented bureaucracy suggests that the experience of front-line service work is centrally informed by the contradictory nature of that work. The final column in Table 10.1 lays out the implications for union strategy of this view, and is elaborated in much of the discussion below.

Who to organise; which interests to prioritise?

The first issue of who to organise has in part already been addressed. As indicated above, the key task for trade unions in the UK is to break through into establishing a presence in non-union workplaces and occupations, particularly in the private services sector. Indeed, while the partnership approach focus on core workers in workplaces with an already-established union presence may make some limited sense for certain manufacturing industries, its relevance for service work, outside the public sector, is likely to be limited.[5] Similarly, a focus on core full-time workers would exclude a large slice of the potential membership in many service industries. As Walsh (1990) notes, such is the level of the use of part-time workers in the retail and hospitality industries that it makes little sense to characterise them as 'peripheral' workers. Just as they are not 'peripheral' to employers, so they should not be to trade unions.

The answer to the question of what unions should do for their members must be informed not only by an understanding of the contradictory nature of front-line work, but also by research into the key factors that promote workers to join trade unions. Waddington and Whitston (1995, p. 191) conclude that two key factors inform workers' decisions to join trade unions: (1) the union role in 'improving pay and conditions', and (2) the union role offering 'support if I had problems at work'. With this in mind, a union priority must remain to challenge low pay. It is difficult to challenge low pay through collective bargaining, however, when the workforce has little bargaining power – as discussed in the preceding chapter. However, with the achievement of the national minimum wage, trade unions in the UK can legitimately present themselves as bodies which have secured better pay for the lowest-paid service workers.[6] As John Edmonds (1986), head of the large UK general union the GMB, noted, the campaign for the national minimum wage put [us] on the side of the oppressed and disadvantaged, which is a side of the argument we haven't actually been on for some time. It also puts us on the side of women... and it puts us on the side of short service and mobile workers in the service sector.

Further, unions can seek better pay levels through neither the straightforward cooperation approach of the partnership model nor the straightforward conflict approach of the organising model, but by engendering cooperation through conflict, and conflict through cooperation (Cobble, 1996). Avoiding conflict where it is likely to be fruitless, that is, where workers have little bargaining power, unions can adopt a cooperative rhetoric of the importance of customer service in order to push for an upgrade in the skill levels of front-line workers – particularly the sort of product-related and problem-solving skills discussed in the preceding chapter. Here, there is also a potential to form coalitions with consumer groups. Recall Jarvis and Prais's (1989) damning indictment: 'the reason British shop assistants so often know hardly anything about what they are selling is that no one has ever taught them'. Trade unions can join with consumer groups to make the case for better-trained front-line staff.

In addition to pay issues, unions can focus on a range of issues that have specific relevance for front-line workers. The false nature of the dichotomy between partnership model and organising model becomes apparent here. An important part of the organising approach is that it seeks to create a union organisation which is close to the workplace and which reflects workers' everyday concerns. It is an attempt to break down the frustrating 'residual industry effect' that seems to block union progress in some service industries. Such a form of union activity has thrown up and will continue to throw up a range of issues stemming from the contradictory nature of front-line service work. However, it is the partnership approach which is the more likely to broaden the formal bargaining agenda of union–management discussions (Heery, 2001). This means that while it is the organising model which is the more likely to unearth these workplace specific issues it is the partnership approach which is the more likely to institutionalise the union role in regulating them. One seems hardly useful without the other. Some important workplace issues that unions may usefully regulate are examined below.

Regulating against negative aspects of emotional labour

Chapter 8 highlighted that the demands for emotional labour are likely to have systematically negative effects for front-line workers. Two key factors were identified as crucial here – the degree to which front-line workers have to follow strict management-imposed feeling rules, and the degree to which they are placed in a position of inequality vis-à-vis the customer. Unions can have a role in both areas. They can argue for greater discretion for workers in the delivery of emotional labour. This is not necessarily an issue of simple conflict with management; nor is it an argument against emotional labour *per se*, but rather is one against emotional labour in the context of a strict managerial imposition of feeling rules. This issue may sound abstract and potentially nebulous, but there is evidence that it can be an important aspect of union activity that can serve to mobilise membership growth. In the union organisation among clerical, often student-facing staff at Harvard University a key spur to membership activity was a training session on 'customer service' which sought to impose management-defined demeaning feeling rules (Eaton, 1996). Eaton states that

> a trainer told workers who were upset by angry students' rebukes to 'think of yourself as a trash can. Take everyone's little bits of anger all day, put it inside you, and at the end of the day, just pour it in the dumpster on your way out of the door.' Not surprisingly, workers found this advice offensive and not helpful. (p. 296)

Cobble (1996) notes that feeling rules have also been a key issue in union–management relations regarding flight attendants. An example she gives is almost a duplicate of the Harvard one: 'a mandatory "Commitment to Courtesy" class in which instructors divided flight attendants into small groups and assigned them to draw pictures on flip charts showing "attendants being nice" particularly galled the women, one activist explained. *"People got livid"* ' (p. 347). Unions contesting strict management imposition of feeling rules may not only speak directly to everyday work concerns of front-line workers, but may also feed into the second important reason for joining a union: 'support if I had a problem at work'. A strict management imposition of feeling rules is likely to result in a number of disciplinary cases brought against front-line workers who have been found to contravene these rules. A key union role is to represent individual workers in disciplinary cases. When these cases centre on feeling rules, unions effectively act to create greater space for the voice of the workforce in defining feeling rules. Importantly, the Employment Relations Act 1999 in the UK has guaranteed the right of union representatives to be present with individual members in disciplinary cases, regardless of whether the union is recognised by the employer for collective bargaining purposes.

Trade unions can also seek to regulate the relationship of the front-line worker with the customer. Unions must walk a fine line here, given that there are systematic reasons that the customer appears to many front-line workers as 'our friend, the enemy' (Benson, 1986). A strategy congruent with this way in which customers are experienced by front-line workers would involve structuring the service encounter to minimise the likelihood of the dark side of the customer surfacing, and to minimise its effect when it does surface. The dark side of the customer potentially emerges when he or she moves from enchantment to disillusionment. If unions can help decrease both enchantment and disillusionment then they will improve the experience of front-line work. The creation of enchantment is a systemic part of consumer capitalism, but this does not mean that it cannot be regulated and altered. Consumers are enchanted primarily through the work of the marketing and advertising part of the service organisation. The images produced serve to enchant customers in specific ways. For instance, advertising images may promote sexualised enchantment; 'I'm Cheryl, Fly Me', ran an advertisement for National Airlines in the USA in the 1970s (Nielsen, 1982). The degree and form of enchantment engendered through advertising will necessarily feed into how often and how deeply the dark side of the customer emerges. Unions can seek to institutionalise a role for the collective voice of the front-line workforce in the creation of advertising images. After all, it is the front-line workforce who 'cop the flak' (Frenkel *et al.*, 1999) from the heightened and sexualised forms of enchantment created by marketing staff.

In addition, unions can seek to minimise the likelihood of customer disillusionment by making the case for the training of front-line staff in deeper, technical and problem-solving skills. Equipped with such skills, front-line workers are more likely to prevent customers becoming so disillusioned as to become irate and abusive. Indeed, training in these sorts of skills appears to be a vital plank in a union strategy in a number of ways. Not only does it minimise customer disillusionment and abuse, but it also creates a way out of a front-line ghetto in organisations. Further, it informs a longer-term approach to tackle low pay, and it helps to erect what some writers have called a 'status shield' (Hochschild, 1983; Leidner, 1993) for front-line workers against the dark side of the customer. The customer–worker relationship is a socially embedded one, with a greater likelihood of customer disillusionment turning to abuse when the worker is in a position of low status. Hochschild, for instance, argues that women flight attendants are more likely to face customer abuse because of their weaker 'status shield' (p. 163). The higher the skill level of front-line workers, the more they have a status shield to militate against manifestations of customer abuse.[7] Wider union strategies focusing on the importance of training are therefore well suited to focusing on front-line workers. Again the approach of the GMB in the UK is notable. As Heery notes, (1993, p. 290), the general secretary of the GMB 'has stated that promotion [of union officials] will increasingly depend on success in recruitment among "the new servant class" and negotiation claims are monitored to ensure they incorporate demands for training and gender equality'. Training certainly tends to be a central aspect of partnership agreements (Knell, 1999). The promotion of training to foster common interests with customer was part of a campaign of the TUC, which proposed a 'Quality Work Assured Servicemark' for the public services. This would be awarded when independent monitoring showed standards of training and staff involvement, equal opportunities, attention to health and safety, and levels of pay to be sufficient to ensure the delivery of high-quality service. The benefit of promoting training is that it makes customers more likely to be the friend and less likely to be the enemy.

However, a union strategy must also be aware that there remain systematic reasons for the emergence of the dark side of the customer to the surface. Therefore, unions should seek to minimise the harmful effects of this on front-line workers. Thus a number of unions have focused on the issue of violence from customers, seeking to ensure that work is organised to minimise the possibilities of this (Heery, 1993). Further, unions in seeking to regulate the feeling rules for service encounters can aim, and have aimed, to ensure that front-line workers are not expected to put up with abusive and disrespectful behaviour from customers (see Simms *et al.*, 2000).

Regulating for the opportunity to deliver meaningful service

An almost constant refrain in research into the experience of front-line work is the desire of front-line workers to give meaningful service to customers, and the frustrations that come from being unable to do so. Trade union activity needs to be informed by this. Most obviously, unions can argue for training and staffing levels that will afford the possibilities for meaningful service. Although management demands to increase the efficiency of service delivery are often presented by writers in terms of the 'intensification of work' (Boyd and Bain, 1999), or a 'speed-up' (Hochschild, 1983), it is not clear that this is the most useful way to conceptualise the issue for union activity. A union strategy and language simply against a work 'speed-up' implicitly contains 'anti-boss' imagery (Cobble, 1996) that rests poorly with many front-line workers' experiences. A language and strategy that speaks to front-line workers' likely deep-rooted 'pro-customer' values and experiences may have more appeal to such workers. Importantly, what others describe as an 'intensification of work' in front-line settings may also be described as a 'rationalisation ' of work. It is not necessarily that workers are working harder, but that they are forced to work differently, emphasising the through-put of customers, rather than the quality of individual service encounters. Their work becomes more bureaucratised and less customer-oriented. Unions can seek to ensure that staffing levels are maintained to allow work in which there is the possibility to deliver meaningful service (for example, see Peters and Merrill, 1998) – in fact, the Royal College of Nursing, the major professional body/union for nurses in the UK, was reported as close to its first industrial action ever primarily because its members felt that the medical service being provided to patients at a particular hospital was not acceptable (Carvel, 2001).

Crucially, the way in which a social order is established in the service workplace is a political process. Management seeking somehow to balance quality and quantity concerns can rarely have a definitive vision of what constitutes such a balance. It must walk its own fine lines, erring on one side and then the other over time, aware that its standards are double. Its ambiguous understanding of what constitutes a balance can be decisively affected by the collective voice of workers expressed through a union. In this, the union can use as a tool the management rhetoric of HRM tied to service quality. This is captured well in a statement from a union seeking to organise customer service representatives at the internet retailers, Amazon.com:

> Quality customer service requires professional well-trained individuals that have job security, compensation that reflects our skills and commitment to the company, respect, career development opportunities, continued education and a voice. Amazon.com cannot sustain the standard of excellence that it has attained with anything less than a true commitment to these core values. (CNN website, 16 November 2000)

Another important way in which unions can pursue this aim of delivering meaningful service is to contest the strict use of sales targets in those jobs involving service and sales elements. A major British union, the Union of Shop, Distributive and Allied Workers, did exactly this by contesting the sales targets imposed by a major insurance sales employer (*Daily Express*, 20 December 1995). Again union activity can be presented not merely as an anti-management stance, but as a pro-customer stance that fits well with the daily experience of front-line workers. Further, this approach can lay the ground for alliances with consumer groups:

> Barclays Bank has been forced to back down from the introduction of heavy-handed 'sell or be fired' techniques after a backlash from employees and their union. Management had called for sales staff to win 60 sales a week of Barclaycards, graduate loans and insurance policies – or face disciplinary action...The bank was attacked by *consumer groups*, saying such pressure could lead to customers being sold products they did not need. (*Guardian*, 2 August 2000) (emphasis added)

In addition, this approach may be closely related to the second key reason people give for joining a union: 'support if I had a problem at work'. In the case above, according to the report, failure by workers to achieve sales targets would have been 'met with a written warning followed by a final written warning and then dismissal'. The union role in contesting disciplinary cases arising from the use of sales targets may prove an important catalyst for union growth (see Bain and Taylor, 2000, regarding call centres).

The means and ideology of organising

Having looked at which workers should be represented, and what interests should be prioritised, the discussion now turns to the question of *how* unions should represent interests and of what sort of sustaining ideology could be developed. Cobble's (1996) call for a form of union structure to match the realities of the service economy emphasises the need for union structures to match their female-dominated service worker constituency. This means that unions must continue to reform the way that they organise themselves along the lines advocated or implied in feminist criticism (Campbell, 1982; Coote and Campbell, 1987; Grint, 1998). Increasingly, the realities of the service economy mean that union structures based on an assumption of a male, full-time, large-workplace-based membership represents organisational suicide. Thus, many unions have increased their representation of women, particularly in laypositions, in addition to providing a proliferation of specific structures, such as conferences, aimed solely at women members. Progress remains slow regarding the appointment up of more women as full-time officials, however (Heery and Kelly, 1988). On the other hand, Heery and Kelly (1989) suggest that female officials are more likely to exist in unions where there is a high proportion of women in membership, and where there is a build-up of pressure from members and activists for female officials. Clearly, this could increasingly be the scenario if unions succeed in recruiting more (predominantly female) service workers.

Many unions have sought to involve and represent members though workplace-based structures, but this approach is based on an assumption of large workplaces. One solution Cobble (1996) offers to this problem is for a rebirth, at least in the USA, of occupational unionism in which unions do not seek to recruit workers by firm, but rather by specific occupation, setting up representational structures in locales rather than around workplaces. She offers the example of the historical unionisation of waitresses in the USA. Unions pursued an occupational strategy and managed to recruit nearly one-quarter of waitresses by the end of the 1940s. Such a strategy, however, does little to match the reality of the increasing demands by employers, in the UK at least, to move away from dealing with multiple unions representing different types of staff (though see Heery *et al.*, 2000, for a discussion of a similar approach adopted by unions for contingent workers). Just as front-line work involves consumption and production simultaneously, unions too must somehow set up representational structures to match the realities of both production and consumption simultaneously.

While service production is decentralised, there is a corresponding trend towards the *centralisation* of certain forms of consumption. Ritzer (1999a) has argued that there has been a revolution in the means of consumption towards the development of large arenas, or 'cathedrals', of consumption. Taking a leading place among these are the new giant shopping malls, chain stores, franchises and fast food restaurants, cruise ships, entertainment complexes, athletic facilities, educational settings and hospitals. One way for unions to cope with decentralised production but centralised consumption is to set up parallel structures around both the employer (decentralised production) and also large, centralised nodes of consumption, for instance, setting up branches for shopping malls. Non-workplace branches, however, can often seem remote to the majority of union members. The challenge for unions is to set up more meaningful structures based around centralised nodes of consumption such as shopping malls and entertainment complexes and districts. Such a level of organisation may become more relevant as unions increasingly come to form coalitions with consumers and consumer groups (Heery, 1993). Such a phenomenon of coalition-forming at a local level has been a characteristic of a number of innovative unionising campaigns for service workers in the USA (Cobble, 1996; Bronfenbrenner *et al.*, 1998; Wever, 1998). Most notably, the coalition formed with clients (and their representatives) was a key element in the successful campaign in 1999 to bring under the union umbrella 74 000 home-care workers in Los Angeles county (Cleveland, 1999) – the largest single union election victory in the USA since the unionisation of Ford in 1941 (Bronfenbrenner, 2000). Coalitions with service recipients have also been a key element in the unionisation of service workers on American college campuses in the late 1990s (Bronfenbrenner *et al.*, 1998; Klein, 2000).

These issues suggest the need for an interplay between representative and participative forms of democracy within unions. The context of small, decentralised service workplaces suggests the need for a representative system within the service organisation, potentially allied to a more participative system constructed around large, centralised nodes of consumption. Further, while participative democracy remains a vital aim in terms of a wider goal of increasing the say people have over their work lives, limitations to it must be recognised. For instance, the organising model's stress on active mobilisation and participation of union members is difficult to marry with a need to unionise part-time service workers, whose ability to spend time participating in union activities is likely to be extremely limited. In addition, lay activists tend to be less concerned with active recruitment than do full-time officials (Kelly and Heery, 1989). It also remains the case that many of the key challenges to male dominance in union structures have come through top-down initiatives (Grint, 1998).

Finally, the sustaining ideology of union activity in front-line-service work needs to be considered. The potential power of ideas in generating union membership and activity should not be underestimated – as Waddington and Whitston (1995) note, from their survey research, white-collar staff ranked a 'belief in trade unionism' as the third most important reason for joining a union. But what set of ideas can create such a 'belief in trade unionism' among service workers? In so far as the organising approach presents an ideology of opposition to employers, of dyadic class conflict, then this approach is likely to speak little to the everyday contradictions and fine lines that front-line workers contend with.[8] Cobble (1996, p. 342), describing the union recruitment of clerical, student-facing staff at Harvard, noted that the union adopted the slogan

> 'You don't have to be anti-Harvard to be pro-union' [and] eschewed an antiboss, antiemployer campaign. They assumed that clerical workers cared about the enterprise in which they worked and about the quality of the service they delivered.

Such a set of assumptions are well supported by the range of research reported on many types of front-line occupations in this book. Further, Heery (1993, p. 292) argues that an anti-employer, radical form of ideology is rooted in the misconception that it is within production that primary identities are formed. As discussed in Chapters 4, 5 and 7, identities within front-line production can revolve as much around consumption as around production. After all, many front-line workers are recruited on the basis of their identification with, and implicitly their identity as, customers.[9]

The sustaining ideology for the partnership approach revolves around the pluralist notion of the stakeholder organisation (Hutton 1995).[10] This vision positions trade unions as a legitimate representative voice for the workforce, who constitute one of many stakeholders – along with customers and other parties such as shareholders – whose voices should be heard in the decision-making process within organisations. One merit in such an ideology is that it points to the importance of trade unions as a collective representative body for the workforce, seeking to create coalitions with consumer groups as *collective* representative bodies for customers. Heery (1993) argues forcibly that the opportunity for coalition-forming to accommodate both worker and consumer interests requires a more active role for the collective, rather than individual, market expression of consumer interests.

However, the vision of the stakeholder organisation must be deemed worthy but rather cold and unaffecting as a sustaining ideology. It is not a vision to win the hearts and minds of union activists and members who work on the front line. The call *to civilise and humanise production and consumption simultaneously*, however, may speak more readily to the experiences and identities of front-line workers. Such a call recognises the interplay between production and consumption that exists in front-line work. It implicitly suggests that the processes of capitalism can create a dehumanised, uncivil production and consumption, but suggests also the potential to civilise these areas together, through active agency. It suggests a defensive agenda, for instance minimising the effects of the dark side of the customer, but also a proactive agenda, for instance regulating to allow the delivery of meaningful service. Such a call for the sustaining ideology of civilising production and consumption simultaneously in part echoes MacDonald and Sirianni's (1996) call for unionism to engender a less servile and more civil society, and a more civic culture. It also fits well with a number of strategies adopted by unions. For instance, the TUC campaign for quality standards, noted above, is one such example. In the USA, Kerchner and Mitchell (1988) argue that teacher unions are moving towards a 'third stage of unionism' in which union activity is based as much around a concern with the welfare of the overall educational system and with giving meaningful education to their clients as it is around the protection of worker interests. It also connects well with the union's key role in the partnership agreement at Tesco, the large UK supermarket, which involves 'the notion that the union should act as the company's conscience, informing Tesco if it fails to live up to its values and commitments' (Marchington, 2001, p. 12). Such a sustaining ideology brings to the fore the crucial 'sword of justice' that has been part of much union activity historically (Flanders, 1970). Crucially, the way it emphasises the connections between production and consumption speaks directly to the new politics of protest so ably articulated by Klein (2000). Klein shows how branded consumption in advanced economies is systematically connected to dehumanising production in impoverished economies. She shows how protests against this element of global capitalism involve making people see *the connection between production and consumption*. Green politics is also based exactly on making people see this connection. All this suggests that unions acting to civilise production and consumption simultaneously can potentially kindle the belief in trade unionism that may be crucial to break through the barriers constraining union growth in many front-line occupations.

Conclusion

Trade unions need not necessarily fade away in the service economy. But if they are to have meaning for front-line workers their strategies must be informed by the daily work experiences of these workers. As much of the rest of this book has stressed, front-line staff experience work in contradictory ways, with tensions and spaces intermingling, and with fine lines constantly to be negotiated. This means that appropriate union strategies are unlikely to fit neatly either the partnership or the organising model of union strategy, but are more likely to be based on an interplay between both approaches. This may appear to create contradictory union strategies. But contradictions are what front-line staff experience every day.

This chapter has examined a number of ways in which unions can organise and have organised themselves in order to better represent front-line staff. In the UK, while there are a few front-line occupations, such as nursing and public welfare work, in which unionisation is high, there are a large number of front-line workplaces in which there is hardly any union presence at all. This means that unions need to seek to recruit outside established areas. They must seek to break down the frustrating 'residual industry effect' that seems to block their progress in a number of key industries. To do this they must prioritise interests that have meaning for workers in their specific contexts. This chapter has argued that a union priority must be to challenge low pay, but that traditional collective bargaining may not necessarily be the best way to accomplish this in some cases. Unions can have a meaningful role for front-line workers in challenging management imposition of feeling rules and in seeking to force management to allow front-line workers the opportunity to deliver meaningful service. Although decentralised service production sets up a daunting barrier to union organisation, there is potential for unions to use the increasing centralisation of some forms of consumption to their advantage. Unions may need to set up parallel organisational structures to deal with this simultaneous decentralisation and centralisation. Such structures may better allow the creation of periodic coalitions with consumer groups. A meaningful sustaining ideology of unionism may emerge from an overall imagery of trade unions as seeking to civilise production and consumption simultaneously. Such imagery speaks to front-line workers' roles as producers but also recognises the degree to which they have a consuming commitment.

This discussion has centred on how far unions can appeal to front-line workers. But it is also the case that unions must reach an accommodation with *employers*. Employers who are cooperative with trade unions may be vital in the many cases where there are decentralised workplaces and relatively high turnover levels. Apparently minor things like an employer being readily willing to include union information in the recruitment pack for newly hired staff, to give union officials easy access to workplaces and to set up an automatic 'check-off' of union membership fees may be crucial in establishing a union presence. The strategy suggested within this chapter has already within it a wide basis for accommodation with management. For instance, the aim of regulating to allow front-line workers to deliver meaningful service is one that immediately speaks to one of the key managerial discourses within the customer-oriented bureaucracy.

It is unlikely that unions will be able to push the employer's hand in all of the areas outlined within this chapter. Accommodations with employers necessarily involve trade-offs. But the overall strategy outlined here allows the possibility of trade-offs between elements in which both unions and management speak the same language.

Notes

1   In both the USA and the UK the main locus of overtly anti-union employer policies has been heavy industries, such as the oil and chemical industries (Kochan *et al.* 1986; Korczynski and Ritson, 2000). This is not to say, of course, that anti-union employers do not exist in service industries (for example, see Royle, 2000, on McDonald's). Further, it should be noted that many service industries are made up of small firms, and it is the case that small employers tend to be to anti-union employers (Bain and Price, 1983). The point is that there are few data to make the case that service employers are more anti-union than other employers simply because they are service employers.

2   There have been a number of attempts to unravel the unidentified industry effect in hotel and catering, for instance. As Wood (1992, p. 103) notes, 'it remains to outsiders one of the great enigmas of the hotel and catering industry that workforce unionisation is low'. This enigma has been explored by Wood and Pedlar (1978), Johnson and Mignot (1982), MacFarlane (1982), Johnson (1983), Mars and Nicod (1984), Riley (1985), Cobble (1991) and Wood (1992).

3   The link between the respective organising approaches in the UK, in Australia and in the USA is clear from the explicit organisational learning that has occurred between the major union federations in the three countries (Heery, 2001).

4   The approaches summarised should be seen as ideal types. In practice, it is clear that no one *definitive* pattern of social relations adheres to either approach (Heery, 2001).

5   It makes sense where unions have established relations with large service employers, such as at Tesco (a supermarket – the largest private employer in the UK) and at Legal & General (an insurance firm), where partnership agreements appeared to have helped to increase union membership density levels (Haynes and Allen, 2001). However, such cases are the minority in most service industries.

6   Of course, there is the real problem of the free rider for trade unions. The national minimum wage is a public good, the consumption of which cannot be withheld from people who are not members of a trade union. However, it should be noted that the free-rider problem has always existed for trade unions regarding negotiated payrises.

7   Sennett and Cobb (1973) and Rothman (1998) note that people tend to rank service occupations as having low status compared with other kinds of jobs. This situation may be altered if unions can systematically upgrade the levels of skills used in these occupations.

8   See Heery (2001) and Hyman (1997a) on 'wildcat cooperation' for arguments about the wider problems of trade unions using an ideology of class conflict.

9   Thus in the service workplaces, workers may not have so much a 'dual commitment' to union and employer (Guest, 1995; Murphy and Olthuis, 1995) as a triple commitment to customer, union and employer.

10   Although see Ackers and Payne (1998) for a discussion of the multiple meanings of partnership in the context of UK employment relations.

CHAPTER 11

Conclusion: reconsidering modern times

Charlie Chaplin's *Modern Times* is rightly regarded by many as a classic film that offers profound insights into the nature of work and society. The film is particularly famous for the lacerating comedy of its portrayal of work on the assembly line. Brilliantly, frighteningly, human beings are portrayed metaphorically, and in one scene, literally, as cogs in a machine. But what is often forgotten is that Chaplin's character in the film has a number of jobs, as he negotiates an uneasy passage through 'modern times'. Not only is he a manufacturing assembly line worker, he is also, later, employed as a front-line service worker, a singing waiter, who, untrained and unaccustomed to either singing or waiting, must somehow do both simultaneously. Pressured by his manager (and chased by the police), he steps out in front of the restaurant audience to sing, with food in hand, and manages somehow, absurdly, comically, to ad-lib his way through a song that he does not know.

Two things centrally relevant to this book resonate from this film and from the common memory of the film. The first is that *the service worker is the forgotten figure of modern times*. Just as the assembly line Chaplin is remembered as the archetypal figure of the film, so the assembly line worker has been cast time and again as the archetypal figure of industrial modernity. But just as the assembly line Chaplin features in only part of the film, so manufacturing workers only constituted around 30 per cent of the US working population when Gramsci coined the term 'Fordism' (Castells, 1996, ch. 4). By the beginning of the twenty-first century, front-line workers appear too numerous to be ignored. Nevertheless, they have been ignored. And so, in certain visions, we jump from the industrial, Fordist economy, to the post-industrial knowledge economy, with a little flexible specialisation production to tie us gently to the manufacturing past. The danger now is that the front-line service worker becomes the forgotten figure of 'late modern times' as well. This is a danger to be avoided because the study of front-line work tells us much about the nature of our times, about production and consumption, about the contradictions of contemporary work and about the dilemmas of trying to manage it.

The second thing that resonates from Chaplin's film is the ambiguity of the scenes featuring his singing waiter set against the clarity of the assembly line scenes. In the factory, the comedy has a simple setting: there is Chaplin as the little man against the hateful manager intent on turning his employees into automatons. But in the restaurant, as Chaplin steps out to sing, food in hand, the structure and dynamic of the comedy is not so clear, and the humour is less comfortable. We, as customers, are absent from the factory; we have no place in the manager–worker dyad. However, we, as customers, are present in the restaurant and have a direct role in the three-sided relationship between workers, management and customers that informs the experience of front-line work. We, as customers, have a more direct complicity in what goes on in the restaurant than in what goes on in the factory. This makes the comedy less comfortable. The ambiguity of the restaurant scene comes also from the fact that it is hard to interpret Chaplin as a singing waiter. We know we do not want him to become another cog in the factory machine, but we are less sure about his restaurant work. Being a singing waiter seems both more liberating and yet more demeaning than working on an assembly line. On the positive side, there is no machine to direct your every action, restaurant work involves more than tightening the next screw on the line, and singing can be a beautiful, meaningful, skilful act. Yet, there is a negative side too. What in one context can have meaning, in another can be demeaning. With food in hand, singing becomes a novelty and the melody, seductive but only on the surface, reminds us of the myth of customer sovereignty. The singer must walk a fine line, close to a position of servility, and close to becoming an object of ridicule. To move away from these demeaning positions, Chaplin the singer must take the restaurant customers with him – he must make them believe in him as a singer. Underlying the ambiguous nature of the comedy, then, is the idea of the customer as a contested terrain. It is testimony to the genius of Chaplin's film that the customer as contested terrain stands as one of the motifs of contemporary work and society.

This book seeks to foreground Chaplin as the waiter rather than Chaplin as the assembly line worker and to foreground the customer as contested terrain. For too long has the front-line worker been the forgotten figure of modern and late modern times. For too long have debates about the nature of employment been constructed without reference to the customer or the sphere of consumption. In examining the existing research on service work this book has put forward a number of central arguments with reference to a number of key concepts. The following section of this concluding chapter summarises the main arguments and concepts of the book. From there, the chapter spells out the implications of this analysis for the study of HRM more generally (that is, for HRM beyond service settings). Finally, the book considers the implications of the analysis for overall characterisations of the service economy.

Summary of main arguments

The introductory chapter argued that the neglect of the study of front-line work was insupportable. Not only are front-line workers too numerous to ignore; it is also the case that *front-line work requires separate analysis, crucially because of the presence of the customer within the labour process.* The service work dimensions of intangibility, perishability, variability, simultaneous production and consumption and inseparability all derive from the presence of the customer. A number of writers have tried to lay out different types of service work by using one or more of these dimensions. It was argued that competition based on both cost and service quality pointed towards the importance of a 'middle' category of service work, the service shop in which a particular type of experience of the service interaction is part of the product for the customer.

The following two chapters examined the major existing and contrasting perspectives on service work. Chapter 2 focused on the new service management school which argues that increasingly service management should leave behind the 'old' production line approach to services. The way of the future involves the application of systematic HRM-related policies involving careful selection and recruitment, well-designed support systems, high-quality training, empowerment, teamwork, appropriate measurement, rewards and recognition, and the overall development of a service culture. These policies and the key idea that workers' and customers' satisfaction mirror each other lay the way open for a win : win : win scenario in service work. Customers win because there is higher service quality and individualised attention, workers win because they are now empowered to deliver the sort of quality service that they want to, and management wins because the satisfied customer becomes the loyal customer, and the loyal customer generates the most profitable revenue streams. These arguments of the influential new service management school were evaluated and found wanting. Despite claims that there is 'concrete evidence' confirming the satisfaction mirror, no such evidence exists. Further, other research into 'exemplar' service firms from which new service management writers pull their examples show a rather different and rather darker side to the nature of employment on the front line. Conceptually, the new service management school was criticised for its central unitarist assumption. Unitarism here appears in the guise of an apparently natural coalescing of interests around the customer. This assumption is flawed.

Some important critical sociological perspectives on service work were reviewed in Chapter 3, specifically Ritzer's McDonaldisation thesis, du

Gay's work on consumption and identity at work, and feminist analyses stressing the servile nature of contemporary service work. In each case it was argued that some important insights from these approaches were unfortunately accompanied by the tendency to see service work through a mono-focus. For instance, regarding the influential McDonaldisation thesis, while it is important to stress the continuing rationalising imperative in service management, it is inadequate to see this as the sole factor driving the organisation of contemporary service work. This chapter also showed that each of the differing perspectives has a different implication for the understanding of HRM in service work. This is an important point that has been central to the book – the idea that it is not possible to understand HRM without a fundamental understanding of the nature of service work itself.

Chapter 4 sought to provide such an understanding of service work. The starting point of the argument is that, given the competitive terrain in which service quality is important, *an understanding of service work requires an understanding of the customer*. A range of literature on the nature of the customer was examined. It was concluded that the contemporary customer should be seen as both formally rational and formally irrational, as seeking satisfaction alongside pleasure. In addition, customers should be seen as constituted both by producing organisations and by their own agency. In the context of front-line work this is played out through customers requiring service which is efficient and which allows the consumption of *the enchanting myth of customer sovereignty* – the feeling that the customer is in charge of the service interaction, that it revolves around him or her. This understanding of the customer implies that the organisation of front-line service work will be underpinned by dual logics, that of rationalisation and that of orientation to the formally irrational aspect of the customer.

Hence the book put forward a model of the *customer-oriented bureaucracy* as capturing the key elements in the organisation of contemporary service work. This model, for instance, suggests that the division of labour comes to be based not just on efficient task completion but also on the creation and maintenance of a relationship with a customer. The concept, therefore, points to a series of dilemmas for management in its organisation of service work. Within the customer-oriented bureaucracy a key management role is the creation of a (*fragile*) *social order* that can generate profit. The concept of the customer-oriented bureaucracy does not suggest exactly how management will seek to resolve these dilemmas, although the discussion did point to key examples of what management does in practice to try to meet the demands of the dual logics. Management actions will vary by context, but their actions in each context are informed by seeking to deal with the dilemmas highlighted by the customer-oriented bureaucracy. The social order that is created should be seen as fragile in the sense that while contradictions might lie latent, (systematically occurring) changes may make them manifest. *Labour-stretching* or *the customer moving from enchantment to disillusionment* and becoming irate may tip a situation of apparent balance into one of overt tension and conflict. The social order of the service workplace is also fragile in the sense that it relies on structuring the behaviour of both front-line workers and customers, each of whom is 'unmanageable' to some degree (Gabriel and Lang, 1995).

Through this approach, *HRM is best understood as operating at two levels*. First, it *promotes the dual, efficient and customer-oriented behaviour that is required from workers*. Second, it *seeks to cope with the inevitable ensuing tensions*. This means that HRM practices are necessarily hard and soft, emphasising both quantitative and qualitative aspects of work. In addition, the rhetorical level of HRM is crucial in seeking to redefine situations of potential tension as areas in which 'balance' is established. The concept of the customer-oriented bureaucracy also has clear implications for the experience of service work. Central here are the concepts of *tensions, spaces* and *fine lines*. While a negative interpretation of the customer-oriented bureaucracy might focus solely on the tensions created for the workforce by the existence of the dual logics underlying their work, my argument was that, as well as tensions, the structures of the customer-oriented bureaucracy also bring spaces and fine lines. Systematically, management may be caught in the ambiguities of the situation of trying to emphasise both efficiency and customer orientation, and this gives workers opportunities to create spaces, both individually and collectively, in their work for meaning and satisfaction. An important space for meaning for many front-line workers is that of relationships with socially embedded customers. Daily, front-line workers have also to walk fine lines in their work in which customer orientation and efficiency are somehow held together. The book's overview of research on the management and experience of hospitality work, call centre work and health care work showed a number of these themes in practice. While for each type of work there is a tendency for some analysts to stress either the rationalising or the customer-oriented imperatives as driving the organisation of the work, more sensitive accounts have analysed their dual existence and how they are played out in practice. Hotels, for instance, have been analysed in terms of their dualistic structures – structures which encompass both rationalisation and customer orientation. The major restructuring of health care work that has occurred in many economies has not simply been about rationalisation and efficiency-seeking, but has also involved significant 'customer'-oriented policies. Call centres are not simple examples of the application of Taylorism, although that is certainly part of the story. Much of the research into the experience of work in these occupations also connects well with the idea of tensions, spaces and fine lines. The contradictory nature of service work is particularly evident in the way the customer becomes 'our friend, the enemy', a simultaneous source of both satisfaction and pain for front-line workers.

While the concept of the customer-oriented bureaucracy, as a heuristic device, can illuminate many types of front-line work it is less useful when considering sales work. Sales work involves front-line workers actively stimulating demand, encouraging the customer to purchase a good or service. At its most extreme, sales work involves sales orientation rather than customer orientation, with the role of the firm and its workers prioritised in defining the customer's interests. It also implies an instrumental relationship between worker and customer. This extreme form of sales work is often managed through a largely contracted-out relationship between a firm and its workforce. HRM systems are often noticeable by their relative absence. It was argued that there are important factors pushing restructuring towards jobs involving both sales and service. Here HRM practices are crucial, not least in their attempts to create a new organisational culture that can uphold the management message that 'sales is service', and 'service is sales', a message that, nevertheless, is likely to be contested at the front line.

Chapters 7 and 8 examined aspects of service work that are central to the debates concerning its nature – empowerment/control, and emotional labour. The discussion of control highlighted its dualistic nature. Bureaucratic measurement of work processes operate alongside the operation of customer-related norms and values. Such a system of control draws on and generates a *consuming commitment*, but this is not all-consuming in its nature. Important, systematic contradictions exist in this system of control. Studies in a range of front-line settings have shown systematic rises in discretion, but it was argued that the overall level of discretion remains relatively limited. The customer-oriented bureaucracy points to systematic reasons for this. The concept also points to systematic reasons for many front-line workers remaining *information-receivers rather than knowledge-creators*. Front-line workers are simultaneously empowered and subservient in relation to customers. Empowerment can give way to an experience of subservience as the irate, disillusioned customer disrupts the fragile social order of the service workplace.

Through the lens of the customer-oriented bureaucracy, emotional labour is best conceptualised in terms of management requirements for *rationalised emotional labour*. Hochschild's path-breaking arguments about the inevitably harmful nature of emotional labour were found to have a number of important flaws. *Crucial to understanding both the positive and negative aspects of emotional labour are two questions: whose feeling rules, and in what sort of relationship with the customer?* The customer-oriented bureaucracy points to ambiguous answers to these questions for many front-line workers. HRM practices have important roles, both in generating committed emotional labour and in seeking to cope with the inevitable ensuing tensions. A key contested terrain here concerns whether coping is directed hierarchically and individually through a discourse of stress management or whether it occurs through front-line workers' *communities of coping*.

For a number of reasons, then, front-line workers cannot rely simply on decisions made by service management to work for their benefit. There is a need for a regulation of service work. This is necessary not least because of the extensive gendered segregation and disadvantage that exists in front-line work. Such segregation and disadvantage is unlikely to simply disappear, for the customer-oriented bureaucracy points to the systematic possibility for the *organisational internalisation of customer prejudices*. Gendered segregation is likely to be perpetuated in part because female service workers are more likely to allow customers to consume the enchanting myth of sovereignty. Women are disadvantaged in front-line work in that the occupations in which they predominate tend to be low-paid, to have a high percentage of part-time employment and to be associated with working unsocial hours, while also being associated with sexualised labour. Further, women in these occupations tend to have extremely restricted career opportunities. Indeed, *it is more likely for strong internal career ladders to function within a traditional bureaucracy than within a customer-oriented bureaucracy*. The ability of the existing legal framework to remedy these factors was examined, and important limitations in this framework highlighted. Certainly, in many areas, for the law to have any real bite it is necessary for trade unions to play a key role.

This begs the question of whether trade unions can be important bodies in the service economy. While it is wrong to see an inevitable link between the rise of the service economy and the decline of trade unions that has occurred in many economies, service work does throw up a number of important obstacles to trade unions. It was argued that trade unions may be able to overcome these obstacles through a creative interplay of organising and partnership approaches, focusing on both pay and work organisation – an interplay that matches the everyday contradictions faced by the service workers whom they must recruit and organise. Unions need to connect with the daily experiences of front-line workers, to put forward both a positive strategy of regulating for the opportunity to deliver meaningful service and a defensive strategy of seeking protection from the disillusioned and irate customer. Trade unions in service work can also tie into wider politics of protests against particularly dehumanised forms of capitalism – *a politics based on making connections between consumption and production*. They can do this by setting forth a sustaining ideology of *humanising and civilising production and consumption simultaneously*. Chaplin the singing waiter needs a trade union to regulate the employment relationship and the service encounter so that his work is less likely to be demeaning and more likely to be engaging and meaningful.

Implications for the wider study of HRM

Human resource management in service work has clearly progressed beyond the approach of the restaurant manager who pushes Chaplin out to sing in front of the customers. This book has argued that to have an adequate understanding of HRM it is necessary first to have an adequate sociological understanding of the work to which and around which HRM is applied. With this wider view of service work as customer-oriented bureaucracy established, the book presented the main role of HRM as attempting to facilitate a (fragile) social order that can generate profit. Both of these points – the way of deriving an understanding of HRM from a wider conceptualisation of the nature of work organisation, and the actual substantive understanding of HRM so derived – have resonance for HRM more generally (that is, for HRM in information-based white-collar work and in manufacturing, as well as in front-line work).

The enduring analyses of the employment relationship and its management have been derived from a profound sociological analysis of the nature of work. Thus, for instance, Fox's (1974) insight – that management attempts to create high-trust employment relations are likely to founder if *the nature of work* is effectively low-trust in nature with workers given little discretion in their jobs – still resounds today. Unfortunately, too many analyses of HRM have been constructed without an attempt to connect with a sociological understanding of the wider nature of work. At its worst, this approach gives rise to simple taxonomic descriptions of HRM practices. Thus one of the great cul-de-sacs in the study of HRM features attempts to create the definitive list of factors that differentiate HRM from personnel management. Some 'models' of HRM do not even feature the nature of work as a relevant factor (Fombrum *et al.*, 1984), while others consider it as only one small aspect among many (Beer *et al.*, 1984; Guest, 1987). Without an understanding of the nature of work, it becomes easy for writers to write blandly about the strategic 'fit' of HRM and business strategy. Such approaches to the study of HRM have little resonance (except, perhaps, in terms of their potential to seduce practitioners), and offer few real insights. Adequate understandings of HRM in specific contexts need to be based on adequate understandings of the nature of work in those contexts. This book has attempted to do this for the context of front-line work.

It may be, indeed, that the way in which HRM is related to the nature of work in service settings finds parallels in other settings. Here I will argue that the idea of HRM working at two levels in seeking to create an (inevitably fragile) social order may indeed help to make sense of some of the key debates on HRM more generally – debates on whether HRM is 'hard' or 'soft', debates on the relationship between rhetoric and reality within HRM and debates on the degree to which HRM is inevitably associated with individualisation within employment.

The contradictory nature of service work finds parallels in studies of manufacturing and information-based white-collar work that stress the increasingly contradictory demands made of workers to deliver both quantity and quality in production. To take the example of manufacturing, a number of theorists of production have pointed to a fundamental break from Taylorist, Fordist mass production because of the rising importance of quality within ever-growing niche markets (Piore and Sabel, 1984; see also Hyman, 1991). More discerning analysts, however, have suggested that the emphasis on quality does not mean the replacement of the rationalising imperative of management (Legge, 1995). In Hyman's (1991) phrase, there is 'change and continuity'. Demands for efficiency are not replaced, but are joined by demands for quality. Insightful analyses similarly show this dualism at the heart of TQM (Wilkinson *et al.*, 1998). If work in front-line, manufacturing and information-based settings is increasingly structured in a dualistic – and potentially contradictory – manner then it may be appropriate to consider the conceptualisation of HRM as attempting to facilitate a (fragile) social order as having general relevance.

Such an analysis would point to *the systematic coexistence of 'hard' and 'soft' elements within HRM policies and practices* (Marchington and Grugulis, 2000). Sisson and Marginson's analysis of HRM in the UK is consistent with this approach. They see that 'the dividing line between "soft" and "hard" versions of HRM is very fine' because management is faced with simultaneously contradictory imperatives: 'faced with ever-increasing demands of competition many managers see themselves engaged in the delicate exercise of simultaneously cutting costs and manufacturing yet greater consent' (1995, p. 110). The simultaneous pressures to deliver quality and quantity efficiently mean that many managers beyond the front-line workplace are turning to HRM as a way of creating a fragile social order out of contradictory pressures. This approach moves analysis away from sterile debates concerning whether to characterise certain HRM practices as 'hard' or 'soft'. Further, it combines Hyman's (1987) concept of the inevitable 'partial failure' of management strategy with an understanding of the dynamic, fluid nature of workplace relations. The concept of a fragile social order suggests that while workforce commitment may be created, the basis of such commitment is systematically subject to potential disruption from the interplay of contradictory forces.[1]

An understanding of HRM as facilitating the establishment of a (fragile) social order also allows for a grounded understanding of the systematic differences between the rhetorics of HRM and its realities that have been picked up by acute observers (Legge, 1989 and 1995; Keenoy and Anthony, 1992; Sisson, 1994). Recall that HRM was analysed as working at two levels. First, it seeks to generate the appropriate quality-conscious *and* efficient behaviour from the workforce. Second, it serves to cope with the inevitable ensuing tensions. A key way in which an organisation may seek to cope with tensions deriving from the contradictory nature of work demands is to create organisational symbols and an organisational language in which tensions and conflict are defined away. Thus, for instance, social situations of potential contradiction, tension and conflict become defined as situations of 'balance'. When tension gives rise to an overt breakdown of the social order (perhaps through a sharp rise in turnover), the key managerial task becomes finding the 'right balance' in the structuring of work and then communicating this to the workforce. The rhetoric of balance and mutuality, and the gap between this and the combination of hard and soft policies pursued, are systematic parts of HRM that flow from seeing its role as attempting to construct a social order amidst contradictory logics in the workplace.

The rise of HRM has coincided with the decline of collective approaches to managing labour. Some authors have suggested that this represents a managerial attempt to bypass, marginalise and weaken trade unions (see the discussion by Legge, 1995), and while this is clearly one part of the story, especially in the USA (Jacoby, 1998), nevertheless an equally important part relates to the aim of HRM in constructing a fragile social order amidst contradictory pressure. Such a social order is likely to be best constructed by identifying, for each *individual* worker, 'points of balance' between the demands of quality and efficiency. If work can be structured around these points of balance then tensions will tend to become manifest less often. If management just sets a general, 'collective point of balance' then tensions may quickly surface for many individual workers, while for other workers such work demands might be easily accommodated with little tension. Thus, the more contradictory the demands placed on the workforce within the labour process, the more likely that individualist HRM practices, such as performance assessment, appraisals, performance-related pay, counselling and stress management are developed by management. Seeing HRM as a key part of managerial attempts to create a (fragile) social order in the workplace, therefore, offers a useful way to analyse HRM more generally.

The service economy

Finally, what kind of economy is the contemporary service economy? This is a difficult question to answer and one that has occasioned a range of responses. On one extreme there are characterisations of the *servile* economy (Gorz, 1989, p. 156; Lipietz, 1989, p. 40), on the other there are implicit arguments that service economy is necessarily becoming the *knowledge-intensive* economy. Somewhere in between there are arguments that we live in a *McDonaldised* society. The analysis in this book contains little to support such approaches. For the vast majority of front-line workers, servility only captures a small part of the social relations of the workplace. Yes, there is an increased tendency for service organisations to place front-line workers in positions where they are expected to put up with abusive behaviour from customers, and this does suggest structured servility to the customer. Similarly, there is rising income inequality between the lower-paid workers (who are often found in female-dominated front-line occupations) and the higher-paid skilled workers and knowledge workers (Herzenberg *et al.*, 1998). However, it is economic determinism of the worst kind to make claims about the servile nature of social relations simply on the basis of income data. Indeed, an understanding of the dual logics of customer orientation and rationalisation informing front-line work highlight important limits to structured servility. Crucially, to be servile to a customer is inefficient. Management needs to serve customers efficiently and they charge and train front-line workers to take control of interaction with customers. Further, the axes of management recruitment and socialisation approaches revolve around empathy and identification with customers rather than servility towards them. As to the view of service society as the McDonaldised society, Chapter 3 offered a summary and critique of Ritzer's arguments. Suffice it to say here that such a view is both contradicted by the research evidence and rests upon the misplaced assumption that customer orientation and moves towards service quality never happened, and that rationalisation remains the sole logic at play in service work.

In contrast to the view of the servile economy and the McDonaldised society is Frenkel *et al.*'s (1999, p. 276) argument that 'in time service . . . work will resemble knowledge work, which combines weak vertical relations with strong lateral relations'. This argument rests on the assumption that 'greater product variety and more frequent policy and procedural changes suggest that service workers will require increasingly better access to information, which they will need to be able to readily convert to usable knowledge' (p. 272). Related arguments were reviewed in Chapter 7's examination of empowerment in front-line work. Here the greater need for information flows and communication to front-line workers were also noted. But there remains a considerable gap between positioning the majority of front-line workers as information-receivers and positioning them as knowledge-creators. Frenkel *et al.* make a huge and unsupported leap in the quotation above by claiming that front-line workers will need access to more *information* which they will then need to convert to *knowledge*. Further, the picture of a gradual metamorphosis of service work into knowledge work rests on assumption that a particular form of customer orientation constitutes the dominant logic structuring service work. Such an assumption is misplaced: an understanding of service work as informed by dual logics leads to the conclusion of Chapter 7 that discretion and informational flows have increased in front-line jobs, but that there exist important limits to further significant increases.

The force of the argument in this book suggests a characterisation of the service economy as a *contradictory* one, and one which is *based upon and reproduces gendered disadvantage*. It is contradictory in the sense that front-line workers are placed in jobs which pull them one way and then the other, which give them both tensions and spaces, and contradictory also in the sense that managers must seek to construct a fragile order out of the dual imperatives of customer orientation and efficiency. Further, customers find themselves wooed by the enchanting myth of customer sovereignty, only to periodically, and systematically, meet disillusionment. Although the rising service economy has brought with it increasing female participation in paid employment, Chapter 9 highlighted systematic ways in which structuring forces of front-line work entrench forms of segregation and disadvantage experienced by women.

The book's analysis has suggested a range of key political economic battles over the nature of the service economy in the medium term. One is likely to relate to attempts to reconstitute regulation to challenge the entrenched segregation and disadvantage within the service workforce. Another crucial issue concerns how far the contradictory service economy leans more towards either the *sales economy* or the *civil society*. Chapter 6 highlighted management moves towards the development of sales aims in many front-line jobs which had been primarily service-oriented. Further, in short-termist, low-trust deregulated economies (Korczynski, 2000), the potential for a quick profit from commission-driven hard sales may be an easy and increasingly popular route to profit creation. Such sales work, in which customers are punters to be manipulated, is hardly the sort of civilised production and consumption that is a fledgling part of some trade union strategies. Trade unions in coalition with collective consumer groups as key institutions of civil society, between the individual and state, may have to play a crucial role in seeking to make the service society a more civil one.

And so as Chaplin and his truelove go walking down the open road arm in arm in late modern times, we can do more than wish them well. Key political economic issues are still to be resolved that will determine the sort of service jobs that they are likely to have in the next town along the road. As citizens, academics, trade unionists, customers, managers and students, we each have a role to play in resolving these issues.

Note

1   While the concept of HRM as seeking to create a (fragile) social order may have general resonance, a strong case can be made that in the front-line workplace the *fragility* of the social order is likely to be greater. The direct presence of the customer within the labour process is the key distinguishing factor here. The discussion in Chapter 7 highlighted that in the service workplace management can develop a process of consuming commitment. As I argue elsewhere (Korczynski, 2002), the customer becomes a means around which to create a new work ethic. But this is not all that is created; it also brings with it *an ethic of work* which can potentially inform resistance to, and/or reinterpretation of, management policies, potentially shattering the careful 'balance' created through sophisticated individualist HRM policies. Further, as Gabriel and Lang (1995) point out,

customers are to an important degree 'unmanageable', and the unpredictable actions of customers can also directly upset the fragile social order. The sudden, unanticipated surge in overall customer demand forces management into the stretching of front-line labour, potentially resulting in tensions bubbling to the surface. Equally, the aggressive and irate behaviour of customers, enchanted but then disillusioned with the myth of customer sovereignty, can constitute an important disruption to the fragility of the front-line workplace. The presence of the customer, then, would appear to increase the fragility of any balance created by management.

References

Abercrombie, N. (1991) 'The privilege of the producer', in Keat, R. and Abercrombie, N. (eds), *Enterprise Culture*, London: Routledge, 43–57.

Acker, J. (1989) *Doing Comparable Worth*, Philadelphia: Temple.

Acker, J. (1990) 'Hierarchies, jobs, bodies: A theory of gendered organisations', *Gender and Society*, 4: 139–58.

Ackers, P. and Payne, J. (1998) 'British trade unions and social partnership: Rhetoric, reality and strategy', *The International Journal of Human Resource Management*, 9, 3: 529–49.

Ackroyd, S. and Bolton, S. (1999) 'It is not Taylorism: Mechanisms of work intensification in the provision of gynaecological services in a NHS hospital', *Work, Employment and Society*, 13, 2: 369–87.

Adkins, L. (1995) *Gendered Work*, Milton Keynes, Open University Press.

Adler, P. (1986) 'New technologies, new skills', *California Management Review*, Fall, 9–28.

Agnew, J. (1993) 'Coming up for air: Consumer culture in historical perspective', in Brewer, J. and Porter, R. (eds), *Consumption and the World of Goods*, New York: Routledge.

Aiken, L. and Sloane, D. (1997) 'Effects of organisational innovations in AIDS care on burnout among urban hospital nurses', *Work and Occupations*, 24, 4: 453–77.

Akehurst, G. and Alexander, N. (1996) *The Internationalisation of Retailing*, London: Frank Cass.

Alferoff, C. and Knights, D. (2000) 'Quality time and "the beautiful call"', Paper presented at Call Centre Workship at Gerhard-Mercator University, Duisburg, December.

Alfino, M., Caputo, J. and Wynard, R. (eds) (1998) *McDonaldization Revisited: Critical Essays in Consumer Culture*, London: Praeger.

Appelbaum, E. and R. Batt. (1994) *The New American Workplace*, Ithaca, New York: ILR Press.

Arzbacher, S., Holtgrewe, U. and Kerst, C. (2000) 'Call centres: constructing flexibility', Paper presented at Call Centre Workship at Gerhard-Mercator University, Duisburg, December.

205

Ashforth, B. and Humphreys, R. (1993) 'Emotional labor in service roles: The influence of identity', *Academy of Management Review*, 18, 1: 88–115.

Ashforth, B. and Tomiuk, M. (2000) 'Emotional labour and authenticity: views from service agents', in S. Fineman (ed.) *Emotions in organisations*, London: Sage, 184–203.

Atkinson, J. (1985) 'Flexibility: Planning for an uncertain future', *Manpower Policy and Practice*, 1 (summer): 26–9.

ASU (Australian Service Union) (2000) *ASU Stress Survey*, Canberra.

Bain, G. and Price, R. (1983) 'Union growth', in Bain, G. (ed.) *Industrial Relations in Britain*, Oxford: Blackwell, 3–34.

Bain, P. and Taylor, P. (2000) 'Worker attitudes, resistance and collective organisation in call centres', Paper presented at Labour Process Conference, University of Strathclyde, April.

Baker, P., Yoels, W. and Clair, J. (1995) 'Emotional expression during medical encounters: social dis-ease and the medical gaze', in James, V. and Gabe, J. (eds), *Health and the Sociology of Emotions*, Oxford: Blackwell, 173–99.

Baldry, C., Bain, P. and Taylor, P. (1998) ' "Bright satanic offices": Intensification, control and team Taylorism', in Thompson, P. and Warhurst, C. (eds) *Workplaces of the Future, Basingstoke*: Macmillan, 163–83.

Ball, K. and Wilson, D. (2000) 'Power, control and computer-based performance monitoring: Repertoires, resistance and subjectivities', *Organisation Studies*, 21, 3: 539–66.

Barbee, C. and Bott, V. (1991) 'Customer treatment as a mirror of employee treatment', *Advanced Management Journal*, 5: 27–31.

Barley, S. (1993) 'What do technicians do?', Philadelphia: National Center on the Educational Quality of the Workforce.

Barlow, J. and Maul, D. (1999) 'Maintaining superior customer service during periods of peak demand', in Zemke, R. and Woods, J. (eds), *Best Practices in Customer Service*, New York: HRD Press, 162–70.

Batt, R. (2000) 'Strategic segmentation in front-line services: Matching customers, employees and human resource systems', *International Journal of Human Resource Management*, 11, 3: 540–61.

Baudrillard, J. (1970/1988) 'Consumer society', in Poster, M. (ed.), *Jean Baudrillard: Selected Writings*. Cambridge: Polity Press.

Bauman, Z. (1988) 'Is there a postmodern sociology?', *Theory, Culture and Society*, 5: 217–37.

Bauman, Z. (1989) *Modernity and the Holocaust*, London: Polity Press.

Baumol, W. (1967) 'Macro-economics of unbalanced growth: The anatomy of urban crisis', *American Economic Review*, 57: 415–26.

Bebbington, D. (1998) 'Speech and Language Therapists, Science and the Health Division of Labour', Paper at the Work, Employment and Society conference, Cambridge, September.

Beer, M., Spector, B. and Lawrence, P. (1984) *Managing Human Assets*, New York: Free Press.

Bell, D. (1973) *The Coming of Post-Industrial Society*, New York: Basic Books.

Bell, D. (1976) *The Cultural Contradictions of Capitalism*, London: Heinemann.

Bellamy, C. (1996) 'Transforming social security beneifts administration for the twenty-first century: Towards one-stop services and the client group principle?', *Public Administration*, 74, 2: 159–79.

Belt, V. (2000) ' "Call girls": Women, work and the telephone', Paper presented at the Labour Process Conference, University of Strathclyde, April.

Belt, V., Richardson, R. and Webster, J. (1999) 'Smiling down the phone: Women's work in telephone call centres', Paper at the call centre conference, London School of Economics, March.

Benner, P. and Wrubel, J. (1989) *The Primacy of Caring*, Menlo Pk, CA: Addison-Wesley.

Benson, S. (1978) 'The clerking sisterhood: Rationalisation and the work culture of saleswomen in American department stores, 1890–1960', *Radical America*, 12: 41–55.

Benson, S. (1986) *Counter Cultures*, Chicago: University of Illinois Press.

Berggren, C. (1993) 'Lean production: The end of history?', *Work, Employment and Society*, 7, 2: 163–88.

Berheide, C. (1988) 'Women in sales and service occupations', in Stromberg, A. and Harkess, S. (eds), *Women Working: Theories and Facts in Perspective*, Mountain View, CA: Mayfield Publishing, 241–57.

Berry, L. and Parasuraman, A. (1991) *Marketing Services*, New York: Free Press.

Beynon, H. (1992) 'The end of the industrial worker?', in Abercrombie, N. and Warde, A. (eds), *Social Change in Britain*, Cambridge: Polity Press, 167–83.

Biggart, N. (1988) *Charismatic Capitalism*, University of Chicago Press.

Bitner, J., Booms, B. and Tetreault, M. (1990) 'The service encounter: diagnosing favourable and unfavourable incidents', *Journal of Marketing*, 54, Jan: 71–84.

Blau, P. (1974) *On the Nature of Organisations*, New York: John Wiley.

Blauner, R. (1964) *Alienation and Freedom*, University of Chicago Press.

Bluestone, B. and Harrison, B. (1988) *The Great U-Turn: Corporate Restructuring and the Polarising of America*, New York: Basic Books.

Boella, M. (1996) *Human Resource Management in the Hospitality Industry*, London: Stanley Thornes Ltd.

Boje, D. (1991) 'The storytelling organisation: A study of story performance in an office-supply firm', *Administrative Science Quarterly*, 36: 106–26.

Bolton, S. (2000) Who's controlling who?: NHS hospital nurses and 'new' management', Paper presented at Labour Process Conference, University of Strathclyde, April.

Bowen, D. (1990) 'Interdisciplinary study of service', *Journal of Business Research*, 20: 71–9.

Bowen, D. (1996) 'Market-focused HRM in service organisations: Satisfying internal and external customers', *Journal of Market-Focused Management*, 1: 31–47.

Bowen, D. and Lawler, E. iii (1992) 'The empowerment of service workers: what, why, how and when', *Sloan Management Review*, 33: 31–9.

Bowen, D. and Lawler, E. (1995) 'Organising for service: Empowerment or production line?', in Glynn, W. and Barnes, J. (eds), *Understanding Service Management*, Chichester: John Wiley, 269–94.

Bowey, A. (1976) *The Sociology of Organisations*, London: Hodder & Stoughton.

Boyd, C. and Bain, P. (1999) ' "Fighting the clock and always rushing": Airline cabin crews and the intensification of work', Paper presented at the Labour Process Conference, Royal Holloway College, University of London.

Bradley, H. (1989) *Men's Work, Women's Work*, Cambridge: Polity Press.

Bradley, H. (1999) *Gender and Power in the Workplace*, Basingstoke: Macmillan.

Bradley, H., Erickson, M., Stephenson, C. and Williams, S. (2000) *Myths at Work*, Cambridge: Polity Press.

Bratton, J. and Gold, J. (1999) *Human Resource Management: Theory and Practice*, Basingstoke: Macmillan.

Braverman, H. (1974) *Labor and Monopoly Capital*, New York: Monthly Review Press.

Bronfenbrenner, K. (2000) 'The American labour movement and the resurgence in union organising', in P. Fairbrother, and C. Yates (eds), *Trade Union Renewal and Organising*, London: Marsell.

Bronfenbrenner, K., Friedman, S., Hurd, R., Oswald, R. and Seeber, R. (eds) (1998) *Organizing to Win*, Ithaca, NY: ILR/Cornell Unviersity Press

Browne, J. (1973) *The Used Car Game*, Lexington: Lexington Books.

Bryman, A. (1995) *Disney and His Worlds*, London: Routledge.

Bryman, A. (1999) 'The Disneyization of society', *Sociological Review*, 47, 1: 25–47.

Burawoy, M. (1979) *Manufacturing Consent*, Chicago: University of Chicago Press.

Burawoy, M. (1981) 'Terrains of contest: factory and State under capitalism and socialism', *Socialist Review* (USA), 11, 4.

Burawoy, M. (1985) *The Politics of Production*, London: Verso.

Burns, T. and Stalker, G. (1961) *The Management of Innovation*, London: Tavistock.

Burrows, R. and C. Marsh (1992) 'Consumption, class and contemporary sociology', in R. Burrows, and C. Marsh (eds), *Consumption and Class*, Basingstoke: Macmillan, 1–14.

Butler, S. and Skipper, J. (1981) 'Working for tips', *Sociological Quarterly*, 22: 15–27.

Butterfield, S. (1985) *Amway: The Cult of Free Enterprise*, Boston: South End Press.

Callaghan, G. and Thompson, P. (2000) 'Edwards revisited: Technical control and call centres', Paper presented at Labour Process Conference, University of Strathclyde, April.

Campbell, B. (1982) 'Women: Not what they bargained for', *Marxism Today*, March.

Campbell, C. (1987) *The Romantic Ethic and the Spirit of Modern Consumerism*, Oxford: Blackwell.

Campbell, C. (1995) 'The sociology of consumption', in Miller, D. (ed.), *Acknowledging Consumption*, London: Routledge, 96–126.

Canning, V. (1999) *Being Successful in Customer Care*, Dublin: Blackhall'.

Carlzon, J. (1987) *The Moment of Truth*, Cambridge, MA: Ballinger.

Carvel, J. (2001) 'Nurses head for first union action', *Guardian*, 2 March.

Castells, M. (1996) *The Rise of The Network Society: The Information Age*, vol. 1, Oxford: Blackwell.

Castells, M. and Aoyama, Y. (1994) 'Paths towards the information society', *International Labour Review*, 133, 1: 5–33.

Child, J. (1972) 'Organisation structure, environment and performance: the role of strategic choice', *Sociology*, 6, 1: 1–22.

Clark, C. (1940) *The Conditions of Economic Progress*, London: Macmillan.

Clarke, M. (2000) *Citizens' Financial Futures*, Aldershot: Ashgate.

Clarke, M., Smith, D. and McConville, M. (1994) *Slippery Customers: Estate Agents, the Public and Regulation*, London: Blackstone.

Cleveland, N. (1999) 'Home-care workers' vote for union a landmark for Labor', *Los Angeles Times*, February, 26.

Cleveland, B. and Mayben, J. (1997) *Call Center Management on Fast Forward*, Annapolis, MD: Call Center Press.

Cobble, D. (1991) 'Organizing the postindustrial work force: Lessons from the history of waitress unionism', *Industrial and Labor Relations Review*, 44, 3: 419–36.

Cobble, D. (1996) 'The prospects for unionism in a service society', in MacDonald, C. and Sirianni, C. (eds), *Working in the Service Society*, Philadelphia: Temple University Press, 333–58.

Cockburn, C. (1985) *Machinery of Dominance*, London: Pluto.

Collinson, D., Knights, D. and Collinson, M. (1990) *Managing to Discriminate*, London: Routledge.

Connelly, M. and Rhoton, P. (1988) 'Women in direct sales', in Statham, A. (ed.), *The Worth of Women's Work*, New York: State University of New York, 245–64.

Coote, A. and Campbell, B. (1987) *Sweet Freedom*, Oxford: Blackwell.

Corrigan, P. (1997) *The Sociology of Consumption*, London: Sage.

Crang, P. (1993) 'A new service society', PhD Thesis, Department of Geography, University of Cambridge.

Cressey, P. and Scott, P. (1992) 'Employment, technology and industrial relations in the UK clearing banks: Is the honeymoon over?', *New Technology, Work and Employment*, 3: 83–96.

Crompton, R. and Sanderson, K. (1990) *Gendered Jobs and Social Change*, London: Unwin Hyman.

Cully, M., Woodland, S., O'Reilly, A. and Dix, G. (1999) *Britain at Work*, London: Routledge.

Curran, M. (1986) *Stereotypes and Selection: Gender and Family in the Recruitment Process*, Equal Opportunities Commission Research Report.

Dann, D. and Hornsey, T. (1986) 'Towards a theory of interdepartmental conflict in hotels', *International Journal of Hospitality Management*, 5, 1: 23–8.

Datamonitor (1998) *Call Centres in Europe*, London.

Daycare Trust (2000) *Shift Parents*, London: Daycare Trust.

Dean, E. and Kunze, K. (1995) 'Bureau of Labor Statistics productivity measures for service industries', in Harker, P. (ed.), *The Service Productivity and Quality Challenge*, Dordrecht: Kluwer, 11–42.

Delaunay, J. and Gardrey, J. (1992) *Services in Economic Thought*, London: Kluwer Academic Publishers.

Dickens, L. (2000) 'Still wasting resources? Equality in employment', in Bach, S. and Sisson, K. (eds), *Personnel Management*, Oxford: Blackwell, 137–70.

DOH (Department of Health) (1987) *Promoting Better Health*, London: HMSO.

Du Gay, P. (1996) *Consumption and Identity at Work*, London: Sage.

Du Gay, P. (2000a) 'Enterprise and its futures: a response to Fournier and Grey', *Organisation*, 7, 1: 165–184.

Du Gay, P. (2000b) *In Praise of Bureaucracy*, London: Sage.

Du Gay, P. and Salaman, G. (1992) 'The cult(ure) of the customer', *Journal of Management Studies*, 29: 615–33.

Dunlop, M. (1986) 'Is a science of caring possible?', *Journal of Advanced Nursing*, 11: 661–70.

DuPuy, F. (1999) *The Customer's Victory*, Basingstoke: Macmillan.

Durr, W. (1996) *A World-Class Inbound Call Center*, Teleprofessional.

Eaton, S. (1996) ' "The customer is always interesting": Unionized Harvard clericals renegotiate work relationships', in MacDonald, C. and Sirianni, C. (eds), *Working in the Service Society*, Philadelphia: Temple Unviersity Press, 291–332.

Eaton, S. (2000) 'Beyond "unloving care": Linking human resource management and patient care quality in nursing homes', *International Journal of Human Resource Management*, 11, 3.

Edmonds, J. (1986) 'New wave unions: An interview with Beatrix Campbell', *Marxism Today*, September.

Edwards, P. K. (1995) 'Introduction' in Edwards, P. K. (ed.), *Industrial Relations*, Oxford: Blackwell.

Edwards, R. (1979) *Contested Terrain*, London: Heinemann.

Edwards, T. (2000) *Contradictions of Consumption*, Milton Keynes: Open University Press.

Elder, L. and Rolens, L. (1985) *Waitress: America's Unsung Heroine*, Santa Barbara, CA: Capra.

Elston, M. (1995) 'The politics of professional power: Medicine in a changing health service', in Gabe, J., Kelleher, D. and Williams, G. (eds), *Challenging Medicine*, London: Routledge.

Equal Opportunities Commission (1999) *Good Practice Guides – Job Evaluation Schemes Free of Sex Bias*, Manchester.

Erickson, R. J. and Wharton, A. (1997) 'Inauthenticity and depression: assessing the consequences of interactive service work', *Work and Occupations* 24, 2: 188–213.

Esping-Andersen, G. (1990) *The Three Worlds of Welfare Capitalism*, Cambridge: Polity.

Etzioni, A. (1961) *A Comparative Analysis of Complex Organisations*. New York: Free Press.

Ewen, S. (1988) *All Consuming Images: The Politics of Style in Contemporary Culture*, New York: Basic Books.

Fairclough, N. (1991) 'What might we mean by "enterprise discourse"?', in R. Keat and N. Abercrombie (eds), *Enterprise Culture*, London: Routledge, 38–57.

Fearfull, A. (1996) 'Clerical workers, clerical skills: Case studies from credit management', *New Technology, Work and Employment*, 11: 55–65.

Ferguson, K. (1984) *The Feminist Case Against Bureaucracy*, Philadelphia: Temple University Press.

Fernie, S. and Metcalf, D. (1997) '(Not) Hanging on the Telephone: Payment Systems in the New Sweatshops', Centre for Economic Performance Paper, London School of Economics.

Filby, M. (1992) 'The figures, the personality and the bums: service work and sexuality', *Work, Employment and Society*, 6, 1: 23–42.

Fine, B. (1995) 'From political economy to consumption', in Miller, C. (ed.), *Acknowledging Consumption*, London: Routledge, 127–63.

Fineman, S. (ed.), (1993) *Emotions in Organisations*, London: Sage.

Fineman, S. (1996) 'Emotion and organizing' in S. Clegg, C. Hardy, W. Nord (eds) *Handbook of Organisation Studies*, London: Sage, 543–564.

Fineman, S. and Sturdy, A. (2001) ' "Struggles" for the control of affect', in Sturdy, A., Grugulis, I. and Willmott, H. (eds), *Customer Service*, Basingstoke: Macmillan.

Fischer, E., Gainer, B. and Bristor, J. (1997) 'The sex of the service provider', *Journal of Retailing*, 73: 361–82.

Fisher, A. (1935) *The Clash of Progress and Security*, London: Macmillan.

Fitchett, J. and McDonagh, P. (2001) 'Relationship marketing' in Sturdy, A. Grugulis, I. and Willmott, H. (ed.), *Customer Service*, Basingstoke: Macmillan/Palgrave.

Fitzgerald, L., Johnstron, R., Brignall, S., Silvestro, R. and Voss, C. (1991) *Performance Measurement in Service Businesses*, Chartered Institute of Management Accounting, UK.

Flanders, A. (1970) *Management and Unions*, London: Faber.

Flynn, R. (1992) *Structures of Control in Health Management*, London: Routledge.

Fombrum, C., Tichy, N. and Devanna, M. (eds), (1984) *Strategic Human Resource Management*, New York: Wiley.

Foner, N. (1994) *The Caregiving Dilemma*, Berkeley: University of California Press.

Ford, M. (1999) *Surveillance and Privacy at Work*, London: Institute of Employment Rights.

Foster, D. and Hoggett, P. (1999) 'Change in the benefits agency: Empowering the exhausted worker?', *Work, Employment and Society*, 13: 19–39.

Foucault, M. (1979) *Discipline and Punish*, New York: Vintage.

Fourastie, J. (1949) *The Great White Hope of the XXth Century*, Paris: Gallimard.

Fournier, V. and Grey, C. (1999) 'Too much, too little, and too often: a critique of du Gay's analysis of enterprise', *Organization*, 6, 1: 107–122.

Fox, A. (1966) 'Industrial sociology and industrial relations', Donovan Commission Research paper 3, London: HMSO.

Fox, A. (1974) *Beyond Contract*, London: Faber.

Freeman, R. and Rogers, J. (1999) *What Workers Want*, Ithaca, NY: ILR Press.

Frenkel, S., Korczynski, M., Shire, K. and Tam, M. (1999) *On the Front Line: Work Orgnization in the Service Economy*, Ithaca, NY: ILR/Cornell University Press.

Frenkel, S., Tam, M., Korczynski, M. and Shire, K. (1998) 'Beyond bureaucracy? Work organisation in call centres', *International Journal of Human Resource Management*, 9: 957–79.

Frenzen, J., Hirsch, P. and Zerillo, P. (1994) 'Consumption, preferences, and changing lifestyles', in Smelser, N. and Swedberg, R. (eds) *The Handbook of Economic Sociology*, Princeton University Press, 403–25.

Friedman, A. (1977) *Industry and Labour*, London, Macmillan.

Friedson, E. (1970) *Medical Dominance: The Social Structure of Medical Care*, New York: Atherton Press.

Fuller, L. and Smith, V. (1991) 'Consumers' reports: management by customers in a changing economy', *Work, Employment and Society*, 5, 1: 1–16.

Gabriel, Y. (1991) 'Turning facts into stories and stories into facts', *Human Relations*, 44, 8: 857–75.

Gabriel, Y. and Lang, T. (1995) *The Unmanageable Consumer: Contemporary Consumption and Its Fragmentations*. London: Sage.

Geary, J. (1992) 'Employment flexibility and human resource management', *Work, Employment and Society*, 6: 251–70.

George, J. and Brief, A. (1992) 'Feeling good – doing good: A conceptual analysis of the mood at work-organisational spontaneity relationship', *Psychological Bulletin*, 112, 2: 310–29.

Gershuny, J. and Miles, I. (1983) *The New Service Economy*, London: Frances Pinter.

Gerth, H. and Mills, C. W. (1958) *From Max Weber: Essays in Sociology*, New York: Oxford University Press.

Geschwender, J. with Geschwender, L. (1999) 'Gender, occupational sex segregation, and the labor process', in Wardell, M., Steiger, T. and Meiskins, P. (eds), *Rethinking the Labor Process*, NY: State University of New York, 149–88.

Glazer, N. (1983) 'Towards a self-service society?', *The Public Interest*, 70: 66–90.

Glazer, N. (1993) *Women's Paid and Unpaid Labor*, Philadelphia: Temple University Press.

Gleick, J. (1987) *Chaos: Making a New Science*, New York: Penguin.

Goffee, R. and Scase, R. (1995) *Corporate Realities: The Dynamics of Large and Small Organisations*, London: Routledge.

Goffman, E. (1983) 'The interaction order', *American Sociological Review*, 48: 1–17.

Gorz, A. (1989) *Critique of Economic Reason*, London: Verso.

Gospel, H. (1983) 'Management structures and strategies', in Gospel, H. and Littler, C. (eds), *Managerial Strategies and Industrial Relations*, London: Heinemann.

Granovetter, M. (1985) 'Economic action and social structure: the problem of embeddedness'. *American Journal of Sociology*, 91: 481–510.

Grant, R. and Higgins, C. (1989) 'Monitoring service workers via computer', *National Productivity Review*, 8, 2: 101–12.

Griffiths, L. (1997) 'Accomplishing teams: Teamwork and categorisation in two community mental health teams', *Sociological Review*, 45, 1: 59–78.

Grimshaw, D., Beynon, H., Rubery, J. and Ward, D. (2000) 'The "Blairing" of the public and the private: towards the "corporate economy"', Paper presented at the Labour Process Conference, University of Strathclyde, April.

Grint, K. (1998) *The Sociology of Work*, Oxford: Polity.

Gronroos, C. (1990) *Service Marketing and Management*, Lexington, MA: Lexington Books.

Guerrier, Y. (1999) *Organisational Behaviour in Hotels and Restaurants*, Chichester: John Wiley.

Guerrier, Y. and Adib, A. (1999) 'Service or servile: issues of gender, ethnicity and sexual identity among hotel workers', paper at EGOS conference, University of Warwick, July.

Guerrier, Y. and Adib, A. (2000) ' "No we don't provide that service": The harassment of hotel employees by customers', *Work, Employment and Society*, 14, 4.

Guest, D. (1987) 'Human resource management and industrial relations', *Journal of Management Studies*, 24, 5: 503–21.

Guest, D. (1990) 'Human resource management and the American dream', *Journal of Management Studies*, 27, 4: 378–97.

Guest, D. (1995) 'Human resource management, trade unions and industrial relations', in Storey, J. (ed.), *Human Resource Management: A Critical Text*, London: Routledge.

Gutek, B. (1995) *The Dynamics of Service*, San Francisco: Jossey-Bass.

Hales, C. (1999) 'Embellishing empowerment: ideologies of management, managerial ideologies and the rhetoric and reality of empowerment programmes', Paper at the Labour Process Conference, Royal Holloway College, University of London.

Halford, S., Savage, M. and Witz, A. (1997) *Gender, Careers and Organisations*, London: Routledge.

Hall, E. (1993) 'Smiling, deferring, and flirting: Doing gender by giving "good service" ', *Work and Occupations*, 20, 4: 452–471.

Hammer, M. and Champy, J. (1995) *Reengineering the Corporation: A Manifesto for Business Revolution*, London: Nicholas Brealey.

Handy, J. (1990) *Occupational Stress in a Caring Profession*, Avebury: Aldershot.

Harrison, S. and Pollitt, C. (1994) *Controlling Health Professionals*, Buckingham: Open University Press.

Haynes, P. and Allen, M. (2001) 'Partnership as union strategy: A preliminary evaluation', *Employee Relations*, forthcoming.

Heckscher, C. (1988) *The New Unionism*, New York: Basic Books.

Heery, E. (1993) 'Industrial relations and the customer', *Industrial Relations Journal*, 24, 4: 284–95.

Heery, E. (2001) 'Social movements or social partner? Alternative futures for British labour', Working paper, Cardiff Business School.

Heery, E. and Kelly, J. (1988) 'Union women: A survey of women full time officials', London School of Economics mimeo.

Heery, E. and Kelly, J. (1989) ' "A cracking job for a woman": A profile of women trade union officers', *Industrial Relations Journal*, 20, 3: 192–202.

Heery, E., Conley, H., Delbridge, R. and Stewart, P. (2000) 'Beyond the enterprise? Trade unions and the representation of the contingent worker', Economic and Social Research Council, Future of Work Programme, Working Paper 7.

Herzenberg, S., Alic, J. and Wial, H. (1998) *New Rules for a New Economy: Employment and Opportunity in Postindustrial America*, Ithaca, NY: Cornell University Press.

Heskett, J., Sasser, E. and Hart, C. (1990) *Service Breakthroughs: Changing the Rules of the Game*, New York: Free Press.

Heskett, J., Sasser, W. and Schlesinger, L. (1997) *The Service Profit Chain*, New York: The Free Press.

Hewer, P. and Campbell, C. (1997) 'Appendix: Research on shopping – a brief history and selected literature', in Falk, P. and Campbell, C. (eds), *The Shopping Experience*, London: Sage, 186–206.

Hey, V. (1986) *Patriarchy and Pub Culture*, London: Tavistock.

Hill, S. and Wilkinson, A. (1995) 'In search of TQM', *Employee Relations*, 17, 3: 8–25.

Himmelweit, S. (1999) 'Caring labor', *Annals of the American Academy of Political and Social Sciences*, 561: 27–38.

Hirschhorn, L. (1985) 'Information technology and the new services game', in Castells, M. (ed.), *High Technology, Space and Society*, Newbury Park, CA: Sage.

Hochschild, A. (1983) *The Managed Heart*, Berkeley: University of California Press.

Hodgson, D. (1999) 'The making of the "born salesman"', Paper at the Labour Process Conference, Royal Holloway College, University of London, March.

Hodgson, D. (2001) '"Empowering customer through education" or governing without government', in Sturdy, A., Grugulis, I. and Willmott, H. (eds), *Customer Service: Empowerment and Entrapment*, Basingstoke: Macmillan/Palgrave.

Hodson, R. and Sullivan, T. (1995) *The Social Organisation of Work*, Washington: Wadsworth.

Holden, P. and Littlewood, J. (eds), (1991) *Anthropology and Nursing*, London: Routledge.

Holtgrewe, U. (2000) 'Recognition, intersubjectivity and service work: Beyond subjectivity and control', Paper presented at Labour Process Conference, University of Strathclyde.

Hook, K. (1998) *The Human Face of Call Centre Management*, Newdigate: Callcraft.

Hopfl, H. (1993) 'Culture and commitment: British Airways', in Gowler, D., Legge, K. and Clegg, C. (eds), *Case Studies in Organisational Behaviour*, London: Paul Chapman, 117–25.

Hoque, K. (2000) *Human Resource Management in the Hotel Industry*, London: Routledge.

Howton, F. and Rosenberg, B. (1965) 'The salesman: Ideology and self-imagery in a prototypic occupation', *Social Research*, 32: 277–98.

Hughes, K. and Tadic, V. (1998) '"Something to deal with": Customer sexual harassment and women's retail service work in Canada', *Gender, Work and Organisation*, 5: 207–19.

Hughes, E., Hughes, H. and Deutscher, I. (1958) *Twenty Thousand Nurses Tell Their Story*, Philadelphia: Lippincott.

Hunter, L. (2000) 'The adoption of innovative work practices in service establishments', *International Journal of Human Resource Management*, 11, 3: 477–96.

Hutton, W. (1995) *The State We're In*, London: Verso.

Hyman, R. (1987) 'Strategy or structure?, Capital, labour and control', *Work, Employment and Society*, 1, 1: 25–55.

Hyman, R. (1991) 'Plus ça change? The theory of production and the production of theory', in Pollert, A. (ed.) *Farewell to Flexibility?*, Oxford: Blackwell, 259–83.

Hyman, R. (1997a) 'Trade unions and interest representation in the context of globalisation', *Transfer*, 3: 515–33.

Hyman, R. (1997b) 'The future of employee representation', *British Journal of Industrial Relations*, 35: 309–31.

Iaffaldano, M. and Muchinsky, P. (1985) 'Job satisfaction and job performance', *Psychological Bulletin*, 97: 251–73.

IDS (Income Data Services) (1999) *Pay and Conditions in Call Centres*, London.

Irvine, D. (2000) 'Medical regulation – modernisation continues', *Consumer Policy Review*, March/April.

Jacoby, S. (1998) *Modern Manors*, Princeton University Press.

James, N. (1989) 'Emotional labour: skill and work in the social regulation of feelings', *Sociological Review*, 37, 1: 15–24.

James, N. (1993) 'Divisions of emotional labour: Disclosure and cancer', in Fineman, S. (ed.), *Emotion in Organisations*, London: Sage, 94–117.

James, V. (1986) *Care and Work in Nursing the Dying*, PhD thesis, University of Aberdeen.

Jarvis, V. and Prais, S. (1989) 'Two nations of shopkeepers: Training for retailing in France and Britain', *National Institute Economic Review*, May, 58–74.

Jenkins, R. (1986) *Racism and Recruitment*, Cambridge Unviersity Press.

Johnson, J. (1996) 'Linking employee perception to customer satisfaction', *Personnel Psychology*, 49, 831–52.

Johnson, K. (1983) 'Trade unions and total rewards', *International Journal of Hospitality Management*, 2, 1: 31–55.

Johnson, K. and Mignot, K. (1982) 'Marketing trade unionism to service industries', *Service Industries Review*, 2, 3: 5–23.

Jones, C., Taylor, G. and Nickson, D. (1997) 'Whatever it takes? Managing "empowered" employees and the service encounter in an international hotel chain', *Work, Employment and Society*, 11, 3: 541–54.

Kaplan, R. and Norton, D. (1993) 'Putting the balanced scorecard to work', *Harvard Business Review*, Sept-Oct: 134–49.

Katz, H. (1996) 'Introduction' in Katz, H. (ed.), *Telecommunications: Restructuring Work and Employment Relations World-wide*, Ithaca, NY: Cornell University Press.

Keat, R. (1991) 'Introduction: Starship Britain or universal enterprise', in R. Keat and N. Abercrombie (eds), *Enterprise Culture*, London: Routledge, 1–17.

Keenoy, T. (1990) 'HRM: Rhetoric, reality and contradiction', *International Journal of Human Resource Management*, 1, 3: 363–84.

Keenoy, T. and Anthony, P. (1992) 'HRM: Metaphor: meaning, and morality', in Blyton, P. and Turnbull, P. (eds), *Reassessing Human Resource Management*, London: Sage.

Keep, E. and Rainbird, H. (2000) 'Towards the learning organisation?', in Bach, S. and Sisson, K. (eds), *Personnel Management*, Oxford, Blackwell, 173–94.

Kelly, J. and Heery, E. (1989) 'Full-time officers and trade union recruitment', *British Journal of Industrial Relations*, 14, 2: 39–54.

Kerchner, C. and Mitchell, D. (1988) *The Changing Idea of a Teachers' Union*, New York: Falmer Press.

Kessler, I. (2000) 'Remuneration systems', in Bach, S. and Sisson, K. (eds), *Personnel Management*, Oxford: Blackwell, 264–86.

Kinnie, N., Hutchinson, S. and Purcell, J. (1998) 'Fun and surveillance: The paradox of high commitment management in call centres', Paper presented at Service Workplace conference, Wharton School of Management.

Klein, N. (2000) *No Logo*, London: Flamingo.

Knights, D. and McCabe, D. (1997) 'How would you measure something like that? Quality in a retail bank', *Journal of Management Studies*, 34, 3: 371–88.

Knights, D. and Morgan, G. (1990) 'Management control in sales forces', *Work, Employment and Society*, 4, 3: 369–89.

Knights, D., Calvey, D. and Odih, P. (1999) 'Social managerialism and the time disciplined subject: Quality-quantity conflicts in a call centre', Paper delivered at the Labour Process Conference, Royal Holloway, University of London.

Kochan, T., Katz, H. and McKersie, R. (1986) *The Transformation of American Industrial Relations*, New York: Basic Books.

Korczynski, M. (1999) 'What a difference a union makes', Paper presented at London School of Economics workshop on call centres.

Korczynski, M. (2000a) 'The political economy of trust', *Journal of Management Studies*, 37, 1: 1–22.

Korczynski, M. (2000b) 'Emotional labour and communities of coping in front-line work', Working paper, Loughborough University.

Korczynski, M. (2001) 'The contradictions of service work: The call centre as customer-oriented bureaucracy', in Sturdy, A., Grugulis, I. and Wilmott, H. (eds), *Customer Service: Empowerment and Entrapment*, Basingstoke: Macmillan/Palgrave.

Korczynski, M. (2002) 'Struggles for legitimacy: Industrial relations in consumer capitalism', in Ackers, P. and Wilkinson, A. (eds) *Reworking Industrial Relations*, Oxford: Oxford University Press.

Korczynski, M. and Ritson, N. (2000) 'Derecognition and centralisation of bargaining: Dualism in the oil and chemical industries', *Work, Employment and Society*, 14, 3: 419–37.

Korczynski, M., Shire, K., Frenkel, S. and Tam, M. (1996) 'Front-line work in the "new model service firm": Australian and Japanese comparisons', *Human Resource Management Journal*, 6, 2: 72–87.

Korczynski, M., Shire, K., Frenkel, S. and Tam, M. (2000) 'Service work in consumer capitalism: Customers, control and contradictions', *Work, Employment and Society*, 14, 4: 669–87.

Kreitzman, L. (1999) *The 24 Hour Society*, London: Profile Books.

Kumar, K. (1996) *From Post-Industrial to Post-modern Society*, Oxford: Blackwell.

Kunda, G. (1992) *Engineering Culture*, Philadelphia: Temple Unviersity Press.

Lachmann, R. (2000) 'Stepping into the kitchen: the implications of clients as co-producers of a professional service for its delivery and staff', *International Journal of Human Resource Management*, 11,3.

Laermans, R. (1993) 'Learning to consume: Early department stores and the shaping of the modern consumer culture (1860–1914)', *Theory, Culture and Society*, 10, 4: 79–102.

Lankshear, G., Cook, P., Mason, D. and Coates, S. (2000) 'Call centres: Something old, something new, what's different, what's true?', Paper presented at Labour Process conference, University of Strathclyde, April.

LaPointe, E. (1992) 'Relationships with waitresses: Gendered social distance in restaurant hierarchies', *Qualitative Sociology*, 15: 377–93.

Larkin, T. and Larkin, S. (1996) 'Reaching and changing frontline employees', *Harvard Business Review*, May-June: 95–104.

Lash, S. and Urry, J. (1994) *Economies of Signs and Space*, London: Sage.

Lashley, C. (1997) *Empowering Service Excellence*, London: Cassell.

Lawson, H. (1996) 'Car saleswoman: expanding the scope of salesmanship' in Lopata, H. (ed.), *Current Research on Occupations and Professions*, Greenwich, CT: JAI Press, 53–73.

Legge, K. (1989) 'Human resource mangement – a critical analysis', in Storey, J. (ed.), *New Perspectives on Human Resource Management*, London: Routledge, 19–40.

Legge, K. (1995) *Human Resource Management*, Basingstoke: Macmillan.

Leidner, R. (1993) *Fast Food, Fast Talk*, Berkeley: University of California Press.

Leidner, R. (1996) 'Rethinking questions of control: Lessons from McDonald's', in MacDonald, C. and Sirianni, C. (eds), *Working in the Service Society*, Philadelphia: Temple University Press, 29–49.

Leverment, Y., Ackers, P. and Preston, D. (1998) 'Professionals in the NHS: A Case Study of Business Process Re-engineering', *New Technology, Work and Employment*, 13, 2: 129–39.

Levitt, T. (1972) 'Production line approach to service', *Harvard Business Review*, Sept/Oct, 41–52.

Levitt, T. (1976) 'Industrialization of service', *Harvard Business Review*, Sept-Oct: 63–74.

Linstead, S. (1995) 'Averting the gaze: Gender and power on the perfumed picket line', *Gender, Work and Organisation*, 2, 4: 192–206.

Lipietz, A. (1989) 'The debt problem, European integration and world crisis', *New Left Review*, 178, 37–50.

Lipsky, M. (1976) 'Toward a theory of street-level bureaucracy', in Hawley, W. and Lipsky, M. (eds), *Theoretical Perspectives on Urban Politics*, Englewood Cliffs, NJ: Prentice-Hall, 196–213.

Lloyd, C. and Newell, H. (1999) 'Selling teams to the sales force', in Proctor, S. and Mueller, F. (eds), *Team Working*, Basingstoke: Macmillan.

Lockwood, A. and Guerrier, Y. (1989) 'Flexible working in the hospitality industry', *Contemporary Hospitality Management*, 1, 1: 11–16.

Lopez, H. (1996) 'The politics of service production: route sales work in the potato-chip industry', in MacDonald, C. and Sirianni, C. (ed.), *Working in the Service Society*. Philadelphia: Temple University Press, 50–73.

Lorence, J. (1992) 'Service sector growth and metropolitan occupational sex segregation', *Work and Occupations*, 19: 128–56.

Lovelock, C. H. and Young, R. (1979) 'Look to customers to increase productivity', *Harvard Business Review*, 57 May-June: 168–78.

Low Pay Commission (1999) *The National Minimum Wage: The Story So Far*, Second Report of the Low Pay Commission, London: HMSO.

Lucas, R. (1995) *Managing Employee Relations in the Hotel and Catering Industry*, London: Cassell.

Lynch, J. (1992) *The Psychology of Customer Care*, Basingstoke: Macmillan.

MacDonald, C. and Sirianni, C. (1996) 'The service society and the changing experience of work', in MacDonald, C. and Sirianni, C. (eds), *Working in the Service Society*, Philadelphia: Temple University Press, 1–28.

MacFarlane, A. (1982) 'Trade union growth, the employer and the hotel and restaurant industry', *Industrial Relations Journal*, 13: 29–43.

McLaughlin, J. (1998) 'Gendering occupational identities and IT in the retail sector', *New Technology, Work and Employment*, 14, 2: 143–56.

Mann, S. (1999) *Hiding What We Feel, Faking What We Don't*, Boston: Element.

Marchington, M. (2001) 'Management-union partnerships in Britain: Who gains what?', Working paper, Manchester Business School.

Marchington, M. and Grugulis, I. (2000) ' "Best practice" human resource management: Perfect opportunity or dangerous illusion?', *International Journal of Human Resource Management*, 11, 6: 905–925.

Marchington, M. and Wilkinson, A. (2000) 'Direct participation', in Bach, S. and Sisson, K. (eds), *Personnel Management*, Oxford: Blackwell: 340–364.

Marshall, J. and Richardson, R. (1996) 'The impact of "telemediated" services on corporate structures: the example of "branchless" retail banking in Britain'. *Environment and Planning*, 28, 1843–58.

Marcuse, H. (1964) *One Dimensional Man*, Boston, MA: Beacon Press.

Mars, G. and Nicod, M. (1984) *The World of Waiters*, London: Allen & Unwin.

Mars, G., Bryant, D. and Mitchell, P. (1979) *Manpower Problems in the Hotel and Catering Industry*, Farnborough: Gower.

Marshall, G. (1986) 'The workplace culture of a licensed restaurant', *Theory, Culture and Society*, 3: 33–48.

Martin, J. (1992) *Cultures in Organisations*, New York: Oxford University Press.

Martin, J., Knopoff, K., and Beckman, C. (1998) 'An alternative to bureaucratic impersonality and emotional labor: Bounded emotionality at the Body Shop', *Administrative Science Quarterly*, 43, 2: 429–69.

Mathews, J. (1994) *Catching the Wave: Workplace Reform in Australia*, Ithaca, NY: ILR Press.

Meek, V. (1988) 'Organisational culture: origins and weaknesses', *Organisational Studies*, 9, 4: 455–73.

Menday, J. (1996) *Call Centre Management*, Newdigate: Callcraft.

Mennerick, L. (1974) 'Client typologies: A method of coping with conflict in the service worker–client relationship', *Sociology of Work and Occupations*: 396–418.

Menzies, I. (1959) 'The functioning of social systems as a defense against anxiety: A report of a study of the nursing service of a General Hospital', *Human Relations*, 13: 95–121.

Merton, R. (1962) 'Bureaucratic structure and personality', in Etzioni, A. (ed.), *Complex Organisations*, New York: Holt, Reinhart & Winston, 48–60.

Metcalf, D. (1999) 'The Low Pay Commission and the national minimum wage', *Economic Journal*, 109: 46–66.

Meyerson, D. (1989) *The Social Construction of Ambiguity and Burnout: A Study of Hospital Social Workers*, Doctoral Dissertation, Stanford University.

Milgram, S. (1974) *Obedience to Authority*, London: Tavistock.

Miller, A. (1949) *Death of a Salesman*, London: Penguin.

Miller, D. (1995) 'Consumption as the vanguard of history', in Miller, D. (ed.), *Acknowledging Consumption*, London: Routledge, 1–57.

Miller, M. (1981) *The Bon Marche: Bourgeois Culture and the Department Store, 1860–1920*, London: Allen & Unwin.

Mills, P. (1986) *Managing Service Industries*, Cambridge, MA: Ballinger

Millward, N, Bryson, A. and Forth, J. (2000) *All Change at Work?*, London: Routledge.

Mohr, L. and Henson, S. (1996) 'Impact of employee gender and job congruency on customer satisfaction', *Journal of Consumer Psychology*, 5, 161–87.

Morgan, G. (1997) *Images of Organisation*, London: Sage.

Morgan, G. and Knights, D. (1992) 'Constructing consumers and consumer protection: The case of the life insurance industry in the United Kingdom', in Burrows, R. and Marsh, C. (eds), *Consumption and Class*, Basingstoke: Macmillan, 32–51.

Morgan, C. and Murgatroyd, S. (1994) *Total Quality Management in the Public Sector*, Buckingham: Open University Press.

Morin, E. and Nair, S. (1997) *Une Politique de Civilisation*, Paris: Arlea.

Morris, J. and Feldman, D. (1996) 'The dimensions, antecedents, and consequences of emotional labour', *Academy of Management Review*, 21, 4: 986–1010.

Mulholland, K. (2000) 'Emotional labour and worker resistance in call centre employment', Paper presented at Labour Process Conference, University of Strathclyde, April.

Murphy, C. and Olthuis, D. (1995) 'The impact of work reorganisation on employee attitudes towards work, the company, and the union', in *Reshaping Work: Union Responses to Technological Change*, Toronto: Ontario Federation of Labour.

Murray, G. (1998) 'Steeling for change: organisation and organizing in two USWA districts in Canada', in Bronfenbrenner, K., Friedman, S., Hurd, R., Oswald, R. and Seeber, R. (eds), *Organizing to Win*, Ithaca, NY: ILR/Cornell University Press, 320–53.

NEDO (National Economic Development Office) (1986) *Changing Working Patterns*, London: HMSO.

Nelson, J. (1994) 'Work and benefits: The multiple problems of service sector employment', *Social Problems*, 41: 240–55.

Neuberger, J. (1999) 'Do we need a new word for patients?', *British Medical Journal*, 318: 1756–58.

Newton, T. with Handy, J. and Fineman, S. (1995) *'Managing' Stress: Emotion and Power at Work*, London: Sage.

Nickson, D., Warhurst, C. and Witz, A. (2000) 'Work, employment and skills: The importance of aesthetics in the interactive service labour process', Paper at the Labour Process Conference, University of Strathclyde, April.

Nickson, D., Warhurst, C., Witz, A. and Cullen, A. (2001) 'The importance of being aesthetic: Work, employment and service organisation', in Sturdy, A., Grugulis, I. and Willmott, H. (eds), *Customer Service: Empowerment and Entrapment*, Basingstoke: Macmillan.

Nielsen, G. (1982) *From Sky Girl to Flight Attendant*, Ithaca: Cornell University Press.

NIESR (National Institute for Economic and Social Research) (1986) *Young People's Employment in Retailing*, London: National Economic Development Office.

Noon, M. and Blyton, P. (1997) *The Realities of Work*, Basingstoke: Macmillan.

Norbeck, J. (1985) 'Coping with stress in critical care nursing', *Focus on Critical Care*, 12, 36.

Normann, R. (1984) *Service Management*, Chichester: John Wiley.

NTO Tele.com (1999) *Analysis and Mapping of the Call Handling Sector*, London,

Oakes, G. (1990) *The Soul of the Salesman: The Moral Ethos of Personal Sales*, London: Humanities Press International.

O'Donovan, O. and Casey, D. (1995) 'Converting patients into consumers: Consumerism and the Charter of Rights for Hospital Patients', *Irish Journal of Sociology*, 5: 43–66.

OECD (1996). *Labour Force Statistics, 1974–1994*, Paris: OECD.

Offe, C. (1985) *Disorganized Capitalism*, Cambridge: Polity Press.

Ogbonna, E. and Wilkinson, B. (1988) 'Corporate strategy and corporate culture: The management of change in the UK supermarket industry', *Personnel Review*, 17, 6: 10–14.

Ogbonna, E. and Wilkinson, B. (1990) 'Corporate strategy and corporate culture: The view from the checkout', *Personnel Review*, 19, 1: 21–9.

Olesen, V. and Bone, D. (1998) 'Emotions in rationalizing organisations', in Bendelow, G. and Williams, S. (eds), *Emotions in Social Life*, London: Routledge, 313–29.

Oliver, M. (1996) *Understanding Disability*, Basingstoke: Macmillan.

O'Reilly, J. (1994) *Banking on Flexibility*, Aldershot: Avebury.

Osborne, D. and Gaebler, T. (1992) *Re-inventing Government*, Reading, MA: Addison-Wesley.

Ostroff, F. (1999) *The Horizontal Organisation*, Oxford University Press.

Ouchi, M. (1979) 'A conceptual framework for the design of organisational control mechanisms', *Management Science*, 25, 9: 833–48.

Packard, V. (1957) *The Hidden Persuaders*, Harmondsworth: Penguin.

Paradise-Tornow, C. (1991) 'Management effectiveness, service quality and organisational performance in banks', *Human Resource Planning*, 14, 2: 129–40.

Parasuraman, A., Berry, L. and Zeithaml, V. (1991) 'Understanding customer expectations of service', *Sloan Management Review*, 32, 3: 39–48.

Parasuraman, A., Zeithaml, V. and Berry, L. (1988) 'SERVQUAL: A multi-item scale for measuring customer perception of service quality', *Journal of Retailing*, 64, 1: 12–40.

Parkington, J. and Schneider, B. (1979) 'Some correlates of experienced job stress: A boundary role study', *Academy of Management Journal*, 22: 270–81.

Paules, G. F. (1991) *Dishing It Out*, Philadelphia: Temple University Press.

Payne, J. (2000) 'The unbearable lightness of skill', *Journal of Education Policy*, 15, 3: 353–69.

Peccei, R. and Rosenthal, P. (2000) 'Front line responses to customer orientation programmes: A theoretical and empirical analysis', *International Journal of Human Resource Management*, 11, 3: 562–90.

Peters, T. (1987) *Thriving on Chaos*, Basingstoke: Macmillan.

Peters, R. and Merrill, T. (1998) 'Clergy and religious persons' roles in organizing at O'Hare Airport and St. Joseph Medical Centre', in Bronfenbrenner, K., Friedman, S., Hurd, R., Oswald, R. and Seeber, R. (eds), *Organizing to Win*, Ithaca, NY: ILR/ Cornell University Press, 164–78.

Peters, T. and Waterman, R. (1982) *In Search of Excellence*, New York: Harper & Row.

Phillips, A. and Taylor, B. (1986) 'Sex and skill', in Feminist Review (ed.), *Waged Work – A Reader*, London, Virago, 54–66.

Philpott, J. (2000) 'Face the ugly truth that "lookism" is all the rage', *Guardian*, 18 December.

Piore, M. and Sabel, C. (1984) *The Second Industrial Divide*, New York: Basic Books.

Pollitt, C. (1990) *Managerialism and the Public Services: The Anglo-American Experience*, Oxford: Blackwell.

Poynter, G. (1999) *Restructuring in the Service Industries*, London: Mansell.

Poynton, C. and Lazenby, K. (1992) *What's in a Word: Recognition of Womens Skills in Workplace Change*, Melbourne: Dept of Employment.

Prais, S., Jarvis, V. and Wagner, K. (1989) 'Productivity and vocational skills in services in Britain and Germany: Hotels', *National Institute Economic Review*, November, 52–73.

Pratschke, J. (2000) 'The work grievances of hospital nurses in Ireland and Southern Italy', Paper presented at Labour Process Conference, University of Strathclyde, April.

Preece, D., Steven, G. and Steven, V. (1999) *Work, Change and Competition*, London: Routledge.

Price, R. (1980) *Masters, Unions and Men*, Cambridge University Press.

Pringle, R. (1989) 'Bureaucracies, rationality and sexuality: The case of secretaries', in Hearn, J., Sheppard, D., Tancrid-Sheriff, P. and Burrell, G. (eds), *The Sexuality of Organisation*, London: Sage.

Proctor, S. and Mueller, F. (eds) (1999) *Team Working*, Basingstoke: Macmillan.

Prottas, J. M. (1979) *People-Processing*, Lexington, MA: Lexington Books.

Prus, R. (1989) *Making Sales*, London: Sage.

Putnam, L. and Mumby, D. (1993) 'Organisations, emotion and the myth of rationality', in Fineman, S. (ed.), *Emotion in Organisations*, London: Sage, 36–57.

Quinn, J. B., (1992) *The Intelligent Enterprise*, New York: Free Press.

Reekie, G. (1992) 'Changes in the Adamless Eden: The spatial and sexual transformation of a Brisbane department store 1930–1990', in Shields, R. (ed.), *Lifestyle Shopping. The Subject of Consumption*, London: Routledge, 170–94.

Regini, M., Kitay, J. and Baethge, M. (eds) (2000) *From Tellers to Sellers*, Cambridge, MA: MIT Press.

Reich, R. (1991) *The Work of Nations*, New York: Knopf.

Reichheld, F. (1996) *The Loyalty Effect*, Boston, MA: Harvard Business School Press.

Reichheld, F. and Sasser, E. (1990) 'Zero defections: Quality comes to service', *Harvard Business Review*, Sept-Oct: 105–11.

Rieder, K., Matuschek, I. and Anderson, P. (2000) 'The workers' and customers' contribution to successful interaction in call center work', Paper presented at Call Centre Workship at Gerhard-Mercator University, Duisburg, December.

Riley, M. (1985) 'Some social and historical perspectives on unionization in the UK hotel industry', *International Journal of Hospitality Management*, 4, 3: 99–104.

Ritzer, G. (1996) *The McDonaldization of Society: An Investigation into the Changing Character of Contemporary Life*, Newbury Park, CA.: Pine Forge Press.

Ritzer, G. (1998) *The McDonaldization Thesis: Explorations and Extensions*, London: Thousand Oaks.

Ritzer, G. (1999a) *Enchanting a Disenchanted World*, California: Pine Forge Press.

Ritzer, G. (1999b) 'Assessing the resistance', in Smart, B. (ed.), *Resisting McDonaldization*, London: Thousand Oaks, 234–55.

Ritzer, G. and Stillman, T. (2001) 'From person to system-oriented service', in Sturdy, A., Grugulis, I. and Willmott, H. (eds), *Customer Service*, Basingstoke: Macmillan/ Palgrave, 102–16.

Robinson, J. (1992) 'Introduction' in Robinson, J., Gray, A. and Elkan, R. (eds), *Policy Issues in Nursing*, Milton Keynes: Open University Press.

Rohantyn, F. (1984) quoted by Shelp, R., 'The service economy gets no respect', *Across the Board*, Feb.

Rose, E. (2000) 'Control and employment relations within a banking services call centre', Paper presented at Labour Process Conference, University of Strathclyde, April.

Rosenthal, P., Hill, S. and Peccei, R. (1997) 'Checking out service', *Work, Employment and Society*, 11, 3: 481–503.

Rosenthal, P., Peccie, R. and Hill, S. (2001) 'Academic discourses of the customer', in Sturdy, A., Grugulis, I. and Willmott, H. (eds), *Consuming Services*, Basingstoke: Macmillan.

Rothman, R. (1998) *Working: Sociological Perspective*, London: Prentice-Hall.

Royle, T. (2000) *Working for McDonald's in Europe: The Unequal Struggle*, London: Routledge.

Rubery, J., Fagan, C. and Humphries, J. (1992) *Occupational Segregation in the UK*, Manchester School of Management Working Paper.

Rubery, J., Horrell, S. and Burrell, B. (1994) 'Part-time work and gender inequality in the labour market', in Scott, A. (ed.), *Gender Segregation and Social Change*, Oxford University Press, 205–34.

Rubery, J., Smith, M., Fagan, C. and Grimshaw, D. (1998) *Women and European Employment*, London: Routledge.

Rubery, J., Smith, M. and Fagan, C. (1999) *Women's Employment in Europe*, London: Routledge.

Ryan, A., Schmidt, M. and Johnson, R. (1996) 'Attitudes and effectiveness: Examining relations at an organisational level', *Personnel Psychology*, 49: 853–82.

Sacks, K. B. (1990) 'Does it pay to care?', in Abel, E. and Nelson, M. (eds), *Circles of Care: Work and Identity in Women's Lives*, Albany: SUNY Press, 188–206.

Samuelson, H. (1991) 'Nurses between disease and illness', in Holden, P. and Littlewood, J. (eds), *Anthropology and Nursing*, London: Routledge.

Satyamurti, C. (1981) *Occupational Survival*, Oxford: Blackwell.

Saunders, K. (1981) *Social Stigma of Occupations*, Farnborough: Gower.

Savage, M. and Witz, A. (eds) (1992) *Gender and Bureaucracy*, Oxford: Blackwell.

Schemmer, R. (1995) *Service Operations Management*, Englewood Cliffs, NJ: Prentice-Hall.

Schlesinger, L. and Heskett, J. (1991a) 'Breaking the cycle of failure in service', *Sloan Management Review*, Spring: 17–28.

Schlesinger, L. and Heskett, J. (1991b) 'Employee satisfaction is rooted in customer satisfaction', *Harvard Business Review*, Sept-Oct: 134–49.

Schlesinger, L. A. and Heskett, J. (1992) 'De-Industrialising the service sector', in T. Swartz, D. Bowen and S. Brown (eds) *Advances in Services Marketing and Management: Research and Practice*, Greenwich CT: JAI Press, 159–76.

Schlesinger, L. and Zornitsky, J. (1991) 'Job satisfaction, service capability and customer satisfaction', *Human Resource Planning*, 14, 2: 141–50.

Schmenner, R. (1995) *Service Operations Management*, Harlow: Prentice-Hall.

Schmidt, M. and Allscheid, S. (1995) 'Employee attitudes and customer satisfaction', *Personnel Psychology*, 48: 521–36.

Schneider, B. (1986) 'Notes on climate and culture', in Venkatesan, M., Schmalensee, D. and Marshall, C. (eds), *Creativity in Services Marketing*, Chicago: American Marketing Association, 63–87.

Schneider, B. (1991) 'Service quality and profits: Can you have your cake and eat it too?', *Human Resource Planning*, 14, 2: 151–8.

Schneider, B. and Bowen, D. (1985) 'Employee and customer perceptions of service in banks: replication and extension', *Journal of Applied Psychology*, 70, 3: 423–33.

Schneider, B. and Bowen, D. (1993) 'Human resource management is critical', *Organizatonal Dynamics*: 39–52.

Schneider, B. and Bowen, D. (1995) *Winning the Service Game*, Boston, MA: Harvard Business School Press.

Schneider, B. and Schechter, D. (1991) 'Development of a personnel selection system for service jobs', in Brown, S., Gummesson, E., Edvardsson, B. and Gustavsson, B. (eds), *Service Quality, Multidisciplinary and Multinational Perspectives*, Lexington, MA: Lexington Books, 217–36.

Schneider, B., Parkington, J. and Buxton, V. (1980) 'Employee and customer perceptions of service in banks', *Administrative Science Quarterly*, 25: 252–67.

Schneider, B., Wheeler, J. and Cox, M. (1992) 'A passion for service: Using content analysis to explicate service climate themes', *Journal of Applied Psychology*, 77: 705–16.

Schneider, B., White, S. and Paul, M. (1998) 'Linking service climate and customer perceptions of service quality', *Journal of Applied Psychology*, 83, 2: 150–63.

Schor, J. (1998) *The Overspent American*, New York: Basic Books.

Scott, A. (1994a) 'Gender segregation and the SCELI research', in Scott, A. (ed.), *Gender Segregation and Social Change*, Oxford University Press, 1–38.

Scott, A. (1994b) 'Gender, segregation in the retail industry', in Scott, A. (ed.), *Gender Segregation and Social Change*, Oxford University Press, 235–70.

Segal-Horn, S. (1989) 'The globalisation of the service firm', in Jones, P. (ed.), *Management in Service Industries*, London: Pitman, 127–45.

Sennett, R. (1998) *The Corrosion of Character: Personal Consequences of Work in the New Capitalism*, London: Norton.

Sennett, R. and Cobb, J. (1973) *Hidden Injuries of Class*, New York: Vintage.

Shackleton, R. (1998a) 'Exploring corporate culture and strategy: Sainsbury at home and abroad during the early to mid 1990s', *Environment and Planning* A, 30: 921–40.

Shackleton, R. (1998b) 'Part-time working in the super-service era: labour force restructuring in the UK food retailing industry during the late 1980s and early 1990s', *Journal of Retailing and Consumer Research*.

Shamir, B. (1978) 'Between bureaucracy and hospitality – some organisational characteristics of hotels', *Journal of Management Studies*, October, 285–307.

Shamir, B. (1980) 'Between service and servility: role conflict in subordinate service roles', *Human Relations*, 33, 10: 741–56.

Shelton, A. (n.d.) 'Writing McDonald's, eating the past: McDonald's as a postmodern space', (unpublished), quoted in Ritzer, G. (1996), The McDonaldization of Society, Newbury Park, CA: Pine Forge Press.

Simmons, D., Shadur, M. and Bamber, G. (1996) 'Optus: New recruitment and selection in an enterprise culture', in Storey, J. (ed.), *Blackwell Cases in Human Resource and Change Management*, Oxford: Blackwell, 147–59.

Simms, M., Stewart, P., Delbridge, R., Heery, E. and Simpson, D. (2000) 'Unionising centre workers: The Communication Workers' Union campaign at TypeTalk', Working paper, Cardiff Business School.

Singleman, J. (1974) 'The sectoral transformation of the labor-force in seven industrial countries, 1920–1960', PhD thesis, University of Texas, Austin.

Sisson, K. (1994) 'Personnel management', in Sisson, K. (ed.), *Personnel Management*, Oxford: Blackwell, 3–50.

Sisson, K. and Marginson, P. (1995) 'Management: Systems, structures and strategy', in Edwards, P. K. (ed.), *Industrial Relations*, Oxford: Blackwell, 89–122.

Smart, B. (1999) 'Resisting McDonaldization: theory, process and critique', in Smart, B. (ed.), *Resisting McDonaldization*, London: Thousand Oaks, 1–21.

Smith, A. (1910) [1776] *The Wealth of Nations*, London: J. M. Dent.

Smith, P. (1992) *The Emotional Labour of Nursing*, Basingstoke: Macmillan.

Smith, S. (1999) 'Airlie Hochschild: Soft spoken conservationist of emotions', *Soundings*, 11: 120–27.

Smith, S. and Lipsky, M. (1993) *Nonprofits for Hire: The Welfare State in the Age of Restructuring*, Cambridge, MA: Harvard University Press.

Snape, E., Wilkinson, A. and Redman, T. (1996) 'Cashing in on quality: Incentive pay and the quality culture', *Human Resource Management Journal*, 6, 4: 5–17.

Snow, G. (1981) 'Industrial relations in hotels', MSc thesis, University of Bath.

Sosteric, M. (1996) 'Subjectivity and the labour process: A case-study in the restaurant industry,' *Work, Employment and Society*, 10: 297–318.

Spradley, J. and Mann, B. (1975) *The Cocktail Waitress: Women's Work in a Man's World*, New York: Knopf.

Stanback, T., Jr. (1979) *Understanding the Service Economy*, Baltimore: John Hopkins University Press.

Stanback, T., Jr. (1990) 'The changing face of retailing', in Noyelle, T. (ed.), *Skills, Wages, and Productivity in the Service Sector*, Boulder, CO: Westview Press, 80–121.

Steinberg, R. J. (1990) 'Social construction of skill', *Work and Occupations*, 17, 4: 449–82.

Steinem, G. (1983) *Outrageous Acts and Everyday Rebellions*, New York: Holt, Rinehart & Winston.

Stenross, B. and Kleinman, S. (1989) 'The highs and lows of emotional labor: Detectives' encounters with criminals and victims', *Journal of Contemporary Ethnography*, 17: 435–52.

Storey, J. (1992) *Developments in the Management of Human Resources*, Oxford: Blackwell.

Storey, J. and Bacon, N. (1993) 'Individualism and collectivism into the 1990s', *International Journal of Human Resource Management*, 4, 3: 665–84.

Stromberg, A. and Harkess, S. (eds) (1988) *Women Working: Theories and Facts in Perspective*, Mountain View, CA: Mayfield Publishing.

Sturdy, A. (1998) 'Customer care in a consuming society: Smiling and sometimes meaning it?', *Organisation*, 5, 1: 27–53.

Sturdy, A., Grugulis, I. and Willmott, H. (eds) (2001) *Customer Service*, Basingstoke: Macmillan/Palgrave.

Sutton, R. (1991) 'Maintaining norms about expressed emotions: The case of bill collectors', *Administrative Science Quarterly*, 36: 245–68.

Tam, M. (1997) *Part-Time Employment: A Bridge or a Trap?*, Aldershot: Avebury.

Taylor, S. (1998). 'Emotional labour and the new workplace', in Warhurst, C. and Thompson, P. (ed.), *Workplaces of the Future*, London: Macmillan.

Taylor, P. and Bain, P. (1999a) ' "An assembly line in the head": Work and employee relations in the call centre', *Industrial Relations Journal*, 30, 2: 101–17.

Taylor, P. and Bain, P. (1999b) 'Trade unions and call centres', MSF paper, London: MSF Centre.

Taylor, S. and Tyler, M. (2000) 'Emotional labour and sexual difference in the airline industry', *Work, Employment and Society*, 14, 1: 77–95.

Terkel, S. (1999) *American Dreams: Lost and Found*, Toronto: Hodder & Stoughton.

Thompson, J. (1967) *Organisations in Action*, New York: McGraw-Hill Co.

Thompson, P. (1984) *The Nature of Work*, London: Macmillan.

Thornley, C. (1996) 'Segmentation and inequality in the nursing workforce', in Crompton, R., Gallie, D. and Purcell, K. (eds), *Changing Forms of Employment: Organisation, Skills and Employment*, London: Routledge, 160–81.

Tilly, C. (1992) 'Short hours, short shrift: The causes and consequences of part-time employment', in Du Rivage, V. (ed.), *New Policies for the Part-Time and Contingent Workforce*, Armonk, NY: Sharpe, 15–43.

Timo, N. (2000) 'From Bravermania to "McDonaldisation"?: Case studies of four service industries', Paper presented at Labour Process Conference, University of Strathclyde, April.

Tisdale, S. (1986) *The Sorcerer's Apprentice: Tales of the Modern Hospital*, New York: McGraw-Hill.

Titmuss, R. (1970) *The Gift Relationship*, London: HarperCollins.

Tolich, M. B. (1993) 'Alienating and liberating emotions at work', *Journal of Contemporary Ethnography*, 22, 3: 361–81

Tornow, W. and Wiley, J. (1991) 'Service quality and management practices', *Human Resource Planning*, 14, 2: 105–16.

Towers, B. (1997) *The Representation Gap*, London: Routledge.

Trades Union Congress (1998) *Polls Apart*, London: TUC.

Trentham, S. and Larwood, L. (1998) 'Gender discrimiantion and the workplace', *Sex Roles*, 38: 1–28.

Troyer, L., Mueller, C. and Osinsky, P. (2000) 'Who's the Boss?', *Work and Occupations*, 27, 3: 406–27.

Twitchell, J. (1997) *AdCult USA*, New York: Columbia University Press.

Ulrich, D., Halbrook, R., Meder, D. and Stuchlik, M. (1991) 'Employee and customer attachment: Synergies for competitive advantage', *Human Resource Planning*, 14, 2: 89–104.

Ungerson, C. (1999) 'Personal assistants and disabled people: An examination of a hybrid form of work and care', *Work, Employment and Society*, 13, 4: 583–600.

URCOT (2000) *Call Centres: What Kind of Future Workplaces?*, Melbourne: Union Research Centre on Organisation and Technology Monograph.

Urry, J. (1990) 'Work, production and social relations', *Work, Employment and Society*, 4, 2: 271–80.

U.S. Deptartment of Labor, Employment and Training Administration, (1991) *Dictionary of Occupational Titles*, 4th edn, Indianapolis, IN: JIST Works.

Van Maanen, J. (1991) 'The smile factory: Work at Disneyland', in Frost, P., Moore, L., Louis, M., Lundberg, C. and Martin, J. (eds), *Reframing Organisational Culture*, Newbury Park, CA: Sage.

Van Maanen, J. and Kunda, G. (1989) ' "Real feelings": Emotional expression and organisational culture', in Cummings, L. and Staw, B. (eds), *Research in Organisational Behaviour*, Greenwich, CT: JAI Press. 43–103.

Veblen, T. (1925) *The Theory of the Leisure Class*, London: Allen & Unwin.

Vidal, J. (1998) *McLibel: Burger Culture on Trial*, London: New Press.

Vogelius, P. and Hagedorn-Rasmussen, P. (2000) 'What is value-adding? Contradictions in the practice of BPR in social service administration', Paper presented at Labour Process Conference, University of Strathclyde, April.

Waddington, J. (1992) 'Trade union membership in Britain', *British Journal of Industrial Relations*, 30, 2: 287–324.

Waddington, J. and Whitston, C. (1995) 'Trade unions: Growth, structure and policy', in Edwards, P. K. (ed.) *Industrial Relations*, Oxford: Blackwell, 151–202.

Walby, S. and Greenwell, J. with others (1994) *Medicine and Nursing*, London: Sage.

Wallace, C., Eagleson, G. and Waldersee, R. (2000) 'The sacrificial HR strategy in call centres', *International Journal of Service Industry Management*, 11, 2: 174–85.

Walsh, T. (1990) ' "Flexible" employment in the retail and hotel trades', in Pollert, A. (ed.), *Farewell to Flexibility*, Oxford: Blackwell.

Walton, R. (1985) 'From control to commitment in the workplace', *Harvard Business Review*, 63, March: 77–84.

Warde, A. (1991) 'On the relationship between production and consumption', in Burrows, R. and Marsh, C. (eds), *Consumption and Class*, London: Macmillan, 15–31.

Weatherly, K. and Tansik, D. (1992) 'Tactics used by customer-contact workers: Effects of role stress, boundary spanning and control', *International Journal of Service Industry Management*, 4, 3: 4–17.

Weber, M. (1921/1978) *Economy and Society*, Berkeley: University of California Press.

Wever, K. (1998) 'International labor revitalization: Enlarging the playing field', *Industrial Relations*, 37, 3: 388–407.

Wharton, A. (1993) 'The affective consequences of service work; Managing emotions on the job', *Work and Occupations*, 20, 2: 205–32.

Whyte, W. F. (1946) 'When workers and customers meet', in Whyte, W. F. (ed.), *Industry and Society*, New York: McGraw-Hill, 123–47.

Whyte, W. F. (1948) *Human Relations in the Restaurant Industry*, New York: McGraw-Hill.

Wial, H. (1993) 'The emerging organisational structure of unionism in low-wage services', *Rutgers Law Review*, 45, Summer: 671–738.

Wicks, D. (1998) *Nurses and Doctors at Work*, Buckingham: Open University Press.

Wiley, J. (1991) 'Customer satisfaction and employee opinion', *Human Resource Planning*, 14, 2: 117–28.

Wilkinson, A., Godfrey, G. and Marchington, M. (1997) 'Bouquets, brickbats and blinkers: Total quality management and empoyee involvement in practice', *Organisation Studies*, 18, 5: 799–820.

Wilkinson, A., Redman, T., Snape, E. and Marchington, M. (1998) *Managing with Total Quality Management*, Basingstoke: Macmillan.

Williams, C. (1987) *Blue, White and Pink Collar Workers in Australia*, Sydney: Allen & Unwin.

Williams, C. (1989) *Gender Differences at Work: Women and Men in Nontraditional Occupations*, Berkeley: University of California Press.

Williams, C. (1995) *Still a Man's World*, Berkeley: University of California Press.

Willman, P. (1989) 'Human resource management in the service sector', in Jones, P. (ed.), *Management in Service Industries*, London: Pitman, 209–22.

Willmott, H. (1995) 'The odd couple? Re-engineering business processes; managing human relations', *New Technology, Work, and Employment*, 10, 2: 89–98.

Winslow, C. D. and Bramer, W. L. (1994) *Futurework*, New York: Free Press.

Witz, A. (1992) *Professions and Patriarchy*, London: Routledge.

Wolf, M. (1999) *The Entertainment Economy*, New York: Times Books.

Womack, J. P., Jones, D. T. and Roos, D. (1990) *The Machine That Changed the World*, New York: Rawson Associates.

Wood, R. (1992) *Working in Hotels and Catering*, London: Routledge.

Wood, R. (1998) 'Old wine in new bottles: critical limitations of the McDonaldization thesis – the case of hospitality services', in Alfino, M., Caputo, J. and Wynard, R. (eds), *McDonaldization Revisited: Critical Essays in Consumer Culture*, London: Praeger, 85–109.

Wood, S. and Pedlar, M. (1978) 'On losing their virginity: The story of a strike at the Grosvenor Hotel, Sheffield', *Industrial Relations Journal*, 9, 2: 15–37.

Woodward, J. (1965) *Industrial Organisation: Theory and Practice*, London: Oxford University Press.

Woody, B (1989) 'Black women in the emerging services economy', *Sex Roles*, 21: 45–67.

Woolf, N. (1990) *The Beauty Myth*, London: Chatto & Windus.

Wouters, C. (1989) 'The sociology of emotions and flight attendants', *Theory, Culture and Society*, 6: 95–123.

Wright Mills, C. (1957) *White Collar*. New York: Oxford University Press.

Zeithaml, V. and Bitner, M. (1996) *Services Marketing*, New York: McGraw-Hill.

Zemke, R. and Schaaf, D. (1989) *The Service Edge: 101 Companies that Profit from Customer Care*, New YorkL: NAL Books.

Zemke, R. and Woods, J. (eds) (1999) *Best Practices in Customer Service*, New York: HRD Press.

Zuboff, S. (1988) *In the Age of the Smart Machine*, New York: Basic Books.

Name Index

Subject Index

235